SOLVED!

SOLVED!

Famous Mystery Writers on Classic True-Crime Cases

Selected, with an Introduction, by
RICHARD GLYN JONES

PETER BEDRICK BOOKS
New York

First American edition published in 1987 by
Peter Bedrick Books
125 East 23 Street
New York, NY   10010

This selection, Introduction and commentary
© Xanadu Publications Ltd., London 1987

BOMC offers recordings and compact discs, cassettes
and records. For information and catalog write to
BOMR, Camp Hill, PA 17012.

Library of Congress Cataloging-in-Publication Data

Solved! : famous mystery writers on classic true crime
   cases.

   1. Crime and criminals—Case studies. I. Jones,
Richard Glyn.
HV6251.S65   1987   364.1   87-47753
ISBN 0-87226-167-0

Contents

Introduction

The gratifyingly warm welcome afforded to my first collection of true-crime stories[1] prompts another, and this one is designed to complement and extend the first — though it can certainly stand on its own feet. In that first collection I gathered together what I considered to be the finest accounts of some of the world's most notorious unsolved murder cases, and I was delighted to be able to include Colin Wilson on Jack the Ripper, Edmund Pearson on Lizzie Borden, Dorothy L. Sayers on the Wallace Case and other such distinguished pairings. Here, my object is to offer equally distinguished *solutions* to some similarly celebrated cases, but they are the solutions not of detectives or criminologists but of mystery writers. Real criminal puzzles tackled by the creators of fictional ones: it ought to be a stimulating mix, and I think that it is.

—For the relationship between murder in fact and in fiction is fascinating. The methods of Sherlock Holmes, the first fictional detective to attain world-wide popularity, had a considerable influence on real police-work, but when his creator tried to take on the rôle of Holmes he found that real crimes were very much less easy to solve, and — even more annoying — real, flesh-and-blood policemen very much less willing to be made fools of, even if some of them were fools. We'll watch Conan Doyle at work in one of these exploits — not a murder case, in fact, but none the less gripping for that — and discover just how different fact can be from fiction, fantasy from brute reality. If Sherlock Holmes had taken on the case of George Edalji he would have looked over the newspaper reports, made a quick excursion to the scene of the crime later the same day, solved it in a brilliant blend of close observation, shrewd deduction and decisive action, then returned to London to the ringing plaudits of everyone except the villain. The real-life cases of George Edalji occupied Conan Doyle on and off for literally years, and although it did reach a solution it proved an

---

[1] *Unsolved! Classic True Murder Cases* (1987)

7

extremely vexing business. Reality turned out to be cruel, inconclusive and above all *messy*, and while we applaud Conan Doyle's fine intentions, his courage and his persistence, we can only — I don't want to give too much away — deplore the wretched state of the real world, which has little room for knight-errants.

If Conan Doyle was at heart a romantic, the same can scarcely be said of Damon Runyon. His completely delightful tales of New York's criminal fraternity are, it is true, fairy tales of a sort, but the author of *Guys and Dolls* was also a hardbitten reporter — one of the greatest of his time — who can have had very few illusions about what went on in the real world. He didn't merely report the seamy side of things, but also played quite a lively part in them. His reports on criminal matters are scarcely remembered today, but how good they were! For this book I have chosen his day-by-day reports of the Snyder-Gray trial: a masterpiece of terse, witty writing, and an extremely shrewd ongoing assessment of Ruth Snyder, the so-called 'Granite Woman'. That she and Gray killed her husband was never in much doubt. What was interesting about this trial, apart from the gradual revelation of its horrors, was who was the instigator and who the executor? Would they turn against one another, and would either of them escape? The problem here is not who-done-it? but what the hell was going on inside these people's heads? This is the grim underside of every romantic triangle you've every heard of, miles away from Mindy's but something that Damon Runyon understood perfectly. His analysis of this case is acute, and absolutely right.

To bring that hero of a couple of hundred courtroom dramas, Perry Mason, to life would need, one might think, the creation of a special fantasy court in which he could spring all those last-minute surprises, for surely real courtrooms are like the one at Queen's County where Ruth Snyder and Judd Gray were put through it, and not mere platforms for handsome and heroic lawyers saving innocent and beautiful defendants? In a word, yes. But if Conan Doyle was the romantic and Damon Runyon the realist, Erle Stanley Gardner was practicality personified, and create a court was precisely what he did. He was a man who Got Things Done, working on up to seven novels simultaneously to make himself (without, let's be honest, any tremendous literary talent) one of the best-selling authors of all time. He was also a lawyer, and when *Argosy* magazine ran his series on possible miscarriages of justice it caught the public's imagination, and the Court of Last Resort came into being. It was a means whereby the innocent could indeed be vindicated, and where verdicts could be reversed by the energy of a right-minded group of people. He did it and it worked, though never quite as decisively as any of Perry Mason's triumphs (messy reality again), and not for very long. But the achievement was extraordinary, and Gardner's fascinating account of the setting-up of the Court and its first major case adds the third major aspect to our theme of writers as righters of wrongs.

These three substantial pieces form the tripartite core of this collection and show the writer as detective, reporter and judge, the three major characters in any criminal investigation, and all the more engaging for being an amateur detective, a deeply cynical reporter and an entirely maverick judge. There are other rôles that can be played, however, and the gallery is filled out with some fine examples from some very famous names indeed. The role of Armchair Detective, for instance, is adopted by Ellery Queen in a rare — possibly unique — excursion into these realms, offering a hypothetical solution to the murder of Grace Roberts, the glamorous 'Silk Stocking Girl' once famous throughout America; Freeman Wills Crofts' own novels specialized in the breaking of seemingly watertight alibis, and here he focusses that penetrating mind of the puzzle of the Gorse Hall murder, one of the England's most famous unsolved cases; and F. Tennyson Jesse, the creator of the remarkable Solange Fontaine and a great authority on true-crime cases, makes up her own mind about the guilt or innocence of the fascinating Madeleine Smith.

Julian Symons eschews the armchair and takes matters into his own hands in the most interesting case of 'The Invisible Man'. Robert Graves (not exactly a mystery writer: forgive me) goes back a couple of thousand years to see if he can discover what really happened to the Emperor Claudius, having left the matter rather unclear at the end of *Claudius the God.* And William le Queux provides a personal introduction to the extraordinary Madame Humbert — but then he claimed to know *everyone,* from Rasputin to the Pope.

These shorter pieces are, if you like, embroideries on the main pattern of the collection, and the solutions they offer are sometimes down-to-earth and sometimes fanciful. But in these too we find that the reality of murder seldom resembles its fiction. To make that match we would have to turn to a more documentary kind of writer such as Dashiell Hammett or Hillary Waugh, but the presentation of reality in fiction is not my concern here. Rather, it is the conflict of the novelist's vision with the world as it is, and the problems that inevitably follow when the one meets the other. Does this mean that I am dismissing these fictions as hopelessly implausible? Not at all. That would be to deny art, but we also need our dreams and our fairy-tales, not just to keep reality at bay but also to give us a notion of the world we would like to inhabit. That writers like Conan Doyle and Erle Stanley Gardner were willing to leave their desks and take on the real world is wholly admirable. Certainly, the results make fascinating reading.

— R.G.J.

ELLERY QUEEN

Death in Silk Stockings

Among great beauties a supreme self-confidence is inevitable.
The world, especially the male world, lies at their feet,
adoring and grateful for small favors. But it is the love goddess'
misfortune if she forgets that not every slave is obedient. And it
takes only one rebel to shatter the idol forever.

This is what happened to Maizie Colbert, or 'Grace
Roberts,' as she called herself professionally. She thought she
could manage Bernard Lewis as safely as she had managed
hundreds of other men in her thrall. By the time she discovered
her mistake, it was uncorrectable.

In 1916 the body and face of Grace Roberts were as widely
known to Americans as, say, those of Woodrow Wilson and
John J. Pershing. That hers was held in far more unanimous
esteem is no depreciation of those historic gentlemen. They
were merely a President and a General; she was 'The Silk
Stocking Girl,' whose delectable legs—displayed on magazines, in newspaper ads, on billboards from coast to coast—had
no enemies or detractors. By the simple process of posing for
lingerie ads she had earned a second title, 'The Girl with the
Divine Figure.' With the legs and figure went a face no less
heavenly.

This perfect flower had come from a humble garden, endear-
ing her further to the American heart. She had been raised in a
grubby little town in north-western Pennsylvania, in a very
much lower-middle-class family. In the most romantic tradi-
tion of rags-to-riches Maizie Colbert had left home at the age of
seventeen to seek fame and fortune in the big city. And in
Philadelphia, as a professional model named Grace Roberts,
she found both.

Manicure sets, dance halls, beauty parlors, skating rinks came to bear the Grace Roberts label. She was the most sought-after belle of her time. Philadelphia's Main Liners contended for her radiant presence at their posh social functions. The newspapers followed her around as if she were a queen. Among her admirers were financiers, judges, sportsmen, politicos. She was the gracious beneficiary of tens of thousands of dollars' worth of furs, diamonds, antiques. All men are brothers, and in the City of Brotherly Love everyone loved her.

Would success spoil Grace Roberts? Her answer was to lift her family out of their dingy surroundings and deposit them luxuriously in a house in West Philadelphia. The superintendent of the exclusive Wilton Apartments at 15th and Poplar, where she lived in swank, described her tenderly as 'the finest tenant' and 'the best tipper' in the building. To numerous poor Philadelphia families who benefited from her frequent acts of charity, she was Lady Bountiful.

Then, abruptly and beyond recall, during Christmas week of 1916, Grace Roberts' fairy-tale career came tumbling down.

As her family had not heard from her for several days, a sister, Bessie Colbert, paid a visit to the Wilton in the late afternoon of Saturday, December 30th. There was no answer to her rings and knocks on the Roberts door.

The superintendent, a man named Benjamin, had to crawl into the Roberts apartment by way of a fire escape. He scuttled out, ashen. 'Don't go in, Miss Colbert! Something terrible has happened.' Benjamin telephoned the police.

What Police Captain James Tate and his men saw when they set foot in the famous beauty's apartment was not beauty, but death in its ugliest form. Grace Roberts lay on her bed, a twisted thing covered by a red and stiffened sheet. The coat of her lilac silk pajamas had been torn to shreds in some wild, unheard struggle. The face that had launched a thousand advertisements was a pulpy ruin, unrecognizable, it had been worked over with a flatiron that lay bloodily nearby. But death had come through a bedsheet; she had been strangled with it.

Christmas gifts, many still unopened, made a huge pile around the tree in the beautiful living room. The names on the attached cards made the detectives' eyes widen. In an escritoire they found bundles of letters and telegrams from admirers, many of them tycoons and socialites. A photograph album was jammed with the autographed likenesses of young men, middle-aged men, old men, famous men, unknowns.

The apartment was filled with expensive things the killer had not touched—jewels, furs, silver, even a large sum of money. But Captain Tate did not need this evidence to decide that robbery had not been the killer's motive. Frustration and fury had tightened the bedsheet around that lovely throat. Homicidal hate and murderous despair had directed the hand brandishing the flatiron.

Perhaps it is not fair, but beauty desecrated arouses outrage not awakened by ordinary murder. And Grace Roberts had had powerful friends. The police knew that this was one homicide they had to solve.

From the building superintendent they got their first lead. He recalled an incident of the previous day. He had been hauled out of bed very early Friday morning by an irate cabdriver who had complained of depositing a fare at the Wilton in the middle of the night, being told to wait, and having waited three hours before the building with his meter going. The fare had never come out, and it looked as if he was nineteen dollars in the hole. At 9:00 a.m. the angry cabbie had given up and driven away.

It took the police several days to locate Elwood Powell, a veteran of the Philadelphia cabstands. And now they had a description of sorts and a hot lead. The man he had taken to the Wilton Apartments, Powell said, was young—about twenty-five—'rather goodlooking,' and he had worn pince-nez eyeglasses.

Powell had picked up the young man and two girls about 1:00 a.m. that morning at the Bellevue-Stratford Hotel. The girls had called him 'Bernie.' Powell had gathered that 'Bernie' hailed from Pittsburgh.

He had driven the trio to the girls' home in Germantown, and then 'Bernie,' after saying good night to the pair, had had Powell drive him to the Wilton, asking Powell to wait. It was the last the hackman had seen of him.

Grace Roberts' photograph album contained a picture of a nice-looking young man which was signed, 'Love, Bernie.' Powell identified the photo as that of his defaulting fare. And in the murdered beauty's address book was noted one Bernard M. Lewis of Pittsburgh.

The Germantown girls turned out to be sisters—Ethel and Mabel Kyle, both schoolteachers. They had met Bernie Lewis of Pittsburgh by chance at the Philadelphia Auto Show in January, they told police. He had said he was a traveling salesman and a bachelor.

They had dated him several times during 1916, on his visits to Philadelphia. They insisted he was 'always a perfect gentleman.'

He had never mentioned Grace Roberts to them; in fact, it was their impression that they were the only girls he knew in town.

On Friday evening, December 29th, Ethel Kyle said, she had had dinner with Lewis. She had noticed some small, rather odd-looking wounds on three fingers of his left hand. Now that she thought of it, they might have been bites—marks of a woman's teeth.

When Captain Tate's men converged on the Hotel Adelphia, where Lewis had been staying, they found their bird flown. He had decamped without paying his bill.

The alarm went out; Lewis was wanted 'for questioning' in the murder that, as the newspapers were saying, 'had shocked the nation'.

The police stayed close to the Kyle sisters. On Thursday, January 4th, they were rewarded. Lewis phoned. He would not say where he was. On police instructions the girls told him to give himself up. He said he would consult a lawyer and hung up.

But he phoned again. The detectives, listening in, had told one of the girls to say, 'Where did you go after you left us last Friday morning?'

'I'll tell you,' Lewis's voice began. Then it faltered. 'I did wrong. I'll give myself up.'

But he did not.

Other investigators traced his flight from the Adelphia to the

Camden ferry. From Camden he had boarded a train for Atlantic City.

The Lewis family had a summer home, the police knew, in Atlantic City. Quietly they pinpointed Bernard Lewis in a hotel opposite his family's home.

On Friday, January 5, 1917 the knuckles of the law rapped on the door of Lewis's room in the Atlantic City hotel.

They were answered with a shot.

The police broke the door down.

The killer of Grace Roberts had not been shooting at them. In the room they found him sprawled on the floor, clutching a .22 caliber rifle, blood streaming from a wound in his temple, dead.

Why had Bernard Lewis murdered America's favorite lingerie model, the darling of millions?

The question is still officially unanswered. Dead men tell no tales. Dead women are silent too.

But, given the cast of characters, it is possible even after almost fifty years to reconstruct the plot and its bloody climax.

Grace Roberts was a famous sex symbol who had kept her pretty head. Essentially she was what one of her innumerable influential friends, a Philadelphia magistrate, called her—'a fine young lady'.

Bernie Lewis was the prodigal, unpredictable son of a wealthy Pittsburgh coal family. By the time he was twenty-five he had squandered a fortune. He had tried marriage and it had failed—he and his wife were separated.

Lewis met the beautiful young model and, like hundreds of men before him, fell in love with her. Poised, sure of her power over men, Grace undoubtedly thought she could handle him. There is evidence that she went out with him several times.

That was her mistake. What she did not know about this particular man was the black depths of his nature. He was a neurotic, perhaps a psychopathic, personality. His fantasies seized on the beautiful girl as the object of his desires. He must have her. For himself alone.

When he came to her in the middle of that night, pressing his possessive desires upon her, Grace Roberts could only have rejected him. She had had plenty of practice rejecting possessive men. And this one could not even offer marriage.

She must have laughed at him.

That was when Bernie Lewis in a blue-black fury wound the bedsheet around her throat and, when she had stopped struggling, seized a flatiron and with it destroyed every vestige of the beauty she had denied him.

Solving crimes from the armchair is one thing; personal involvement quite another. Arthur Conan Doyle was at the height of his success in 1906 when, after years of struggle as an unsuccessful doctor, his writing had finally supplanted medicine as a career and brought him worldwide fame, especially for his creation of Sherlock Holmes. Yet with the death of his wife and other personal crises his life was in tatters, and when the chance of immersing himself in a new and worthwhile venture appeared he plunged himself into it — the matter of George Edalji.

'It was late in 1906 that I chanced to pick up an obscure paper called The Umpire, *and my eye caught an article which was a statement of his case, made by himself. As I read, the unmistakeable accent of truth forced itself upon my attention and I realized that I was in the presence of an appalling tragedy…' So wrote Conan Doyle afterwards, but in fact it was Edalji himself who had sent* The Umpire *to him ('I knew him only as the author of the Sherlock Holmes detective stories and as the man most likely to be able to unravel the mystery'), when he had been languishing in jail for a series of horrible crimes that might have seemed to be possible only as the work of an out-and-out lunatic. But Edalji was a practicing solicitor, and the mildest of men: what could have happened?*

In true Holmesian style, Conan Doyle made a flying visit to the scene of the outrages, gathered all the evidence he could, and then made his views known publicly in a series of articles in The Daily Telegraph, *which were specified to be free of copyright and which were widely reprinted elsewhere; it is from these articles that the following account of the case is taken.*

SIR ARTHUR CONAN DOYLE

The Case of Mr George Edalji

The first sight which I ever had of Mr George Edalji was enough in itself to convince me both of the extreme improbability of his being guilty of the crime for which he was condemned, and to suggest some at least of the reasons which had led to his being suspected. He had come to my hotel by appointment, but I had been delayed, and he was passing the time by reading the paper. I recognised my man by his dark face, so I stood and observed him. He held the paper close to his eyes and rather sideways, proving not only a high degree of myopia, but marked astigmatism. The idea of such a man scouring fields at night and assaulting cattle while avoiding the watching police was ludicrous to anyone who can imagine what the world looks like to eyes with myopia of eight dioptres—the exact value of Mr Edalji's myopia according to Mr Kenneth Scott of Manchester-Square. But such a condition, so hopelessly bad that no glasses availed in the open air, gave the sufferer a vacant, bulge-eyed, staring appearance, which, when taken with his dark skin, must assuredly have made him seem a very queer man to the eyes of an English village, and therefore to be naturally associated with any queer event. There, in a single physical defect, lay the moral certainty of his innocence, and the reason why he should become the scapegoat.

Before seeing him I had read the considerable literature which had been sent to me about his case. After seeing him I read still more, saw or wrote to everyone who could in any way throw light upon the matter, and finally visited Wyrley and had a useful day's work upon the spot. The upshot of my whole research has been to introduce me to a chain of circumstances which seem so extraordinary that they are far beyond the

invention of the writer of fiction. At all times in my inquiries I
have kept before my mind the supreme necessity of following
truth rather than any preconceived theory, and I was always
prepared to examine any point against the accused with as
much care as if it made for his innocence, but I have felt at last
that it was an insult to my intelligence to hold out any longer
against the certainty that there had been an inconceivable
miscarriage of justice.

Let me now tell the strange story from the beginning. I hope
that the effect of my narrative will be to raise such a wave of
feeling in this country as will make some public reconsideration
of his case inevitable, for I am convinced that such reconsideration can only end in his complete acquittal and to his restoration to the ranks of that honourable profession from which he
has been most unjustly removed.

The story begins as far back as the year 1874, when the Rev
S. Edalji, a Church of England clergyman of Parsee origin, was
married to Miss C. Stoneham. An uncle of the bride, as I
understand it, held the gift of the living of Great Wyrley, which
was a parish, half agricultural and half mining, about six miles
from Walsall, in Staffordshire. Through this uncle's influence
Mr Edalji became vicar of Great Wyrley, a cure which he has
now held for thirty-one years, living a blameless life in the sight
of all men. Placed in the exceedingly difficult position of a
coloured clergyman in an English parish, he seems to have
conducted himself with dignity and discretion. The only time
that I can ever find that any local feeling was raised against him
was during elections, for he was a strong Liberal in politics, and
had been known to lend the church school-room for meetings.
Some bitterness was aroused among the baser local politicians
by this action.

There were three surviving children from this union—
George, who was born in 1876, Horace in 1879, and Maud in
1882. Of these Horace received a Government post, and was
absent at the time when the long persecution to which the
family had been subjected culminated in the tragedy which
overwhelmed his brother.

In the year 1888, George Edalji being at that time twelve
years of age, a number of threatening anonymous letters were

received at the vicarage. The aid of the police was called in, and an arrest was made. This was of the servant-maid at the vicarage, one Elizabeth Foster, who was accused, among other things, of writing up ribald sentences about her employers on outhouses and buildings. She was tried at Cannock in 1889, but her solicitor pleaded that it was all a foolish joke, and she was bound over to keep the peace. An attempt has been made since to contend that she was not guilty, but I take it that no barrister could make such an admission without his client's consent. She and her friends were animated afterwards by bitter feelings of revenge; and there is good reason to believe that in this incident of 1888 is to be found the seed which led to the trouble of 1893–95 and the subsequent trouble of 1903. The 1892–95 letters openly championed Elizabeth Foster; the 1903 ones had no direct allusion to her, but a scurrilous postcard on Aug. 4 contained the words, 'Why not go on with your old game of writing things on walls?' this being the very offence Elizabeth Foster was charged with. The reader must remember that in 1888 George Edalji was a schoolboy of twelve, and that the letters received at that date were in a formed handwriting, which could not possibly have been his.

In 1892 the second singular outbreak of anonymous letters began, some of which were published in the Staffordshire papers at the time by Mr Edalji, in the hope that their style or contents might discover the writer. Many were directed to the vicarage, but many others were sent to different people in the vicinity, so malevolent and so ingenious that it seemed as if a very demon of mischief were endeavouring to set the parish by the ears. They were posted at Walsall, Cannock, and various other towns, but bore internal evidence of a common origin, and were all tainted with the Elizabeth Foster incident. They lasted for three years, and as they were accompanied by a long series of most ingenious and elaborate hoaxes, it is really wonderful that they did not accomplish their proclaimed purpose, which was to drive their victim off his head.

On examination of such of these letters as I have been able to see their prevailing characteristics are:

1 A malignant, diabolical hatred of the whole Edalji family,

Mr. George Edalji without his spectacles.

the 16–17–18-year-old George coming in for his fair share of the gross abuse. This hatred is insane in its intensity, and yet is so coldly resolute that three years of constant persecution caused no mitigation. Here are extracts to illustrate the point: 'I swear by God that I will murder George Edalji soon. The only thing I care about in this world is revenge, revenge, revenge, sweet revenge, I long for, then I shall be happy in hell.' 'Every day, every hour, my hatred is growing against George Edalji.' 'Do you think, you Pharisee, that because you are a parson God will absolve you from your iniquities?' 'May the Lord strike me dead if I don't murder George Edalji.' 'Your damned wife.' 'Your horrid little girl.' 'I will descend into the infernal regions showering curses upon you all.' Such are few of the phrases in which maniacal hatred of the Edalji family is shown.

2   The second characteristic of the letters is a frantic admiration, real or feigned, for the local police. There was a Sergeant Upton on duty in Cannock, who is eulogised in this way: 'Ha, ha, hurrah for Upton! Good old Upton! Blessed Upton. Good old Upton! Upton is blessed! Dear old Upton!

> Stand up, stand up for Upton,
> Ye soldiers of the Cross.
> Lift high your Royal banner,
> It must not suffer loss.'

'The following in this district we love truly—the police of Cannock in general.' Again: 'I love Upton. I love him better than life, because for my sake he lost promotion.'

3   The third characteristic of these letters, besides hatred of Edalji and eulogy of the police, is real or simulated religious mania, taking the form, in some portions of the same letter, that the writer claims to be God, and in others that he is eternally lost in hell. So consistent is this that it is hard to doubt that there was a real streak of madness in the writer.

4   A fourth remarkable characteristic of the letters is the intimacy of the writer with the names and affairs of the people in the district. As many as twenty names will sometimes be given, most of them with opprobious epithets attached. No one can read them and doubt that the writer lived in the immediate neighbourhood, and was intimately acquainted with the people of whom he spoke.

One would imagine that under these circumstances there would be little difficulty in tracing the letters to their source, but, as a matter of fact, the handwriting was never recognised, nor was the culprit discovered. The opinion was strongly held, however, by those who were most concerned, that there was a connection with the former incident, and that the letters were done by some male ally or allies of the discharged maid.

Whilst these letters had been circulating the life of the Edaljis had, as I have already said, been made miserable by a series of most ingenious and daring hoaxes, many of which might have seemed comic had it not been for the tragedy of such a persecution. In all sorts of papers the curious wants of the Rev S. Edalji, of Great Wyrley, broke out by letter and by advertisement. Forgery caused no qualms to the hidden conspirator. Mr Edalji became in these effusions an enterprising matrimonial agent, with a number of ladies, their charms and fortunes most realistically catalogued, whom he was ready to dispose of to any eligible bachelor. His house was advertised to be let for the most extraordinary purposes. His servant-girl was summoned over to Wolverhampton to view the dead body of a non-existent sister supposed to be lying at a public-house. Tradespeople brought cartloads of unordered goods to the vicarage. An unfortunate parson from Norwich flew across to Great Wyrley on the urgent summons of the Rev Shapurji Edalji, only to find himself the victim of a forgery. Finally, to the confusion of anyone who imagines that the youth George Edalji was annoying himself and playing heartless tricks upon his own people, there came a forged apology in the public Press, beginning with the words: 'We, the undersigned, G.E.T. Edalji and Fredk. Brookes, both residing in the parish of Great Wyrley, do hereby declare that we were the sole authors and writers of certain offensive and anonymous letters received by various persons during the last twelve months.' The apology then goes on to express regret for utterances against the favourite protégé of the unknown, Upton, the sergeant of police at Cannock, and also against Elizabeth Foster. This pretended apology was, of course, at once disowned by the Edaljis, and must, I think, convince any reasonable man, if there were already any room for doubt, that the Edaljis were not persecuting themselves in this maddening fashion.

Before leaving this subject of the anonymous letters of 1893, which breathe revenge against the Edalji family, I should like to quote and strongly emphasise two expressions which have a lurid meaning when taken with the actual outcome of the future.

On March 17, 1893, this real or pretended maniac says in a letter to the father: 'Before the end of this year your kid will be either in the graveyard or disgraced for life.' Later, in the same letter, he says: 'Do you think that when we want we cannot copy your kid's writing?' Within ten years of the receipt of that letter the 'kid', or George Edalji, had indeed been disgraced for life, and anonymous letters which imitated his handwriting had played a part in his downfall. It is difficult after this to doubt that the schemer of 1893 was identical with the writer of the letters in 1903.

Among the many hoaxes and annoyances practised during these years was the continual laying of objects within the vicarage grounds and on the window-sills, or under the doors, done with such audacity that the culprit was more than once nearly caught in the act. There was one of these incidents which I must allude to at some length, for though it was trivial in itself, it has considerable importance as forming a link between the outrages of 1893 and of 1903, and also because it shows for the first time the very strong suspicion which Captain the Honourable G.A. Anson, Chief Constable of Staffordshire—influenced no doubt by those reports of his subordinates, which he may or may not have too readily believed—has shown towards George Edalji. Personally I have met with nothing but frankness and courtesy from Captain the Hon G.A. Anson during the course of my investigation, and if in the search after truth I have to criticise any word or action of his, I can assure him that it is with regret and only in pursuit of what seems to me to be a clear duty.

On Dec. 12, 1892, at the very beginning of the series of hoaxes, a large key was discovered lying upon the vicarage doorstep. This key was handed to the police, and was discovered in a few days to be a key which had been taken from Walsall Grammar School. The reason why I say that this incident has an important bearing upon the connection between the outrages of 1893 and those of 1903 is that the very first letter in the latter series proclaimed the writer to be a scholar at Walsall Grammar School. Granting that he could no longer be a scholar there if he were concerned in the hoaxes of 1893, it is still an argument that the same motive power lay behind each, since we find Walsall Grammar School obtruding itself in each case.

The incident of the key was brought before the chief constable of the county, who seems at once to have concluded that young George Edalji was the culprit. George Edalji was not a scholar at the Walsall School, having been brought up at Rugeley, and there does not appear to have been the slightest reason to suppose that he had procured a key from this six miles' distant school and laid it on his own doorstep. However, here is a queer-looking boy, and here are queer doings, and here is a zealous constable, the very Upton whose praises were later to be so enthusiastically voiced by the writer of the letters. Some report was made, and the chief constable believed it. He took the course of writing in his own hand, over his own name, in an attempt to bluff the boy into a confession. Under date Jan. 23, 1893, he says to the father, in a letter which now lies before me: 'Will you please ask your son George from whom the key was obtained which was found on your doorstep on Dec. 12? The key was stolen, but if it can be shown that the whole thing was due to some idle freak or practical joke, I should not be inclined to allow any police proceedings to be taken in regard to it. If, however, the persons concerned in the removal of the key refuse to make any explanation of the subject, I must necessarily treat the matter in all seriousness as a theft. I may say at once that I shall not pretend to believe any protestations of ignorance which your son may make about this key. My information on the subject does not come from the police.'

Considering the diabolical ingenuity of the hoaxer, it would seem probable that the information came directly or indirectly from him. In any case, it seems to have been false, or, at least, incapable of proof, as is shown by the fact that after these threats from the chief constable no action was taken. But the point to be noted is that as early as 1893, when Edalji was only

Sir Arthur Conan Doyle at the time of the Edalji case.

seventeen, we have the police force of Staffordshire, through the mouth of their chief, making charges against him, and declaring in advance that they will not believe any protestation of innocence. Two years later, on July 25, 1895, the chief constable goes even further. Still writing to the father he says: 'I did not tell Mr. Perry that I know the name of the offender' (the writer of the letters and author of the hoaxes), 'though I told him that I had my suspicions. I prefer to keep my suspicions to myself until I am able to prove them, and I trust to be able to obtain a dose of penal servitude for the offender; as although great care has apparently been exercised to avoid, as far as possible, anything which would constitute any serious offence in law, the person who writes the letters has overreached himself in two or three instances, in such a manner as to render him liable to the most serious punishment. I have no doubt that the offender will be detected.'

Now, it must be admitted that this is a rather sinister letter. It follows after eighteen months upon the previous one in which he accuses George Edalji by name. The letter was drawn from him by the father's complaint of gossip in the neighbourhood, and the allusion to the skill of the offender in keeping within the law has a special meaning, in view of the fact that young Edalji was already a law student. Without mentioning a name, he assures Edalji's father that the culprit may get a dose of penal servitude. No doubt the chief constable honestly meant every word he said, and thought that he had excellent reasons for his conclusions; but the point is that if the Staffordshire police took this attitude towards young Edalji in 1895, what chance of impartiality had he in 1903, when a culprit was wanted for an entirely new set of crimes? It is evident that their minds were steeped in prejudice against him, and that they were in the mood to view his actions in the darkest light.

At the end of 1895 this persecution ceased. Letters and hoaxes were suddenly switched off. From that date till 1903 peace reigned in Wyrley. But George Edalji was resident at the vicarage all the time. Had he been the culprit there was no reason for change. But in 1903 the troubles broke out in a far more dangerous form than ever.

It was on Feb. 2, 1903, that the first serious outrage occurred at Wyrley. On that date a valuable horse belonging to Mr Joseph Holmes was found to have been ripped up during the night. Two months later, on April 2, a cob belonging to Mr Thomas was treated in a similar fashion; and a month after that a cow of Mrs Bungay's was killed in the same way. Within a fortnight a horse of Mr Badger's was terribly mutilated, and on the same day some sheep were killed. On June 6 two cows suffered the same fate, and three weeks later two valuable horses belonging to the Quinton Colliery Company were also destroyed. Next in order in this monstrous series of barbarities was the killing of a pony at Great Wyrley Colliery, for which George Edalji was arrested and convicted. His disappearance from the scene made no difference at all to the sequence of outrages, for on Sept. 21, betwixt his arrest and his trial, another horse was disembowelled, and, as if expressly to confute the views of those who might say that this outrage was committed by confederates in order to affect the trial, the most diabolical deed of all was committed, after Edalji's conviction upon Nov. 3, when a horse and mare were found mutilated in the same field, an additional touch of horror being added by the discovery of a newly-born foal some little distance from the mare. Three months later, on Feb. 8, 1904, another horse was found to be injured, and finally, on March 24, two sheep and a lamb were found mutilated, and a rough miner named Farrington was convicted, upon entirely circumstantial evidence, and condemned to three years. Now here the results of the police are absolutely illogical and incompatible. Their theory was that of a moon-lighting gang. Edalji is condemned as one member of it, Farrington as another. But no possible connection can be proved or was ever suggested between Edalji and Farrington; the one a rude, illiterate miner, the other the son of the vicar and a rising professional man; the one a loafer at public-houses, the other a total abstainer. It is certainly suggestive, presuming that Farrington did do the deed for which he was convicted, that he was employed at the Wyrley Colliery, and may have had to pass in going to his work that very pony which Edalji was supposed to have injured. It is also, it must be admitted, suggestive that while Edalji's imprisonment had no effect upon the outrages, Farrington's was at once followed by their complete cessation. How monstrous, then, to contend, as the Home Office has done, that no new facts have arisen to justify a revision of Edalji's case. At the same time, I do not mean to imply Farrington's guilt, of which I have grave doubts, but merely that, as compared with Edalji, a strong case could be made out against him.

Now let me, before examining the outrage of Aug. 17, 1903, which proved so fatal to Edalji, give some account of the fresh epidemic of letters which broke out in the district. They were synchronous with the actual outrages, and there were details in them which made it possible, though by no means certain, that they were written by someone who was actually concerned in the crimes.

It cannot be said that there is absolute proof that the letters of 1903 were by the same hand as those of 1895, but there are points about their phrasing, about their audacity and violence of language, finally, about the attentions which they bestow upon the Edalji family, which seem to point to a common origin. Only in this case the Rev Edalji escapes, and it is the son—the same son who had been menaced in the first series with disgrace for life—who receives some of the communications, and is referred to in the others. I may say that this series of letters presents various handwritings, all of which differ from the 1895 letters, but as the original persecutor was fond of boasting that he could change his handwriting, and even that he could imitate that of George Edalji, the variance need not be taken too seriously.

And now for the letters. They were signed by various names, but the more important purported to come from a young schoolboy, named Greatorex. This youth denied all knowledge of them, and was actually away in the Isle of Man when some of them were written, as well as on Aug. 17, the date of the Wyrley outrage. It is a curious fact that this youth, in going up to Walsall every day to school, travelled with a certain number of schoolfellows upon the same errand, and that the names of some of these schoolfellows do find their way into these letters. In the same carriage travelled young Edalji upon some few occasions. 'I have known accused by sight for three or four years,' said Greatorex at the trial, 'he has travelled in the same compartment with me and my schoolmates, going to Walsall. This has not occurred many times during the last twelve months—about a dozen times, in fact.' Now, at first sight, one would think this was a point for the police, as on the presumption that Edalji wrote these anonymous letters it would account for the familiarity with these youths displayed in them. But since Edalji always went to business by the 7.30 train in the morning, and the boys took the same train every day, to find himself in their company twelve times in one year was really rather more seldom than one would expect. He drifted into their compartment as into any other, and he seems to have been in their company but not of it. Yet the anonymous writer knew that group of boys well, and the police, by proving that George Edalji might have known them, seemed to make a distinct point against him.

The 'Greatorex' letters to the police are all to the effect that the writer is a member of the gang for maiming cattle, that George Edalji is another member, and that he (Greatorex) is prepared to give away the gang if certain conditions are complied with. 'I have got a dare-devil face and can run well, and when they formed that gang at Wyrley they got me to join. I knew all about horses and beasts and how to catch them best . . . they said they would do me in if I funked it, so I did, and caught them both lying down at ten minutes to three, and they roused up; and then I caught each under the belly, but they didn't spurt much blood, and one ran away, but the other fell . . . Now I'll tell you who are in the gang, but you can't prove it without me. There is one named —————, from Wyrley, and a porter who they call —————, and he's had to stay away, and there's Edalji, the lawyer . . . Now I have not told you who is at the back of them all, and I shan't unless you promise to do nothing at me. It is not true we always do it when the moon is young, and the one Edalji killed on April 11 was full moon.' (It is worth mentioning here that there was no outrage at all within a week of that date.) 'I've never been locked up yet, and I don't think any of the others have, except the Captain, so I guess they'll get off light.'

I would draw attention in passing to the artistic touch of 'ten minutes to three.' This is realism overdone, as no mutilator on a dark night could readily consult his watch nor care to remember the exact hour to a minute. But it corresponds closely to the remarkable power of imaginative detail—a rather rare gift—shown in the hoaxes of 1893–95.

In the next letter, also to the police, the unknown refers to his previous communication, but is a good deal more truculent and abusive than before. 'There will be merry times at Wyrley in November,' he says, 'when they start on little girls, for they will do twenty wenches like the horses before next March. Don't think you are likely to catch them cutting the beasts; they go too quiet, and lie low for hours, till you men have gone . . . Mr Edalji, him they said was locked up, is going to Brum on Sunday night to see the Captain, near Northfield, about how it's to be carried on with so many detectives about, and I believe they are going to do some cows in the daytime instead of at night . . . I think they are going to kill beasts nearer here soon, and I know Cross Keys Farm and West Cannock Farm are the two first on the list . . . You bloated blackguard, I will shoot you with father's gun through your thick head if you come in my way or go sneaking to any of my pals.'

This letter was addressed, like the last, to:

> The Sergeant,
> Police Station, Hednesford,
> Staffordshire.

bearing a Walsall post mark of July 10, 1903. Edalji is openly accused of the crimes in the letters, and yet the police put forward the theory that he himself wrote them, and founded upon the last sentence of them, which I have quoted, that second charge, which sounded so formidable in his indictment, viz., of threatening to murder Sergeant Robinson.

A few days previously a second police officer, Mr. Rowley, of Bridgtown, had received another letter, evidently from the same hand. Here the detail as to the method of the crime is more realistic than ever, though no accusations against others are made. I quote this letter in extenso:

'Sir—A party whose initials you'll guess will be bringing a new hook home by the train from Walsall on Wednesday night, an he will have it in his special long pocket under his coat, an if you or your pals can get his coat pulled aside a bit you'll get sight of it, as it's an inch and half longer than the one he threw out of sight when he heard someone a slopin it after him this morning. He will come by that after five or six, or if he don't come home tomorrow he is sure on Thursday, an you have made a mistake not keeping all the plain clothes men at hand. You sent them away too soon. Why, just think, he did it close where two of them were hiding only a few days gone by. But, sir, he has got eagle eyes, and his ears is as sharp as a razor, and he is as fleet of foot as a fox, and as noiseless, and he crawls on all fours up to the poor beasts, an fondles them a bit, and then he pulls the hook smart across 'em, and out their entrails fly, before they guess they are hurt. You want 100 detectives to run him in red-handed, because he is so fly, and knows every nook and corner. You know who it is, and I can prove it; but until £100 reward is offered for a conviction, I shan't split no more.'

There is, it must be admitted, striking realism in this account also, but a hook—unless it were a billhook or horticultural hook—could not under any circumstances have inflicted the injuries.

It seems absurd enough that these letters incriminating himself in such violent terms should be attributed to young Edalji, but the climax is reached when a most offensive post-card, handed in at Edalji's own business office, is also sworn to by the expert employed by the police as being in Edalji's own writing. This vile effusion, which cannot be reproduced in full, accuses Edalji of guilty relations with a certain lady, ending up with the words, 'Rather go back to your old game of writing anonymous letters and killing cows and writing on walls.'

Now this postcard was posted at Wolverhampton upon Aug. 4, 1903. As luck would have it, Edalji and his sister had gone upon an excursion to Aberystwyth that day, and were absent from very early morning till late at night. Here is the declaration of the station official upon the point:

'On the night of 4th of August, 1903, and early morning of the 5th I was on duty at Rugely Town Station, and spoke to Mr George Edalji and his sister, who were in the train on their return from Aberystwyth. *William Bullock, Porter-Signalman, Rugeley Town Station*.'

The station-master at Wyrley has made a similar declaration.

It is certain, then, that this postcard could not have been by him, even had the insulting contents not made the supposition absurd. And yet it is included in that list of anonymous letters which the police maintained, and the expert declared, to be in Edalji's own handwriting. If this incident is not enough in itself to break down the whole case, so far as the authorship of the letters goes, then I ask, what in this world would be sufficient to demonstrate its absurdity?

Before leaving this postcard, let me say that it was advanced for the prosecution that if a card were posted at certain country boxes to be found within two and a half miles of Wyrley they would not be cleared till evening, and so would have the Wolverhampton mark of next day. Thus the card might have been posted in one of these out-of-the-way boxes on the 3rd, and yet bear the mark of the 4th. This, however, will not do. The card has the Wolverhampton mark of the evening of the 4th, and was actually delivered in Birmingham on the morning of the 5th. Even granting that one day was Bank Holiday, you cannot stretch the dislocation of the postal service to the point that what was posted on the 3rd took two days to go twenty miles.

Now, during these six months, while Edalji was receiving these scurrilous letters, and while the police were receiving others accusing the young lawyer, you will naturally ask why did he not take some steps himself to prove his innocence and to find out the writer? He did, as a matter of fact, everything in his power. He offered a reward of £25 in the public Press—a reward, according to the police theory, for his own apprehension. He showed the police the letters which he received, and he took a keen interest in the capture of the criminals, making the very sensible suggestion that bloodhounds should be used. It seems hardly conceivable that the prejudice of the police had risen to such a point that both these facts were alleged as suspicious circumstances against him, as though he were endeavouring to worm himself into their confidence, and so find out what measures they were taking for the capture of the offender. I am quite prepared to find that in these dialogues the quick-witted youth showed some impatience at their constant blunders, and that the result was to increase the very great malevolence with which they appear to have regarded him, ever since their chief declared, in 1895, 'I shall not pretend to believe any protestations of ignorance which your son may make.'

And now, having dealt with the letters of 1903, let me, before I proceed to the particular outrage for which Edalji was arrested and convicted, say a few words as to the personality of this unfortunate young man, who was, according to the police theory, an active member, if not the leading spirit, of a gang of village ruffians. Anyone more absurdly constructed to play the rôle could not be imagined. In the first place, he is a total abstainer, which in itself hardly seems to commend him to such a gang. He does not smoke. He is very shy and nervous. He is a most distinguished student, having won the highest legal prizes within his reach, and written, at his early age, a handbook of railway law. Finally, he is as blind as the proverbial bat, but the bat has the advantage of finding its way in the dark, which would be very difficult for him. To find a pony in a dark field, or, indeed, to find the field itself, unless it were easily approached, would be a hard task, while to avoid a lurking watcher would be absolutely impossible. I have myself practised as an oculist, but I can never remember correcting so high a degree of astigmatic myopia as that which afflicts Mr Edalji. 'Like all myopics, Mr Edalji,' says an expert, 'must find it at all times difficult to see clearly any objects more than a few inches off, and in dusk it would be practically impossible for him to find his way about any place with which he was not perfectly familiar.' Fearing lest it might be thought that he was feigning blindness, I asked Mr Kenneth Scott, of Manchester-Square, to paralyse the accommodation by atropine, and then to take the result by means which were independent of the patient. Here is his report:

Right eye—8.75 Diop Spher.
—1.75 Diop cylind axis 90°.
Left eye —8.25 Diop Spher.

'I am prepared to testify as to the accuracy of the above

The Edalji home (top), and one of the thickets that George Edalji would have had to negotiate on his way to the scene of the crimes (bottom).

under oath,' says Mr Kenneth Scott.

As to what such figures mean, I will bring it home to the uninitiated by saying that a glass made up to that prescription would cause the normal healthy eye to see the world as Edalji's eyes always see it. I am prepared to have such a glass made up, and if any defender of the police will put it on at night, and will make his way over the route the accused is alleged to have taken inside of an hour, I will admit that what seems to me absolutely impossible could be done. I may add that this blindness is a permanent structural condition, the same in 1903 as in 1906.

I appeal to the practising oculists of this country, and I ask whether there is one of them who would not admit that such a condition of the eyes would make such a performance practically impossible, and that the circumstance must add enormously to a defence which is already overwhelmingly strong. And yet this all-important point was never made at the trial.

It is this studious youth who touches neither alcohol nor tobacco, and is so blind that he gropes his way in the dusk, who is the dangerous barbarian who scours the country at night, ripping up horses. Is it not perfectly clear, looking at his strange, swarthy face and bulging eyes, that it is not the village ruffian, but rather the unfortunate village scapegoat, who stands before you?

I have brought the narrative down to the Aug. 17 outrage. At this period twenty constables and detectives had been brought into the district, and several, acting, I presume, upon orders from higher quarters, watched the vicarage at night. On Aug. 17 Edalji, following his own account, returned from his day's work at Birmingham—he had started in practice there as a lawyer—and reached his home about 6.30. He transacted some business, put on a blue serge coat, and then walked down to the bootmaker's in the village, where he arrived about 8.35, according to the independent evidence of John Hands, the tradesman in question. His supper would not be ready before 9.30, and until that hour he took a walk round, being seen by various people. His household depose to his return before supper-time, and their testimony is confirmed by the statement of Walter Whitehouse, who saw the accused enter the vicarage at 9.25. After supper Edalji retired to bed in the same room as his father, the pair having shared an apartment for seventeen years. The old vicar was a light sleeper, his son was within a few feet of him, the whole house was locked up, and the outside was watched by constables, who saw no one leave it. To show how close the inspection was, I may quote the words of Sergeant Robinson, who said, 'I saw four men observing it when I was there . . . I could see the front door and side door. I should say no one could get out on the side I was watching without my seeing.' This was before the night of the outrage, but it is inconceivable that if there was so close a watch then, there was none on the 17th. By the police evidence there were no less than twenty men scattered about waiting for the offender. I may add at this point some surprise has been expressed that the vicar should sleep in the same room as his son with the door locked. They slept thus, and had done for many years, so that the daughter, whose health was precarious, might sleep with the mother, and the service of the house, there being only the one maid, should be minimised. Absurd emphasis has been placed by the police upon the door being locked at night. I can only suppose that the innuendo is that the vicar locked the door to keep his son from roving. Do we not all know that it is the commonest thing for nervous people to lock their doors whether alone or not, and Mr Edalji has been in the habit of doing so all his long life. I have evidence that Mr Edalji always locked his door before he slept with his son, and that he has continued to lock his door after his son left him. If, then—to revert to the evidence—it is possible for a person in this world to establish an alibi, it was successfully established by Edalji that night from 9.30 onwards. Granting the perfectly absurd supposition that the old vicar connived at his son slipping out at night and ripping up cattle, you have still the outside police to deal with. On no possible supposition can George Edalji have gone out after 9.30.

And yet upon that night a pony had been destroyed at the Great Wyrley Colliery. Sergeant Parsons gave evidence that he saw the pony, apparently all right, at eleven o'clock at night. It was very dark, but he was not far off it. It was a wild night, with rain coming in squalls. The rain began about twelve, and cleared about dawn, being very heavy at times. On the 18th, at

6.20, a lad, named Henry Garrett, going to his work at the colliery, observed that the pony was injured. 'It had a cut on the side,' he said. 'The blood was trickling from the wound. It was dropping pretty quickly.' The alarm was at once given. Constables appeared upon the scene. By half-past eight Mr Lewis, a veterinary surgeon, was on the spot. 'The wound,' he deposed, 'was quite fresh, and could not have been done further than six hours from the time he saw it.' The least learned of laymen might be sure that if the pony was standing bleeding freely at six it could not have been so all night, as the drain must have exhausted it. And here, on the top of this obvious consideration, is the opinion of the surgeon, that the injury was inflicted within six hours. Where George Edalji was during those six hours has already been shown beyond all possible question or dispute. So already the whole bottom has dropped out of the case; but, none the less, the indefatigable police went on with their pre-arranged campaign.

That it was pre-arranged is evident, since it was not on account of evidence, but in search of evidence, that the constables raided the vicarage. The young lawyer had already started for his day's work in Birmingham. The startled parents were ordered to produce all the young man's clothing. The mother was asked for his dagger, but could produce nothing more formidable than a botany spud. A hunt was made for weapons, and a set of razors belonging to the vicar were seized. Some were said to be wet—a not uncommon condition for razors in the morning. Dark spots were perceived upon the back of one, but they proved upon chemical examination to be rust stains. Twelve men quartered the small garden, but nothing was found.

The clothes, however, were a more serious matter. One coat was seized by the police and declared to be damp. This is vigorously denied by the vicar, who handled the coat before it was removed. Damp is, of course, a relative term, and all garments may give some feeling of dampness after a rainy night, when the whole atmosphere is humid; but if the condition had been caused by being out in the wild weather which prevailed that night, it is certain that the coat would have been not damp, but sopping wet.

The coat, however, was not one which Edalji used outside, and the evidence of Mr Hands was called to show that he had not worn it the night before. It was an old house-coat, so stained and worn that it is not likely that an ambitious young professional man would, even in the lamplight, walk in the streets and show himself to his neighbours in such a garment. But it was these very stains which naturally attracted the attention of the police. There were some whitish stains—surely these must be the saliva of the unfortunate animal. They were duly tested, and proved to be starch stains, probably from fish sauce or bread and milk. But there was something still more ominous upon this unhappy coat. There were, according to Inspector Campbell, 'dark red or brown stains, right cuff much more stained than the left. There were other stains on each sleeve, further up, reddish brown or white. The coat was damp . . . There are other spots and stains upon it.'

Now the police try to make two points here: that the coat was damp, and that there were stains which might have been the traces of the crime upon it. Each point is good in itself; but, unfortunately, they are incompatible and mutually destructive. If the coat were damp, and if those marks were blood-stains contracted during the night, then those stains were damp also, and the inspector had only to touch them and then to raise his crimson finger in the air to silence all criticism. But since he could not do so it is clear that the stains were not fresh. They fell twelve hours later into the capable hands of the police surgeon, and the sanguinary smears conjured up by the evidence of the constable diminished with absurd swiftness until they became 'two stains in the centre of the right cuff, each about the size of a threepenny bit.' This was declared by Dr Butter to be mammalian blood. He found no more blood at all. How these small stains came there it is difficult to trace—as difficult as to trace a stain which I see now upon the sleeve of my own house-jacket as I look down. A splash from the gravy of underdone meat might well produce it. At any rate, it may most safely be said that the most adept operator who ever lived would not rip up a horse with a razor upon a dark night and have only two threepenny-bit spots of blood to show for it. The idea is beyond argument.

But now, having exhausted the white stains and the dark

stains, we come to the most damning portion of the whole indictment, though a careful consideration may change one's view as to who it is who is damned by it. The police claimed that they discovered horse-hairs upon the coat. 'On the sleeve,' says Inspector Campbell, 'I found brownish hairs, which look like horse-hairs. There are some on now.' Now, let us listen to the very clear statement of the vicar upon the subject. I transcribe it in full:

'On Aug. 18, 1903, they called at the vicarage at about eight o'clock in the morning, and in compliance with their request Mrs Edalji showed them a number of garments belonging to her son, George Edalji. As soon as they saw the old coat they began to examine it, and Inspector Campbell put his finger upon one place and said that there was a hair there. Mrs Edalji told him that it was not a hair, but a thread, and Miss Edalji, who was present then, remarked that it looked like a 'roving.' This was all that Inspector Campbell had said to them about the hair before I came down. When I saw him he told me that he had found horse-hairs upon the coat. The coat was then spread out upon the desk in the study. I asked him to point out the place where the hairs were to be seen. He pointed out a lower part of the coat, and said, "There's a horse-hair there." I examined the place and said, "There is no hair here at all." Some further conversation followed, and then suddenly he put his finger upon another place on the coat nearer to where I was standing, and, drawing two straight lines with his finger, he said, "Look here, Mr Edalji, there's horse-hair here." I looked at the place for a moment, and in order to have more light upon it, I took up the coat with both my hands and drew nearer to the window, and after carefully examining it I said to him, "There is, to be sure, no hair here, it is a clear surface." He then said that he wanted to take the coat with him, and I said, "You can take the coat. I am satisfied there is no horse-hair upon it."

'Now I have said it over and over again, and I say it here once more, that there was absolutely no horse-hair upon the coat. If there had been any I could not have failed to see it, and both Mrs Edalji and Miss Edalji looked at the coat at the same time, and saw no hair of any sort upon it.' Incidentally it may be mentioned in connection with this statement, in which Miss

Edalji entirely concurs, that we have the evidence of Miss
Foxley, formerly of Newnham College, and then head mistress
of the High School, that Miss Edalji was an exceedingly
competent scientific observer. She adds, 'Wilful mis-statement
on her part is as impossible in itself as it is inconsistent with her
high principles and frank, straightforward character.'

Now, here is a clear conflict of evidence between two groups
of interested people—the constables on the one hand, eager to
build up their case; the household on the other, eager to confute
this terrible accusation. Let us suppose the two statements
balance each other. But is it not evident that there was only one
course open for the police now to establish their point, and that
if they did not avail themselves of it they put themselves out of
court? Their obvious course was then and there to send for a
referee—the police doctor, or any other doctor—and picking
samples of the hair from the coat to have sealed them in an
envelope, calling the new-comer to witness when and where
they had been obtained. Such a proceeding must silence all
doubt. But they did nothing of the kind. What they actually did
was to carry off the coat upon which three reputable witnesses
have sworn there were no hairs. The coat then disappears from
view for twelve hours. In the meantime the pony has been put
out of its pain, and a portion of its hide was cut off with the hairs
attached, and also secured by the police. The coat had been
taken at eight in the morning. It was seen by Dr Butter, the
police surgeon, at nine in the evening. At that hour Dr Butter
picked twenty-nine undoubted obvious horse-hairs from its
surface.

The prosecution have here to break their way through two
strong lines of defence, each within the other. On the one hand,
if Edalji had done the crime the evening before, it was his blue
serge coat, and not his house-coat, that he wore, as is shown by
the independent evidence of Mr Hands. In the second line of
defence is the oath of the family that there were no hairs in the
morning, which is strengthened by the failure of the police to
demonstrate there and then a fact which could have been so
easily and completely demonstrated. But now we are faced by
the undoubted fact that the hairs were there, upon the cuffs and
the left breast, by evening. Why was the coat not taken straight

THE CASE OF MR GEORGE EDALJI

to the surgeon? Why was a piece of the animal's hide sent for before the coat was shown to Dr Butter? One need not fly to extreme conclusions. It is to be remembered that the mere carrying of hide and coat together may have caused the transference of hairs, or that the officers may themselves have gathered hairs on their clothes while examining the pony, and so unconsciously transferred them to the coat. But the fact that the hairs were found just on the cuffs and breast will still recur in the mind. It would be sad indeed to commit one injustice while trying to correct another, but when the inevitable inquiry comes this incident must form a salient point of it.

There is one test which occurs to one's mind. Did the hairs all correspond with the type, colour, and texture of the hairs on the sample of hide? If they did, then they were beyond all question conveyed from that sample to the coat. The cut was down the belly, and the portion taken off was from the side of the cut. The under hair of a horse differs greatly from the longer, darker, harsher hair of the sides. A miscreant leaning against a horse would get the side hairs. If all the hairs on the coat were short belly hairs, then there is a suggestive fact for the inquiry. Dr Butter must have compared their appearance.

Since writing the above I have been able to get the words of Dr Butter's evidence. They are quoted: 'Numerous hairs on the jacket, which were similar in colour, length, and structure to those on the piece of skin cut from the horse.' In that case I say, confidently—and all reflection must confirm it—that these hairs could not possibly be from the general body of the pony, but must have been transferred, no doubt unconsciously, from that particular piece of skin. With all desire to be charitable, the incident leaves a most unpleasant impression upon the mind.

If one could for a moment conceive oneself performing this barbarity, one would not expect to find hairs upon one's coat. There is no necessary connection at all. Anxious to avoid the gush of blood, one would imagine that one would hold off the animal with the flat of one hand and attack it with the other. To lean one's coat against its side would be to bring one's trousers and boots in danger of being soaked in blood.

So much for the saliva stains, the blood stains, and the hairs.

There remain the questions of the trousers and the boots. The trousers were said by the police to be damp, and stained with dark mud round the bottom. The boots were very wet. The boots were the same ones which Edalji had admittedly used during his sixty-minutes' walk upon the evening before. It was fine in the evening, but there had been heavy rain during the day, and puddles everywhere. Of course his boots were wet. The trousers were not a pair used the evening before, according to the family. No attempt was made to show blood marks on boots or trousers, though Mr Sewell, a well-known veterinary surgeon, deposed afterwards that in making such an incision a skilled operator would wear an apron to prevent his clothes from being soaked. It is an interesting point, brought out by the evidence of some of the witnesses of the prosecution, that the mud at the place of outrage was yellow-red, a mixture of clay and sand, quite distinct from the road mud, which the police claim to have seen upon the trousers.

And now we come to the farce of the footprints. The outrage had occurred just outside a large colliery, and hundreds of miners going to their work had swarmed along every approach, in order to see the pony. The soft, wet soil was trampled up by them from six o'clock onwards; yet on four o'clock of that afternoon, eight hours after the seizure of the boots, we have Inspector Campbell endeavouring to trace a similarity in tracks. The particular boot was worn at the heel, a fairly common condition, and some tracks among the multitude were down at the heel, and why should not the one be caused by the other? No cast was taken of the tracks. They were not photographed. They were not cut out for purpose of expert comparison. So little were they valued by Inspector Campbell that he did not even mention them to the magistrates on the 19th. But in retrospect they grew more valuable, and they bulked large at the trial.

Now, once again, the police are trying to make a point which in itself would help them, but which is incompatible with their other points. Their original theory was that the crime was done before 9.30. There was heavy rain on and off all night. It is perfectly clear that any well-marked footsteps must have been left after the rain stopped, or when it had nearly stopped. Even granting that the earth was soft enough, as it was, to take footprints before then, this heavy rain would blur them to a point that would make identification by a worn-down heel absurd. What becomes then of all this elaborate business of the footmarks? Every point in this case simply crumbles to pieces as you touch it.

How formidable it all sounds—wet razor, blood on razor, blood and saliva and hair on coat, wet boots, footmark corresponding to boot—and yet how absolutely futile it all is when examined. There is not one single item which will bear serious criticism. Let us pass, however, from these material clues to those more subtle ones which the bearing or remarks of the youth may have furnished. These will bear examination even less than the others. As he waited upon the platform for the 7.30 train an ex-constable, now an innkeeper, named Markhew, came up to him and asked him to stay, as Inspector Campbell wished to see him. At the same moment someone announced that a fresh outrage had been committed, upon which Markhew says that Edalji turned away and smiled. Now, it is perfectly clear that a guilty man would have been much alarmed by the news that the police wished to see him, and that he would have done anything but smile on hearing of the outrage. Edalji's account is that Markhew said, 'Can't you give yourself a holiday for one day?' on which Edalji smiled. Which is the more probable version I leave to the reader. The incident was referred to by the prosecuting counsel as 'the prisoner's extraordinary conduct at the station.'

He went to his office in Birmingham, and there, later in the day, he was arrested by the police.

On the way to the station, after his arrest, this unfortunate youth made another deadly remark: 'I am not surprised at this. I have been expecting it for some time.' It is not a very natural remark for a guilty man to make, if you come to think of it; but it is an extremely probable one from a man who believes that the police have a down on him, and who is aware that he has been accused by name in malignant anonymous letters. What else would he have said? Next day and the following Monday he was before the magistrates, where the police evidence, as already set forth, was given. The magisterial proceedings lasted till Sept. 4, off and on, when a prima facie case was made out, and the prisoner committed to the Staffordshire Quarter Sessions. How far a case of this importance should have been referred to any less tribunal than the assizes I leave to legal opinion. Again the criminal made a remark which rose up in judgment against him. 'I won't have bail,' said he to Police-constable Meredith, 'and when the next horse is killed it will not be by me.' In commenting upon this, Mr Disturnal, the prosecuting counsel, said, 'In refusing bail the prisoner made use of a very significant observation, and it went to suggest that the prisoner knew perfectly well what he was about when he refused bail.' The inference here is that it was pre-arranged that a friend of Edalji's would do a fresh crime, in order to clear him. Was ever a more unfair utterance! It was, 'Heads I win, tails you lose!' If no crimes occur, then it is clear we have the villain under lock and key. If crimes do occur, then it is clear that he is deep in conspiracy with others. As a matter of fact, both Edalji's decision to remain in gaol and his remark were the most proper and natural things in the world. He believed that there was a strong conspiracy against him. In the face of the letters he had every reason to believe so. So long as he was in his cell he was safe, he thought, from this conspiracy. Perhaps another crime would be committed, and in that case, he thought, in the innocence of his heart, that it would clear him. In his wildest dreams he could never have imagined that such a crime would be fitted in as a link in the chain against him.

A crime was committed, and it occurred upon Sept. 21, between Edalji's committal and trial, whilst he lay in Stafford Gaol. The facts are these: Harry Green was the nineteen-year-old son of a farmer who lived somewhere between the vicarage and the scene of the outrage for which Edalji was convicted. He and Edalji knew each other slightly, as neighbours in the country must do, but how slight was their acquaintance may be shown by the fact that when, in the course of my inquiry, I asked Edalji what Green's writing was like, he had to admit that he had never seen it. Consider the utter want of common ground between the two men, the purblind, studious teetotal young lawyer of twenty-seven, and the young Yeomanry trooper of nineteen, one of a set of boisterous young fellows, who made a centre of mirth and also of mischief at each annual training. Edalji entered no public-house, and was at work from early morning to late at night. Where was there room for that blood-brotherhood which would make the one man risk any danger and sacrifice his own horse for the sake of the other?

Green's charger was found disembowelled. It was not a very valuable animal. In one estimate it is placed at five pounds. Whether it was insured or not there is a conflict of evidence. For days there was scare and conjecture. Then, at the end of that time, it was known that Green had signed a confession which admitted that he had himself killed his own horse. That confession undoubtedly exists, but Green, having had a week or two to think things over, and having in the meantime got a ticket to South Africa, suddenly went back on his own confession, and declared, with much circumstantiality of detail, that he had not done it, and that the confession had been bullied out of him by the police. One or other statement of Green's must be a falsehood, and I have sufficient reason myself, in the shape of evidence which has been set before me, to form a very clear opinion what the actual facts of the case were. When a final clearing of the case arrives, and there is a renewed inquiry on the basis that Edalji is innocent, and that the actual perpetrators have never been punished, there are many facts which may be laid before the authority who conducts it. Meanwhile the task which lies immediately before me is not to show who did do the crime—though that, I think, is by no means an insuperable problem—but that Edalji did not and could not have done them. I will leave young Green there, with his two contradictory statements, and I will confine myself to his relation with the case, whichever of the statements is true.

And, first of all, here are the police who claim to hold his written confession. Then why did they not prosecute? It will not do to say that it is not a crime to kill your own horse. It is not a crime to shoot your own horse from humane motives, but it is at all times a crime, as the Society for the Prevention of Cruelty to Animals would very quickly show, to disembowel a horse on a dark night, be it fifty times your own. Here is an outrage of the same sort which has convulsed the countryside for so many months, it is brought home by his own confession to the offender, and yet the police refuse to prosecute, and connive at the man's flight from the country. But why? If it was not that the prosecution of Green would bring out facts which would interfere with the successful prosecution of Edalji, then, again, I ask, why? Far be it from me to be unjust to the police, but again it is their own really extraordinary behaviour which drives one to seek for hypotheses. The Home Office says that all inquiry has been made in this case, and that everything has been investigated and the matter closed. That is the official answer I received only a fortnight ago. Then can the Home Office give any good reason why Green was not prosecuted? The point is a very vital one.

Green was present at Edalji's trial, was not called, and left afterwards for South Africa. He had been subpœnaed by the police, and that, no doubt, was what prevented the defence from calling him. But had they done so, and had he spoken in public as he has spoken in private, there would have been an end of all possibility, according to my information, of the great miscarriage which ensued. It may be noted before leaving this extraordinary incident that the reason given by Green in his confession was that the horse had to be killed, having been injured in the Yeomanry training, but nowhere has he ever said a word to suggest that he was acting in collusion with George Edalji.

And now at last we come to the trial. Here, as at every point of this extraordinary case, there are irregularities which will be more fitly dealt with by a lawyer. Suffice it that though the case was of such importance that it is generally thought that it should not have been at Quarter Sessions at all, it was at the lesser of the courts which make up that tribunal that it was at last tried. In Court A a skilled lawyer presided. Sir Reginald Hardy, who conducted Court B, had no legal training. I have not a word to say against his desire to be impartial and fair, but here was a young man, accused of one of a series of crimes for which the whole county was longing to find someone who might be made an example of. The jury would naturally have the same feelings as their fellow-citizens. Hence it was peculiarly necessary to have a cold legal mind to cool their ardour and keep them on firm ground of fact, far from prejudice and emotion. Yet it was in the court of the layman that the case was tried.

The ground over which the prosecution advanced is already familiar to the reader. We have the clothes which have now become 'wet'. They were merely 'damp' in the previous inquiry, and we have the word of the vicar that this dampness was imperceptible to him, coupled with the fact that any bloodstains would then have been liquid. We have the down-at-heel boot, which was fitted into impressions which must have been made after rain, whereas the whole police theory was that the crime was committed before the rain. We have the bloodstains which sank from smears into two threepenny-bit patches, and we have the hairs which made their appearance thirteen hours after the coat had been in the hands of the police, and after it had been associated with the strip of horse's hide. Then came the letters. There was a strong probability that whoever wrote the letters knew something of the crimes. What matter that the letters actually accused Edalji himself and vilified him in all sorts of ways? What matter that one villainous postcard in the same writing as the others was posted at Wolverhampton when he was at Aberystwyth? What matter that in the original series of anonymous letters the writer had said, 'Do you think we cannot imitate your kid's writing?' None of these things weighed as compared with the expression of opinion by an expert that the letters were in George Edalji's own writing. As the unfortunate prisoner listened to such an opinion he must have felt that he was in some nightmare dream. And who was the expert who expressed these views which weighed so heavily with the jury? It was Mr Thomas Gurrin. And what is the record of Mr Thomas Gurrin? His nemesis was soon to come. Within a year he had to present himself before the Beck Committee, and admit the terrible fact that through his evidence an innocent man had suffered prolonged incarceration. Does this fact alone not convince my readers that an entire reconsideration of the Edalji case is a most pressing public duty?

There is absolutely the whole evidence—the coat-boot-razor business, the letter business, the so-called incriminating expressions which I have already analysed, and the one fact,

which I admit did really deserve consideration, that a group of
schoolboys with whom once a month young Edalji may have
travelled were known also to the writer of the letters. That is all.
I have shown what each link is worth. And on that evidence a
young gentleman, distinguished already in an honourable
profession, was torn from his family, suffered all the indignities
of a convict, was immured for three of the best years of his life,
was struck from the roll on which with such industry and
self-denial he had written his name, and had every torture
made ten-fold more bitter by the thought of the vicar at home,
of his mother and of his sister, so peculiarly sensitive, from their
position in the church, to the scoff and the derision of those
around them. It is a tale which makes a man hot with indignation as he reads it.

One word as to the evidence of the family, upon which so
much depends. It has been asserted that it was given in a
peculiar way, which shook the confidence of the jury. I have
had some experience of the Edaljis, and I can say with confidence that what seemed peculiar to the jury arose from extreme
anxiety to speak the absolute, exact truth. An experienced
barrister who knew them well remarked to me that they were
the most precisely truthful people he had ever met—'bad
witnesses,' he added, 'as they are so conscientious that they lay
undue stress upon any point of doubt.'

It must be admitted that the defence was not as strong as it
might have been made, which does not seem to have been due
to any shortcomings of the counsel so much as to a deficiency in
the supply of information. The fact is that the consciousness of
innocence was in this case a danger, as it caused some slackness
in guarding every point. So far as I can find, the whole story of
the early persecutions of 1888 and of 1893–5 was not gone into,
nor was their probable connection with that of 1903 pointed
out. The blindness of Edalji, a most vital fact, was not supported by an array of evidence; indeed, I think that it was
hardly mentioned at all. At all points one finds things which
might have been better, but even granting that, one cannot but
feel the amazement, which Sir George Lewis has voiced, when
the jury brought in 'Guilty,' and Sir Reginald Hardy sentenced
the prisoner to seven years.

Now, once again, let me state the double dilemma of the police, before I leave this portion of my statement. Either Edalji did the crime before ten o'clock that night or after ten o'clock that night. The latter case must be laughed out of a common-sense court by the fact that his father, the vicar, spent the night within a few feet of him, that the small vicarage was bolted and barred, no one being heard to leave it, and that the police watchers outside saw no one leave it. If that does not establish an alibi what could? On the other hand, supposing that he did it before ten, or rather before 9.30, the time of his return home. You have to face the supposition that after returning from a long day's work in Birmingham he sallied out in a coat which he was only known to wear in the house, performed a common-place mission at the boot-shop in the village, then, blind as he was, hurried off for three-quarters of a mile, through difficult, tortuous ways, with fences to climb and railway lines to cross (I can answer for it, having myself trod every foot of it), to commit a ghastly and meaningless crime, entirely foreign to his studious and abstinent nature; that he then hurried back another three-quarters of a mile to the vicarage, arrived so composed and tidy as to attract no attention, and sat down quietly to the family supper, the whole expedition from first to last being under an hour. The mere statement of this alternative supposition seems grotesque enough, but on the top of the gross, inherent improbability you are up against the hard facts that the pony was bleeding freely in the morning, and could not have so bled all night, that the veterinary surgeon deposed that the wound could not possibly be more than six hours old, no other veterinary surgeon being called to contradict this statement, and that the footprints on which the police relied were worthless unless left after the rain, which began at twelve. Add to this that the pony was seen standing apparently all right by the police themselves at eleven o'clock, and the case then seems to me to be overpoweringly convincing. Take whichever supposition you like, and I say that it is demonstrably false, and an insult to common-sense, to suppose that George Edalji committed the crime for which, through the action of the Staffordshire police, the error of an expert, and the gross stupidity of a jury, he has been made to suffer so cruelly.

I do not know that there is much to add, save a bare recital of the events which have occurred since then. After Edalji's conviction the outrages continued unabated, and the epidemic of anonymous letters raged as ever. The November outrage upon Mr Stanley's horses was never traced, but there was some good local information as to the author of that crime, and a widespread conviction in the district, which may have been utterly unjust, that the police were not too anxious to push the matter, as any conviction would certainly disturb the one which they had already obtained. This incident, also, will furnish some evidence for the coming inquiry. Finally, in March, 1904, a man, named Farrington, was convicted for injuring some sheep. No attempt has ever been made to trace any connection between this man and Edalji. In the Green case not only was there no attempt to prove complicity between Green and Edalji, but I have evidence to show that the police had a most positive statement from Green that he had nothing to do with Edalji, obtained under circumstances which make it perfectly convincing. And yet, in face of this fact, Mr Disturnal, the mouthpiece of the police at the trial, was permitted to say, referring to this outrage: 'The letters which would be read would show that the writer of them was not acting alone, but in conjunction with some other people, and he put it to the jury, what was more likely than that, if there was a gang operating in the way suggested, one of its members would commit a similar outrage in order to create evidence for the defence?' Counsel, no doubt, spoke according to his instructions; but what are we to think of those from whom such instructions issued, since they had the clearest proof that there was no connection between Green and Edalji? Such incidents shake one's confidence in British justice to the very foundations, for it is clear that the jury, already prejudiced by the nature of the crimes, were hoodwinked into giving their conviction.

A few words as to the sequel. The friends of the prisoner, organised and headed by Mr R.D. Yelverton (late Chief Justice of the Bahamas), to whose long, ceaseless, and unselfish exertions Edalji will owe so much when the hour of triumph comes, drew up a memorial to the Home Secretary, setting forth some of the facts as here recorded. This petition for reconsideration was signed by ten thousand people, including hundreds of lawyers and many K.C.'s, and was reinforced by the strongest letters testifying to Edalji's character from men who must have known him intimately, including Mr. Denning, his schoolmaster; Mr Ludlow, the solicitor with whom he was for five years articled; the Honorary Secretary and Reader of the Birmingham Law Society, and many others. Now every man of the world will admit that the schoolmaster's testimony is of very great importance, for any traits of cruelty will show themselves most clearly at that age. This is what Mr. Denning says: 'During the five years your son George was here I have never known him commit any acts of cruelty or unkindness. I have always found him a thoroughly upright and well-principled youth, in whom I could place every confidence.' Grier, his school-mate, writes: 'He was several years older than myself, but always treated me with great kindness. I never knew him cruel to any animal, and from what I knew of him then—for I came to know him well—I should say he was quite incapable of any act of cruelty.' How foolish the loose gossip and surmise of Stafford seem in the face of page after page of testimonials such as these.

The memorial had no effect, and some inquiry should certainly be made as to how its fate was determined. It would be indeed a vicious circle if a police prosecution, when doubted, is referred back again to the police for report. I cannot imagine anything more absurd and unjust in an Oriental despotism than this. And yet any superficial independent investigation, or even a careful perusal of the memorial, must have convinced any reasonable human being. The friends of Edalji, headed by Mr Yelverton, naturally demanded to see the dossier at the Home Office, but, as in the Beck case, the seekers after justice were denied access to the very documents which they needed in order to prove their case and confute their opponents.

I have said it was as in the Beck case. I might well have gone to a more classic example, for in all its details this seems to me to form a kind of squalid Dreyfus case. The parallel is extraordinary close. You have a Parsee, instead of a Jew, with a young and promising career blighted, in each case the degradation from a profession and the campaign for redress and restoration,

in each case questions of forgery and handwriting arise, with
Esterhazy in the one, and the anonymous writer in the other.
Finally, I regret to say that in the one case you have a clique of
French officials going from excess to excess in order to cover an
initial mistake, and that in the other you have the Staffordshire
police acting in the way I have described.

And that brings me to what is the most painful part of my
statement, and the one which I would be most glad to shirk
were it possible for me to do so. No account of the case is
complete which does not deal with the attitude taken up by
Captain Anson, Chief Constable of Staffordshire, against this
unhappy young man. It must, I suppose, have taken its root in
those far-off days from 1892 to 1895, when Edalji was little
more than a boy, and when Sergeant Upton, for reasons which
make a tale by themselves, sent reports against him to his
superior at Stafford. It was at that early date that Captain
Anson delivered those two memorable dicta: 'You may tell
your son at once that I will not believe any profession of
ignorance,' and 'I will endeavour to get the offender a dose of
penal servitude.'

Now, I have no doubt Captain Anson was quite honest in his
dislike, and unconscious of his own prejudice. It would be folly
to think otherwise. But men in his position have no right to
yield to such feelings. They are too powerful, others are too
weak, and the consequences are too terrible. As I trace the
course of events this dislike of their chief's filtered down until it
came to imbue the whole force, and when they had George
Edalji they did not give him the most elementary justice, as is
shown by the fact that they did not prosecute Green at a time
when his prosecution would have endangered the case against
Edalji.

I do not know what subsequent reports prevented justice
from being done at the Home Office—(there lies the wicked-
ness of the concealed dossier)—but this I do know, that, instead
of leaving the fallen man alone, every possible effort was made
after the conviction to blacken his character, and that of his
father, so as to frighten off anyone who might be inclined to
investigate his case. When Mr Yelverton first took it up, he had
a letter over Captain Anson's own signature, saying, under

date Nov. 8, 1903: 'It is right to tell you that you will find it a simple waste of time to attempt to prove that George Edalji could not, owing to his position and alleged good character, have been guilty of writing offensive and abominable letters. His father is as well aware as I am of his proclivities in the direction of anonymous writing, and several other people have personal knowledge on the same subject.'

Now, both Edalji and his father declare on oath that the former never wrote an anonymous letter in his life, and on being applied to by Mr Yelverton for the names of the 'several other people' no answer was received. Consider that this letter was written immediately after the conviction, and that it was intended to nip in the bud the movement in the direction of mercy. It is certainly a little like kicking a man when he is down.

Since I took up the case I have myself had a considerable correspondence with Captain Anson. I find myself placed in a difficult position as regards these letters, for while the first was marked 'Confidential,' the others have no reserve. One naturally supposes that when a public official writes upon a public matter to a perfect stranger, the contents are for the public. No doubt one might also add, that when an English gentleman makes most damaging assertions about other people he is prepared to confront these people, and to make good his words. Yet the letters are so courteous to me personally that it makes it exceedingly difficult for me to use them for the purpose of illustrating my thesis—viz., the strong opinion which Captain Anson had formed against the Edalji family. One curious example of this is that during fifteen years that the vicarage has been a centre of debate, the chief constable has never once visited the spot or taken counsel personally with the inmates.

For three years George Edalji endured the privations of Lewes and of Portland. At the end of that time the indefatigable Mr Yelverton woke the case up again, and *Truth* had an excellent series of articles demonstrating the impossibility of the man's guilt. Then the case took a new turn, as irregular and illogical as those which had preceded it. At the end of his third year, out of seven, the young man, though in good health, was suddenly released without a pardon. Evidently the authorities were shaken, and compromised with their consciences in this fashion. But this cannot be final. The man is guilty, or he is not. If he is he deserves every day of his seven years. If he is not, then we must have apology, pardon, and restitution. There can obviously be no middle ground between these extremes.

And what else is needed besides this tardy justice to George Edalji? I should say that several points suggest themselves for the consideration of any small committee. One is the reorganisation of the Staffordshire Constabulary from end to end; a second is an inquiry into any irregularity of procedure at Quarter Sessions; the third and most important is a stringent inquiry as to who is the responsible man at the Home Office, and what is the punishment for his delinquency, when in this case, as in that of Beck, justice has to wait for years upon the threshold, and none will raise the latch. Until each and all of these questions is settled a dark stain will remain upon the administrative annals of this country.

I have every sympathy for those who deprecate public agitations of this kind on the ground that they weaken the power of the forces which make for law and order, by shaking the confidence of the public. No doubt they do so. But every effort has been made in this case to avoid this deplorable necessity. Repeated applications for justice under both Administrations have met with the usual official commonplaces, or have been referred back to those who are obviously interested parties.

Amid the complexity of life and the limitations of intelligence any man may do an injustice, but how is it possible to go on again and again reiterating the same one? If the continuation of the outrages, the continuation of the anonymous letters, the discredit cast upon Gurrin as an expert, the confession of a culprit that he had done a similar outrage, and finally the exposition of Edalji's blindness, do not present new fact to modify a jury's conclusion, what possible new fact would do so? But the door is shut in our faces. Now we turn to the last tribunal of all, a tribunal which never errs when the facts are fairly laid before them, and we ask the public of Great Britain whether this thing is to go on.

Arthur Conan Doyle
Undershaw, Hindhead. January, 1907.

That was the main evidence that Conan Doyle presented as proof of George Edalji's innocence: over-argued in some place and rather dubious in others (Edalji's supposed near-blindness, for instance, must surely have hindered his career as a solicitor and writer if it was as bad as all that), but convincing nonetheless, and further evidence was offered in a detailed analysis of handwriting samples. Edalji was free but not pardoned, and this was what outraged him and his defender: so if George Edalji was not guilty of the crimes, who was? Conan Doyle thought he knew, and sent the following statement to the authorities.

At the time of the outrages, roughly July, 1903, Royden Sharp had a conversation alone with Mrs Greatorex, who is the wife of Mr W.A. Greatorex, Littleworth Farm, Hednesford, who was appointed Trustee at the time of the death of Peter Sharp, the father, in November, 1893. To this gentleman, Mr Greatorex, I owe much assistance in working out the case. In the course of the conversation referred to above, Royden Sharp—after alluding to the outrages—went to a cupboard, and produced a horse lancet of unusual size. He showed this to Mrs Greatorex, saying, 'This is what they kill the cattle with.' Mrs Greatorex was horrified, and told him to put it away, saying, 'You don't want me to think you are the man, do you?' The possession by Sharp of this unusual instrument of so huge a size is to be explained by the fact that he served for ten months of 1902 on board a cattle boat between Liverpool and America. No doubt he took this lancet when he left the boat. I suggest that the instrument is still in the house, and could be secured in case of an arrest.

The fact that this was true, and that this actually was the instrument with which the crimes were committed is corroborated by the following considerations:—

That the wounds in all the earlier outrages up to August 18th were of a peculiar character, which could not have been inflicted by any other weapon. In every case there was a shallow incision which had cut through the skin and muscles, but had not penetrated the gut. Had any knife been plunged in and drawn along it must almost certainly have cut the gut with its point.

The blade in question is like this:

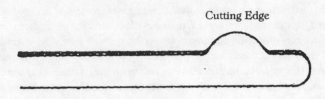

Cutting Edge

It is very sharp, but could not penetrate further than super-ficially. The witnesses who could testify most clearly as to the nature of the wounds are Mr Sambrook, a butcher, who has now removed from Wyrley to Sheffield, but can, I understand, be easily traced, and Mr Forsyth, a veterinary surgeon, of Cannock. I know that Mr Sambrook was struck by the peculiarity of the cuts.

Royden Sharp was in all respects peculiarly fitted to have done these crimes, and there is, apart from this incident, much evidence both before the time of the crimes, during the time and after the time to cause him to be regarded with gravest suspicion. I will, for the moment, put on one side the persecution of the Edaljis (in which he was concerned with his elder brother Wallie in 1892–95) and confine the evidence entirely to that which bears upon the outrages and the anonymous letters of 1903. I will first trace his early career.

EVIDENCE OF HIS CHARACTER BEFORE THE CRIMES

Royden Sharp was born in 1879. He very early showed marked criminal tendencies which took a destructive form. When he was 12 years of age he was found to have set a rick on fire at a Cannock Farm (Hatton's Farm at West Cannock) and his father was forced to pay a considerable compensation.

He was sent at the age of eleven to Walsall Grammar School, where his brother Wallie was an elder scholar at the time. His record at the school was as follows: this is an extract which I got from the school books through the courtesy of Mr Mitchell, the present headmaster.

Xmas, 1890.   Lower 1. Order, 23rd out of 23.
                     Very backward and weak. French and Latin not attempted.

Easter, 1891.	Lower 1. Order, 20th out of 20.
	Dull, homework neglected, begins to improve in Drawing.
Midsummer, 1891.	Lower 1. Order, 18th out of 18.
	Beginning to progress, caned for misbehaviour in class, tobacco chewing, prevarication, and nicknaming.
Xmas, 1891.	Lower 1. Order, 16th out of 16.
	Unsatisfactory, often untruthful. Always complaining or being complained of. Detected cheating, and frequently absent without leave. Drawing improved.
Easter, 1892.	Form 1. Order, 8th out of 8.
	Idle and mischievous, caned daily, wrote to father, falsified school-fellows' marks, and lied deliberately about it. Caned 20 times this term.
Midsummer, 1892.	Played truant, forged letters and initials, removed by his father.

It will thus be seen that forgery, which played a part in the anonymous letters of 1903 was familiar to him as a school boy.

Apart from the forgery which the school records show to have been done by him, the disposition to brutal violence was very marked, and so was that of foisting upon others, often with considerable ingenuity, the misdeeds of his own doing. Out of the anonymous letters which are certainly from his hand at this school period 1892–95, I take the two following expressions:

'I will cut your bowels out,'
'I will open your belly,'

showing curiously how his own thoughts were already turning. If he were left in a railway carriage he would turn up the cushion and slit it on the lower side, so as to let out the horse hair. This evidence is given by Mr Wynne, painter, of 'Clovelly,' Cheslyn Hay, who was at school with him. He adds the following anecdote illustrative of his destructiveness, of his bearing false witness, and of his writing vindictive anonymous letters, all of them qualities which came out 10 years later, in 1903.

During the time that the Edalji family had been deluged with anonymous letters from 1892 to 1895 (which letters I have good reason to believe were from the Sharps), another family in the same village, the Brookes, were plagued in the same way, and in the same handwriting, especially the young son, Fred Brookes. I had failed to find any cause, save colour hatred, in the case of the Edaljis, so I hoped I might get something more definite in the case of young Brookes. This is Wynne's story:—

MR WYNNE'S STATEMENT

'R.S.,' known as 'Speck,' was a small built youth with sharp features. Generally in a sailor's suit, he was the worst scholar in the school for about three years, and remained at the bottom of the first form. He was very fond of chewing tobacco, and I think it was in the Summer holiday of 1892 that he set a rick on fire near Hednesford . . . One evening we were returning by the usual evening train. F.G. Brookes and myself got in the train when Speck came running into the same compartment straight to the end of the carriage, and put his head through the carriage window smashing it all to bits. We all made our way into another compartment. In a day or two after Brookes and myself were charged by one of the railway officials of breaking the carriage window. We found out that Sharp had told of us, that it was us, not himself. Then we sought the station master, and told him how it happened, and Sharp had to pay for it, and he was also caught cutting the straps of the window, and had to pay, I think, more than once; his father was asked to take him away from the school as they could not do any good with him. He was always into mischief and getting others into trouble. The next I heard was he was sent to sea.

'If my memory serves me right the first letters that I heard of were sent to Mr W.H. Brookes, some time after the railway carriage incident, in a large school handwriting, saying that 'Your kid and Wynn's kid have been spitting in an old woman's face on Walsall station,' and requesting monies to be sent to Walsall Post Office. The second one was threatening to prosecute if the money was not sent.'

Thus the receipt of the anonymous letters by Brookes immediately followed a cause of feud between young Brookes and Royden Sharp.

Having been expelled from school, Royden Sharp was apprenticed to a butcher, thus learning to use a knife upon animals. The butcher's name was Meldon, I think, he still lives at Cannock. In November, 1893, the father died, and W.A. Greatorex, of Littleworth Farm, became Royden's Trustee.

This gentleman is an excellent witness, and ready to help the ends of justice in any way. It was to his wife that the implied confession was made. For two years, 1894 and 1895, this gentleman had much trouble with the lad. Finally he sent him to sea. He went to sea from Liverpool on December 30th in the ship 'General Roberts,' belonging to Lewis Davies & Co., 5, Fenwick Street, Liverpool. He went as apprentice.

From the time he left the letters, hoaxes, &c., which had kept the countryside in a turmoil, ceased completely, and were not renewed until his return in 1903. I may remark in passing that Edalji was at home all this time, and that this fact alone would, one would have thought, have awakened the suspicions of the police and shown them who was the author of the troubles. I am told, but have not verified the fact, that the last anonymous hoax on the Edaljis was an advertisement in a Blackpool paper, about the end of December, 1895—Blackpool being the pleasure resort of Liverpool.

Royden Sharp does not, so far as my enquiries go, appear to have acted badly aboard ship. He finished his apprenticeship in 1900, and afterwards gained a third Mate's certificate. He came home late in 1901, but shortly after got a billet on board a cattle ship to America, where his natural brutality was probably not lessened, and where he, no doubt, got the huge horse lancet which Mrs Greatorex can depose to having seen in his hand.

The Wyrley outrages upon cattle were begun while Royden Sharp was at home, and he was in the district during the whole time of their continuance. Whoever committed the outrages must have been in a position to get into and out of his house at all hours of the night without being observed either by the police or by the other inmates of the house, if they were not conniving at the crimes. Royden Sharp's house was peculiarly well situated for this. He lived alone with his mother and his sister, his brother Wallie coming and going. There was no servant or stranger to check his doings. The back door opened into a garden which led into the fields, so that he could get right away without going down any road or running any risk of being seen. The man who did the outrages must certainly have been a man of cosiderable nerve and activity—able to handle animals, with an almost reckless daring which prompted him to do these outrages under the very nose of the police. As an ex-sailor and an ex-butcher Royden Sharp united all these qualities. Compare him with the purblind and studious young lawyer, Edalji.

The crimes were accompanied by a series of anonymous letters, some of which point straight to the Sharp family. They were so designed as to implicate young Edalji on the one hand, and Wilfred Greatorex on the other. Now Edalji has always been a butt of the Sharp family (Edalji does not know Sharp, so that the origin of this hatred may be mere colour prejudice), and on the other hand the Sharps bore a grudge against their own trustee who had regulated their money matters in a business-like way which was not always to their mind. Therefore, in implicating Edalji and Greatorex, Sharp was bringing down two birds with one stone, and gratifying a double animosity. The second letter of the Greatorex series says, 'I know Holton and Lyndop, Guy, Harvey, Phillips, and many a score.'

Now, these people were as follows:—Holton was the Little-worth doctor, Lyndop the local timekeeper at the Colliery, Guy the local butcher, Harvey an official in the Colliery, Phillips a shopkeeper hard by. They were the people who were not, and could not, be known to young Edalji, living miles away from him; but they belonged to the immediate group who surrounded the Sharp and Greatorex families. They lived two stations down the line from Edalji, whom everyone describes as a very retiring man who made no friends. How could he know these people? But they were put in by Sharp because they were the people whom Greatorex knew, and in putting them in he really proved his own guilt, for he and his family were the only people who could know exactly the same circle. This piece of internal evidence alone must convince any independent and intelligent observer that Edalji could not have written these 'Greatorex' letters, and that if Greatorex did not, which all admit to be true, then all the evidence points to the Sharps, who were accomplished forgers and mystifiers as already shown.

Apart from the letters bearing upon the crimes, other anonymous letters of an obscene description were circulating in the district at this period. I have seen a letter from one who was present dated August 3rd, 1903, saying that a conference was held as to the authorship of these letters that day in the presence of Mr Greatorex, now dead (no relation of the other), who was a local bank manager, and Inspector Campbell, now living at Cannock. The letter wound up, 'I believe that Royden Sharp will be arrested before evening.' From this I infer that the local police had evidence of Sharp's writing anonymous letters at this time. This evidence should be available at the trial, and should show that this was a habit of his. I believe that August 3rd did mark a cessation of letters for some time.

There are many points of internal evidence in the letters (the so-called 'Greatorex' letters) which point to Royden Sharp, apart from the fact that they appeared after his return to the district, and that they deal with a number of people well known to him (and unknown to Edalji). In all the 1892–95 letters there is, so far as I have seen, no mention of the sea. In the very first of the 'Greatorex' letters in 1903 there are two or three allusions to the sea, most natural for anyone who had just left it. He advises in his letter that some boy be sent to sea as an apprentice which was, as I have shown, Royden Sharp's own experience.

The writer uses the curious expression that a hook did the crimes. The instrument which Sharp showed to Mrs Greatorex has a hooky appearance, and could be carried shut in the pocket, as the writer asserts that the 'Hook' actually was. A sharp hook in the ordinary sense of a hook could not be so carried without cutting the cloth.

The writer says that he feels inclined to put his head on the rails where the train runs from Hednesford to Cannock. This is the actual stretch of rail near the Sharp's [sic] house (and is some distance from Wyrley where Edalji lives).

In June, 1903, a letter (still preserved) was received with the Rugeley post mark, signed 'A Lover of Justice,' and addressed to George Edalji. It was asking him to leave the district for a time, so as to be away when the next crime was done, as otherwise he would be in danger of being taken for it. The writer of this letter I identify as being the same as the former anonymous letters of 1895; which I also identify as having been done by Wallie Sharp. There would be no difficulty in getting expert evidence as to the hands being the same. Wallie Sharp was acting as apprentice to an electrical engineer at the time, and was much in the small neighbouring towns of which Rugeley is one. It is to be observed that in the letter in question occurs the phrase 'you are not a right sort.' This phrase occurs also in one of the Greatorex letters. This points to Wallie's complicity in the Greatorex letters, or his brother's phrase may have lingered in his mind. It could hardly be coincidence that the same phrase could occur in both letters. Wallie Sharp died in South Africa in November, 1906.

I now come to what I look upon as a very important piece of evidence, indeed, I think it is conclusive as regards the anonymous letters. Some time after Edalji's arrest there began a series of anonymous letters, signed 'G.H. Darby,' the writer claiming to be Captain of the Wyrley Gang. These letters— many of which I have seen—are all in the same writing and, though very roughly done, contain some of the characteristics of Royden Sharp's writing, especially an r made like x and sometimes so exaggerated as to be almost x which occurs from boyhood in Royden Sharp's writing. About November, 1903, some of these letters arrived from Rotherham, near Sheffield. The police, I think, had some, and others were received by a local paper, the Wolverhampton *Star*. The writer was evidently a Cannock man, and I should think few Cannock men would at any time visit Rotherham. Now, I have found the porter, whose name is A. Beenham, Drayman, near Baptist Chapel, Cannock Road, Chadsmoor, near Cannock, who in November carried Royden Sharp's box to the station, and observed that it was addressed to Rotherham. The Darby letters said that the Captain would return before Xmas, and I believe Sharp actually did so. This seems to me perfectly conclusive, as regards the identity of Royden Sharp with G.H. Darby, and the latter boasted that he was the author of the outrages.

Another significant fact is as follows:—On September 29th, 1903, there was an anonymous notice that 'it was decided to "slice up" ten wenches between November 1st and 20th and 10 after Xmas,' repeating a threat which had already been uttered in the second 'Greatorex' letter. The dates are curious in view of the fact that Royden Sharp would be away as already shown from November to Xmas. The announcement caused much terror in the district, which was increased by the following incident:—A woman and little girl (Mrs Jarius Handley, Great Wyrley, is [the] woman's name) were coming from Wyrley station one evening, soon after, where they had been buying some papers for sale. They met two men in the road. One of them caught the girl by the throat, and held in his hand something that gleamed. They both screamed, on which the man ran away, crying to his comrade who had gone on: 'All right, Jack, I am coming.' I suggest that this man was Royden Sharp, and that his companion was Jack Hart, a dissolute butcher, of the neighbourhood, and a friend of Sharp's. The little girl declared to her mother that she had been stopped once before by the same young man, and proceeded to give a minute description of him. She said that he had a round face, no moustache, about 5ft. 8in. in height, a dark suit, and a shiny peaked cap, which was exactly Royden Sharp's sailor-like costume. I suggest that after Sharp's arrest this girl be allowed an opportunity of identifying him. I am informed that from the time that his description got about Sharp gave up wearing this style of dress.

There was another of the series of anonymous letters which came from London, and was said by the writer to have been written in a Lockhart's coffee-house there. It was dated '———— ——19th' (month can be found by further search) and the writer said he had gone up to London from Birmingham that day. On enquiry Mr Beaumont, of Wolverhampton Road, Cannock,—who has assisted me much—discovered that Royden Sharp had actually left Cannock for Birmingham upon the morning of that same day—19th. Mr Hunt, the local station master, was his informant.

I will now recapitulate in condensed form the statement which has been here set out at length. Royden Sharp can be shown to have been the culprit:

1   Because of his showing the weapon to Mrs Greatorex.

2   Because the wounds could only be produced by such an instrument as he showed.

3   Because only such an instrument fits in with the description in the letters.

4 Because being a butcher and a man from a cattle ship he was able to do such crimes which would be very hard for any ordinary man.

5 Because in many points of the anonymous letters there is internal evidence pointing to Royden Sharp.

6 Because he had a proved record of writing anonymous letters, of forgery, of diabolical mischief, and of bearing false witness, all of which qualities came out here.

7 Because he went to Rotherham at the time when letters bearing on the crimes came from Rotherham.

8 Because he is correctly described by a girl, who saw a man endeavouring to carry out, or pretend to carry out, the threats in the letters.

9 Because the actual handwriting in many of the letters bears a resemblance to Royden Sharp's own old writing. It is impossible now to get any specimen of his actual writing, as he is most guarded in writing anything. Why should he be if he is innocent?

10 I am informed (but have not yet verified the fact) that in one of the anonymous letters occurs the phrase, 'I am as Sharp as Sharp can be.'

This seems to me to be in itself a complete case, and if I—a stranger in the district—have been able to collect it, I cannot doubt that fresh local evidence would come out after his arrest. He appears to have taken very little pains to hide his proceedings, and how there could have been at any time any difficulty in pointing him out as the criminal is to me an extraordinary thing.

If further evidence were needed in order to assure a conviction, there are two men who could certainly supply it. These men are:—

Harry Green, formerly of Wyrley Farm, Wyrley, now in South Africa.

The other is Jack Hart, Butcher, Bridgtown, near Cannock.

Either of these men, if properly handled, would certainly turn King's evidence. They both undoubtedly knew all about

Sharp. Others who know something, but possibly not enough, as they were only on the edge of the affair, are Fred Brookes (formerly of Wyrley, now in Manchester), Thomas and Grinsell, all of the local Yeomanry. It seems to me that Sharp did no more outrages with his own hands after the arrest of Edalji in August. The next outrage was admittedly done by Harry Green, who can be shown, when in doubt as to what he should do, to have sent a note to someone else, which note was answered from London in a letter written on telegram forms, now to be seen in the Home Office. This answer was, I believe from the writing, from Royden Sharp. It is worth noting on the evidence of Mr Arrowsmith, of the Cannock Star Tea Company, who has done most excellent work on this case, that Green accepted all Arrowsmith's remarks good-humouredly, but on the latter saying 'Sharp should be where Edalji now is,' he at once became very angry. The November outrage was done upon Stanley's horses by Jack Hart, the butcher, acting in collusion with Sharp. This makes really a separate case.

If it should be found possible to get Mrs Sharp in the box, she would depose as she has told Mrs Greatorex, that Royden Sharp is strangely affected by the new moon, and that on such occasions she had to closely watch him. At such times he seems to be a maniac, and Mr Greatorex has himself heard him laughing like one. In this connection it is to be observed that the first four outrages occurred on February 2, April 2, May 3, and June 6, which in each case immediately follows the date of the new moon. The point of a connection between the outrages and the moon is referred to in one of the 'Greatorex' letters, so it was present in the mind of the writer.

I cannot end this statement without acknowledging how much I owe to the unselfish exertions of Mr Greatorex, of Littleworth Farm, Mr Arrowsmith, of the Star Tea Company, Cannock, and Mr Beaumont, of Wolverhampton Road, Cannock, without whose help I should have been powerless.

(Signed) *Arthur Conan Doyle.*

Undershaw, Hindhead

AFTERWORD

Did this bring about the immediate arrest of Royden Sharpe, and a trial for these offences, followed by a Free Pardon and compensation for George Edalji, and complete vindication for Conan Doyle? No. And the blank refusal of the authorities to even consider these matters soured Doyle for life. He was never taken into the police's confidence, and became convinced that the case had been mishandled and the resultant mess glossed over: what we would now call a cover-up.

'The mistake that I made, so far as my own interests were concerned,' he wrote later, 'was that having got on the track of the miscreant I let the police and the Home Office know my results before they were absolutely completed.' Whether the case against Sharpe would have stood up in court, founded as it was on hearsay and with little in the way of direct evidence, is a moot point, for likelihood is very different from proof. No writer on the case has disputed George Edalji's innocence, however, and someone *committed these crimes, which continued sporadically until 1914.*

So messy reality spoiled the neat detective-story ending, though it saved Edalji, and helped Conan Doyle pull his life together again. George Edalji, indeed, was a guest at the reception when Conan Doyle married his second wife, and practised successfully as a solicitor for the rest of his long life.

Now John D. MacDonald tells us just how confusing witnesses *can be...*

JOHN D. MACDONALD

Coppolino Revisited

Here is a direct quote from the testimony of Doctor Charles J. Umberger, Toxicologist with the office of the Chief Medical Examiner in New York City. He and the late Dr Milton Helpern had gone to Naples, Florida, in April of 1967 to testify for the Prosecution in the trial of Carl Coppolino, anesthesiologist, at which he was convicted of second-degree murder for killing his wife with an injection of succinylcholine chloride, a paralyzing compound used to stop the patient from breathing on his own during major surgery on the lungs or heart.

With the glazed eyes of the jurors upon him, Umberger said, 'Now this case was treated as a general unknown, and when the analysis was started, tissue was set up to cover all categories. For example, one of the first things that was done was to take a piece of kidney. The kidney was ashed and a sample was put on a spectrograph. The purpose of the spectrograph is to determine whether there were any metal compounds. With the spectrographic plate, all but three of the metals can be excluded. Another sample was subjected to what we call a digestion, using an old-fashioned Reinsch Test, plating out the metal on copper. Arsenic, antimony, and mercury, along with silver and bismuth plated out on copper, and from that one can subject the copper plate to an X-ray fluorescent machine and determine whether any of those three metals are there. That is necessary, because in spectrographic analysis there is what is called the volatile metals and these distill out of the crater or the arc and would not produce the spectrum . . .'

As if that wasn't enough, a little further along he got into the procedures by which his lab had isolated and identified the components of the succinylcholine chloride which had killed Carmela Coppolino.

He said, 'The one [test] depends upon the formation of what we call ferric hydroxamic imides. That happens to be what we call a generic test for esters, which is another type of organic structure. Succinic acid is an acid and shouldn't react with this reagent. In working with it, what we discovered is if the succinic acid is sublimed at ordinary atmospheric pressure that as a result of that heating it is turned into the anhydride. In other words the two acid groups kind of lock together and water is lost, and then subsequent to that we found that if we put in a little phosphorous pentoxide in that tube and carried out sublimation we could convert the succinic acid without a lot of manipulation over the anhydride.'

What sort of people were soaking up all this great information?

The jury was composed of twelve men—a retired naval officer, a refrigerator repairman, a construction-crew foreman, two motel owners, a retired clothing salesman, a furniture salesman, a mortgage broker, a maintenance engineer, a fisherman, an air-conditioner serviceman, and a semiretired plumber.

F. Lee Bailey brought on his team of experts to refute the testimony of Helpern and Umberger. I quote from the Naples newspaper the following weekend: 'One of the most fascinating and immediate impressions received by all was the paradox of conclusions reached by these highly qualified scientists in their efforts to determine what happens to the drug after it is injected into a muscle or vein of the human body.'

A Dr Moya, Chairman of the Department of Anesthesiology at the University of Miami, had testified, in just as much stupifying detail as Umberger, that Umberger's experiments were flawed and his conclusions improper. He said that the compounds found in Carmela Coppolino's body were there in normal amounts and had been released for measurement by the embalming fluid.

The newspaper item ends: 'You pays your money and you takes your choice. And a man's life rests on the choice made by the 12 good men and true who listened intently all week from the jury box.'

What do we have then, in this and in other trials where contemporary expert testimony is given by both sides? Not one of those twelve jurors knew diddly about anesthesiology, toxicology, biochemistry, and pharmacology. They could *not* follow and comprehend the expert testimony. The prosecution lawyers and the defense lawyers knew that the jurors could not follow the expert testimony and evaluate it upon its scientific merits. The experts knew this also.

So it is a charade.

Recognizing the fact of charade, one realizes that the jurors will side with that expert who has the best stage presence, who radiates a total confidence in his grasp of the subject at hand, who speaks crisply, with dignity, confidence, and charm, who is neatly and properly dressed and has no distressing mannerisms.

In short, the expert must be precisely the sort of person an advertising agency would select to talk about a new deodorant on national television.

The expert who mumbles, slouches, grimaces, stares into space, and keeps ramming his little finger into his ear and inspecting what he dredges up *might* be a far better scientist than the television commercial chap. But there is no real correlation here. The impressive presence is more likely to be the result of the number of appearances as an expert than the result of academic credentials.

In January of 1977 Melvin M. Belli, sometimes known as the King of Torts, published a syndicated defense of the jury system which appeared op-ed in scores of newspapers.

He wrote:

> After arguing hundreds of cases, both civil and criminal, I do not believe that I have ever seen a jury that did not give the case under submission its honest judgment and deliberation. Contemporary jurors are not swayed by old-fashioned oratory or legal theatrics; thus jury trials have become a precise, orderly business.
>
> Today, jurors take detailed notes during testimony and ask probing questions about the facts and the law. Frequently they will return from their deliberations and ask the judge to have crucial testimony reread or to repeat his instructions on the applicable statutes. Juries do not want to make mistakes—and seldom do.

The question is obvious. How can jurors make honest judgments about a body of knowledge beyond their capacity to comprehend? Are they going to take notes on the ferric hydroxamic imides, and come back out to ask what a Reinsch Test might be?

Trial by jury, using expert witnesses to clarify the testimony of others and add to the body of the case, worked beautifully in a world which was far simpler in all technologies. In a village culture a scout could be called in to testify as to the origin of the arrow which struck the deceased, showing to the jury those points of difference in fletching and notching which indicated the tribe where it had been made.

In a world more compartmentalized, knowledge becomes increasingly impossible to communicate to anyone who has not had a substantial background in the discipline at hand.

A friend of mine has spent most of his life in pure mathematics, in abstractions as subtle as music. He tells me that up until perhaps fifteen years ago it was still possible to explain what he was doing, in rather rough outline, to a bright layman, using analogy, models, little drawings, and so on. But now he tells me that he cannot explain to me where he is and where he is going. He has gone beyond analogy, beyond models and drawings and comprehensible statements. Think of that. What he is doing is out of my reach. And yours. Other disciplines are becoming ever less easy to explain. Computers are playing an ever more active and forceful role in the designing of computers. IBM had a computer exhibit in New York City long ago, a big room full of winking tubes and chuckling sounds. You can hold in one hand a computer that will do everything that one did, and faster.

We have all become that Naples fisherman, wondering at the difference between an ester and an oyster.

Jury trials are becoming ever longer. In notorious trials, the jurors are sequestered for weeks and months. Deadlocked juries are more common. Giving expert testimony has become a profession for scientists who have reason to be disappointed in the rewards from their career alone.

It is possible that the jury system could be saved from its own excesses by a revision of the expert-testimony folkdance.

When it appears that medical or scientific testimony will be a key factor in any case, I would suggest that the prosecution select a single expert to present its side, and the defense do the same. These two gentlemen would then select a third man in their field, satisfactory to both of them. After the third man had listened to the scientific evidence and had a chance to read the documentation and do whatever research might be necessary, there would be a meeting between the experts, the judge, and the attorneys for both sides. The selected expert would give his opinion, and it would be binding on both sides. If, for example, in the Coppolino case, the selected expert backed Umberger's procedures and said that he believed that it had been proven that succinylcholine chloride had been injected into the upper outer quadrant of the left buttock in sufficient quantity to cause death, then the defense would be forced to stipulate that this was indeed so, and it would then be up to the defense to change the plea, or try to show that it would not have been done by the defendant.

If such a procedure were to be instituted in civil and criminal trials we would see trials of less duration. Juries would be more prone to reach agreement on the verdicts. Expenses to both the state and the accused would be dramatically reduced in criminal cases, and reduced for the plaintiff and defendant in civil cases.

I would imagine it would make Mr Belli's court appearances of far less duration and hence not quite so burdensome to the insurance companies and to the patients of the doctors who must pass along the high malpractice premiums to their patients in the form of higher charges for office visits.

I have taken my samples of expert-witness jargon from the Coppolino trial only because I happen to have a complete transcript in my files, and not because I have any feeling that Coppolino was done any disservice by this oppressive conflicting testimony. At this writing he has been a prisoner of the state of Florida for over ten years.

By the time the long days of scientific testimony and the direct and cross and redirect examinations of the seven or eight expert witnesses had gone droning on and on, the twelve jurors had already decided that it was of no moment to them whether or not the succinylcholine chloride was detectable or not.

Here is how the state of mind came about. During the prosecution's direct examination of its leading expert, Dr Milton Helpern, there came an opportunity to project onto a large white wall behind and to Judge Lynn Silvertooth's right, some very sharp-focus slides taken by the Medical Examiner's office. The courtroom was darkened. There were a dozen of these slides. The very first one brought a sick gasping sound from the spectators and press. It showed, in about a five-by-eight-foot projection, Carmela Coppolino, clothing removed, face down, full length, after three and a half months in a New Jersey cemetery.

Successive slides moved in closer and closer, focusing on the left buttock, then on the upper outer quadrant of the left buttock to show a tiny crater and, near it and below it, the dark stains of five bruise marks. States Attorney Frank Schaub had asked Dr Helpern, 'Could they be the type consistent with the use of human force, the fingers? Could they be caused by a hand pressing down on the body?' In his quiet clinical voice Helpern testified that they could be consistent, and testified as to how he had proven through micro-examination that the bruises had been inflicted shortly before death.

The final slides showed magnified photographs of the incision Helpern had made adjacent to the crater, showing that it was indeed a puncture wound along with a needle track deep into the subcutaneous fat of the buttock.

Now then, because Helpern had testified that he could find no other cause of death, and because the defense offered no plausible alternative reason for the needle track, and because the jurors could readily believe that Coppolino as a nonpracticing anesthesiologist would have access to the substance in question, and because a reasonably satisfactory motive and a provable opportunity had been established by the State, the jurors did not care whether or not the presence of that suck-something could be proven beyond the shadow of a doubt. They had seen the unforgettable pictures, the fingermark bruises, and the needle track, and nobody had stepped up to show she had died of anything else.

And so they drowsed through a lot of it.

So let us imagine a similar case where there is no needle track, no pitiful and ghastly slides of the slim dead lady, a case where it really *does* hang on the technical evidence presented.

Want to be a defendant? Want to take your chances in a forum where charm rather than fact is the persuader? Want to pay an additional $50,000 to $150,000 for the transportation, housing, fees, and sustenance of your team of experts, plus the additional legal costs of the preparation and the additional days in court?

Or will you choose arbitration?

Final question. *If* it is known that arbitration of conflicting expert testimony *is* available, and the defendant elects to finance a battle of the experts, will it be more difficult to preserve the presumption of innocence?

One solution to the problem posed by the messy nature of evidence is, simply and blandly, to claim inside knowledge. As I remarked earlier, William Le Queux claimed to have known everyone; here is a little story related by Alan Hynd that is perhaps revealing:

'Le Queux had, while prowling a second-hand book store in Stockholm, come upon a rare book, published in 1869, entitled Secrets of the States of Venice. *The volume, printed in Latin and old Italian, both of which Le Queux understood, gave detailed formulas for the slow, lethal and undetectable poisons by which upper-class Venetians abbreviated associations with enemies, friends and chance acquaintances. In one of his novels, Le Queux made casual reference to* Secrets of the States of Venice, *mentioning that the volume detailed the formulas for ancient, and undetectable poisons without dwelling on the formulas themselves.*

'When Dr Crippen, reading Le Queux in his attic retreat, came upon the reference to the rare old book, his professional curiosity was piqued. Having been grounded in the basic poisons during his studies at the Hospital College in Cleveland and at Ophthalmic Hospital in New York, the doctor wondered what the Venetians had had that modern poisoners did not have. Was it possible that the rare book to which Le Queux referred contained the key to some long-lost knowledge that the medical profession could put to advantage — or, more to the point, knowledge that Dr Crippen himself, ever on the qui vive for a stray pound could, monetize?

'Crippen began to spend his spare time in the second-hand book stalls, trying to track down a copy of Secrets of the States of Venice. *Failing to locate the book,*

he wrote to Le Queux, in March of 1908, for an appointment. For some reason or other, perhaps so that his motives wouldn't be misunderstood, Dr Crippen used the name of Dr Adams in writing to the author. Le Queux made an appointment for Dr Adams to have some Scotch and soda with him at the Devonshire Club. Crippen opened the conversation by saying that he liked LeQeux's mysteries even better than those of Conan Doyle — a remark that didn't exactly offend the author — and then got around to the subject of poisons. He wondered if Le Queux might be so kind as to lead him to the whereabouts of that copy of Secrets of the States of Venice *so casually mentioned in one of his books. Le Queux said he would be happy to oblige but the book was in storage in Italy. Crippen seemed deeply disappointed. 'Well', he said, can you tell me anything about those formulas that are in the book — those formulas for poisons that left not the slightest trace?' Le Queux recalled that the volume had mentioned several such poisons, but of course he didn't remember sufficient details to deal them off the cuff now. Anyway, he doubted that many of the so-called undetectable poisons of ancient Venice would be quite so undetectable if subjected to modern toxicological analysis...*

'Crippen decided he might pick up some extra money by contriving a plot for a mystery story and selling it to Le Queux. He immersed himself in volumes on poisons. He read practically everything that was in print on the subject of toxicology; he became an authority on the Manual of Dr Rudolph August Witthaus, the American toxicologist whose conclusions were being generally accepted as standard, particularly at murder trials. Crippen, still calling himself Dr Adams, saw Le Queux several times late in 1908 and early in 1909. At each meeting, the little doctor had a plot for the novelist that turned on a murder by poison. The basic plot was always the same: A man poisoned his wife, secreted her body, and ran off with a mistress. The man in the Crippen plot always got away with murder so that the plot had, from one point of view, a happy ending.

'Le Queux would remonstrate that this was not good, that the reader wanted to have the mystery solved and the guilty man punished. The doctor's answer to that was the chief entertainment to be derived from one of his plots would be to show how easy it was for a man who really knew poisons to get away with murder.'

Convincing? The following story, told by Le Queux himself, is supported by other writers too.

WILLIAM LE QUEUX

The Mysterious Treasure of Mme Humbert

One of the most colossal frauds of modern times was that which was finally exposed on May 9th, 1902, and was known as 'The Humbert Millions.'

Before the great swindle had been disclosed it had been the means of ruining some thousands of people, at least five of whom committed suicide, and there were three other deaths which have never been satisfactorily explained.

As I had some personal knowledge of the perpetrators of this gigantic imposture it may, perhaps, be of interest if I relate the circumstances in which I became acquainted with them.

One day in August 1900, at the invitation of Madame Sarah Bernhardt, I went to a luncheon party at her big white villa close to the lake at Enghien-les-Bains, just outside Paris. Before lunch I, with two other men, took a vivacious, dark-haired girl—whom I had met at a country house near Tours a few months before, and whose name was Marie d'Aurignac—out for a row upon the picturesque lake. We had arrived from Paris a little too early, and as the lawn sloped to the lake we paddled about till lunch was ready.

At the meal I sat next to my old friend Madame Zola. On my right was a stout, rather overdressed, and by no means prepossessing woman to whom I had not been introduced. We began to chat. To me she appeared to be a rather unintelligent and uncultivated woman, for she spoke with a distinctly provincial accent, and her conversation was interlarded with words of Parisian argot.

Presently Madame Zola said:

75

'I do not think you have been introduced,' and she told the stout, well-preserved woman who I was, adding that I was a friend of her husband, 'dear Emile,' and also a writer.

In a moment her attitude towards me entirely changed. From formal frigidity she became all smiles and geniality. I learnt that she was Madame Thérèse Humbert. But to me it then conveyed no unusual meaning. One meets many people at luncheon parties, and at those given by Sarah Bernhardt celebrities were present by the dozen; and several Parisian operatic stars.

The assembly in that long, old-fashioned dining room, the open French windows of which looked out upon the lake sparkling in the summer sunlight, was a brilliant one, and the chatter was equally vivacious and entertaining. The Divine Sarah was then at the zenith of her popularity, and had just returned from a long tour in the United States and Canada. But the stout woman on my right seemed morose and thoughtful. At last she said:

'What are your movements, Monsieur? I know your name very well. Your father was introduced to me long ago. Sarah told me all about you! You are a friend of Emile Zola, our greatest novelist. And you write too! Ah! I wish you all success. I envy you writers. It is all so clever to publish a book. You know my sister Marie. You took her out on the lake before lunch. So now you know who I am.'

Later, when we walked out upon the lawn and sat beneath the shadow of the trees at the lake-side, I asked Madame Zola about the stout lady who had been my companion at table.

'Oh!' she exclaimed. 'She's a widow—one of the richest women in Paris. She is Madame Humbert. If she invites you to her house in the Avenue de la Grande Armée you must go. All Paris goes there to her dinners and receptions. Frederic Humbert, her husband, was son of the late Minister of Justice, Gustave Humbert; who died five years ago. She is not chic by any means—but she is immensely wealthy.'

'I know her sister, Mademoiselle d'Aurignac, very slightly,' I said. 'But I did know that she was related to Madame Humbert.'

Who in Paris had not heard the fame of the great hostess of

the Avenue de la Grande Armée? Hardly a day passed but one read in the newspapers lists of her guests, which included persons in the most exclusive sets in Parisian society, with diplomats, cabinet ministers, writers, lawyers, dramatists, and the like. If Madame was not in Paris she entertained at her fine old Château de Vellexon, near Vesoul, or at the Villa des Cyclamens, on the road between Beaulieu and Monte Carlo.

Possibly it was through Madame Zola's good offices that a week later I received a card for Madame Humbert's reception.

The great mansion was profusely decorated with choice flowers, and the spacious *salons* were filled with the élite of Paris. I sat in a corner with Emile Zola, Henri Lamorre, Préfet of the Puy de Dôme, and Jules Guyon, the famous painter, and we chatted. Presently, Lamorre, a thin, grey-haired man, mentioned something about a safe.

'What safe?' I asked in my ignorance.

'Why, the safe in the next room,' he replied. 'The safe which contains over four millions sterling! Come and see it,' and he led me to a smaller apartment wherein a few people were seated near the open window, for it was a hot, close night. In a corner against the wall I saw a great fireproof safe about seven feet high and four feet across. There were three keyholes, each being sealed with huge red seals upon broad tapes which had once been white but were now discoloured with age.

I asked my friend what it meant. Whereupon, in an awed voice, he told me of the great fortune therein contained, a mysterious story which, I confess, greatly impressed me as a writer of romance.

As we stood there passed by us the President of the Court of Appeal, chatting with the famous lawyer, Maître Waldeck-Rousseau, and the Italian Ambassador and his wife. Truly Madame Humbert's receptions were the most wonderful in Paris since the downfall of the Empire.

That autumn I was Madame Humbert's guest at the famous old Château de Vellexon, and there again met her sister, Mademoiselle Marie d'Aurignac, and her brother Romain, who was three years her senior. There were some sixteen others of the house-party, and as at that time I was a fair shot—before my eyesight played me false—I enjoyed some good sport in the great woods surrounding the splendid Château.

I

From the first the secret of that great safe with its three big seals laid hold of my imagination. Indeed, that safe, with the mysterious millions it was thought to contain, had captured the imagination of all Paris; as it would naturally attract any novelist.

I am now going to tell the beginning of one of the most impudent frauds ever imposed upon a credulous public. So strange were the whole circumstances that, if written in the form of fiction, they would have been dismissed as being absolutely incredible. But what is here related is actual fact, as was afterwards proved in the Assize Court of the Seine.

It seems that two years after the Prussian invasion there was living at Bauzelles, a village near Toulouse, a young country girl of commonplace appearance. Her father, whose name was Aurignac, was a drunken, incorrigible old peasant, who in his elated moments was fond of declaring himself to be of noble birth. In his cups in the village *estaminet* each night he assumed the self-styled title of Count d'Aurignac. His cronies always addressed him as Monsieur le Comte, and his fame spread far and wide, even into Toulouse itself. At that time there were many scions of noble houses ruined by the Prussian invasion and reduced to beggary, therefore it was not considered very remarkable.

'The Count' lived with his daughters, Thérèse and Marie, and his sons, Romain and Emile. Thérèse did the housework, and the two boys worked in the fields and did odd jobs for anyone who liked to employ them. But the father, obsessed with the idea of his noble ancestry, one day bought for ten francs in the Rue St. Etienne, in Toulouse, an old oak chest studded with brass nails. It was that purchase which was the beginning of the extraordinary sham of the Humbert millions.

The old peasant, who had for years boasted of his noble ancestry, now exhibited to his neighbours the old carved chest, which he had locked and sealed, and which he solemnly declared contained the title-deeds of the great Château d'Aurignac, in Auvergne, and proofs which, upon his death, would entitle his children to a fortune. His friends, ignorant as are most French peasants, were much impressed by his story, but it brought in no money except a few odd francs as loans, so Thérèse was compelled by her father to accept the lowly position of laundry-maid to a family named Humbert, who had befriended the queer old fellow. The family in question consisted of Monsieur Gustave Humbert, Mayor of Toulouse, his wife, and their son Frederic, a slim, impressionable young man with a sloping forehead. Old Madame Humbert took Thérèse into their service out of charity a week after her father died, in January 1874. He did not possess one sou, and when the famous oak box was broken open, only a brick was found in it!

But Thérèse, though not in any way prepossessing, had a sly manner about her, and her eyes were ever open for the main chance. She had been educated to the belief that she was of noble birth, and at length she succeeded in attracting the attention of Frederic, her employer's son, who was then a law student in Toulouse.

All this time the Aurignacs were being laughed at by their neighbours, who knew of the discovery of the sealed-up brick, but so persistent were they all to their claim to nobility that the countryside began to wonder whether, after all, they were not descendants of the great house of d'Aurignac, in Auvergne.

The legend thus born was now to grow, thanks to 'La Grande Thérèse'—as she was later dubbed by the Paris press. She started to carry on the fiction of her absinthe-drinking father and evolved, in her imagination, a great ancestral home, the Château de Marcotte, in the Tarn. In strictest secrecy she disclosed to her lover that the octogenarian Mademoiselle de Marcotte, a very wealthy old lady, who was owner of the château, had bequeathed her entire fortune to her, together with her vast estate. The château, however, never existed, except in Thérèse's imagination, but the story impressed the Humbert family and especially Frederic's father, the Mayor of Toulouse.

Soon afterwards Monsieur and Madame Humbert left Toulouse for Paris, to take up their abode there, where a month later, to their chagrin, they learnt that their son Frederic intended to marry their ex-washerwoman, the girl Thérèse! Frederic had been left in Toulouse to conclude his law studies, and the wily girl had very cleverly entrapped him.

So far the facts all read like a sensational novel. But the events which followed and the *dénouement* are far more amazing still.

II

Monsieur Gustave Humbert had, by dint of hard work and considerable shrewdness—some say that his conduct as a lawyer was not altogether above suspicion—come to the fore in politics, and certain of his friends had hinted at his appointment as Minister of Justice. In such circumstances it was but natural that he should be horrified at the suggestion of a laundry-maid becoming his son's wife. He travelled post-haste to Toulouse, and there was a heated scene between father and son. The father threatened to cut off Frederic's allowance, but was only met with defiance. The young man was determined, and so cleverly did Thérèse play her cards that, despite all entreaties, Frederic married her.

There was a queer circumstance on the day of the wedding. Just as she was going to the Hôtel de Ville an official of the Court of Toulouse arrived with a warrant for the arrest of the adventurous Thérèse on account of a debt incurred with a hairdresser. Mademoiselle met the man with perfect sangfroid and told him that she was about to be married, and that in an hour's time if he returned she would obtain the money from her husband and discharge the debt. Thus assured, the warrant was not executed. Indeed, the official could not bring himself to arrest a bride on the eve of her marriage. But on returning at the appointed hour he found that the pair had been registered as man and wife and were already on their way to Paris.

From the first moment of Thérèse's married life her whole career became one of amazing duplicity and adventure. She possessed a subtle cunning, a wheedling manner, a vivid imagination and an utter disregard of honesty or fair dealing. From her reprobate father she seems to have, with her brothers, inherited that same idea of pretence of nobility, an all-absorbing ambition and the gain of money from the credulous. The sealed oak box which was supposed to contain proofs which would secure for his heirs a title and valuable estates and which had only contained a brick—but which had during its existence brought in petty loans from neighbours—had impressed itself upon the mind of 'La Grande Thérèse,' so gradually she evolved from her fertile brain a greater and much more grandiose scheme.

For a time Frederic Humbert and his wife lived in humble circumstances in Paris, occupying a three-roomed flat *au troisième* in the Rue Provence. Her husband, who had now passed his examinations, managed to earn a modest income at his profession, and for several years their existence was quiet and uneventful. From time to time Frederic questioned his wife about the £5000 a year which was coming to her from Mlle de Marcotte, but she was always evasive concerning it, as she well might be. Thérèse had entered the Humbert family and was daughter-in-law of Monsieur Gustave, who had now been appointed Minister of Justice, therefore she had taken a considerable step forward. But, alas! there was no money.

Creditors pressed them in the Rue Provence, so they moved to another flat in the Rue Monge, where her plausible story to the local grocer concerning her expectations from the owner of the mythical Château de Marcotte quickly spread about the neighbourhood, and because of it the pair existed for quite a long time upon credit.

The Marcotte myth proved a very profitable one, but without any tangible proof and no substantiation except the word of the amazing Thérèse it was soon doomed to failure. The local tradesmen began to question the locality in which the Château de Marcotte was situated. The Prefect of the Department was written to, and his reply was that he had no knowledge of any such estate within his jurisdiction. The farm, it may be mentioned, adjoins the Haute Garonne, the capital of which is Toulouse. Sometimes Thérèse had told people that the Château was near Albi, and at others she had mentioned Carmaux and Castres as the nearest towns. The creditors were bewildered, though greatly intrigued. So one of them, who was a native of a village near Castres, went on his summer vacation to his home, and on his return declared that there was no such estate in the Tarn.

Upon that things grew very ugly for the pair. Threats of prosecution for swindling if bills were not paid arrived in a crop, and so serious was the position that Thérèse was compelled to admit to her husband that the whole story was a fabrication. Frederic, greatly alarmed, went to his father, the Minister of Justice, told him the truth, and His Excellency—who could not afford the scandal of his son being arrested for swindling—paid the whole of their debts, much to the relief of 'La Grande Thérèse.'

The latter was sly, unscrupulous and highly ambitious. The sealed oak box with its brick was ever in her mind. For three or four years she slowly evolved plans by which she might, just as her father had done in his own small way to obtain money for drink, impose upon an ever credulous public but on a grander scale.

By this time she had gauged the mind of the French public to a very fine degree. She knew that persons dealing in high finance could not be imposed upon except by some great scheme with enticing profits, and if a little romance were mixed with it then the more certain of success it would be. It was proved in Court that Frederic Humbert had no knowledge that the Marcotte fortune had no foundation until his domineering wife confessed, and that it was he who implored his father to save the family from disgrace.

Yet a few months after the episode, in March 1881, astounding whispers went around Paris—whispers that were not to be repeated. At the salons each evening Paris society discussed the romantic story that M. Gustave Humbert, Minister of Justice, had told his friends vainly that his daughter-in-law had met with a most romantic adventure while travelling on the Ceinture Railway, and that by her brave conduct towards a perfect stranger, an American she had inherited eighty thousand pounds.

His Excellency the Minister had dined at the Elysée, at several of the houses of the great hostesses of Paris, and at one of the Embassies, and had told the story. His son's wife had come into a fortune by reason of her courage and sympathy. The affair at once became the gossip of all Paris. Like all such stories it was not reduced in the telling, so its embroidery increased day by day, just as Thérèse had hoped, until all Paris was gossiping regarding the mysterious fortune of His Excellency's daughter-in-law.

It now became a question, never satisfactorily settled, by the way, whether the Minister of Justice really believed it, or whether in order to increase his own social advancement he readily accepted Thérèse's story, yet believing it to be untrue. He knew the Marcotte myth to have no foundation in fact, therefore it seems incredible that he, a very accomplished lawyer, should have swallowed the strange, romantic tale which the imaginative ex-laundry-maid should have told him.

III

Briefly related, the story, as told by 'La Belle Grande Thérèse,' was as follows: About two years after her marriage she had one hot September afternoon entered a train on the Ceinture Railway in Paris at the Grenelle station to go to Bel-Air. She was in a compartment alone when she heard groans in an adjoining compartment just after they had left Montsouris. She shouted, but there was no response. The cries were of a man in agony. Therefore, at great risk to herself, she got out of the carriage, climbed along the footboard, and in the adjoining compartment found a white-haired old gentleman who had been taken ill. She gave him her smelling-salts, unloosened his collar, and lifting him from the floor dragged him into a corner where, in a sitting position, he soon regained consciousness. He had apparently suffered from a severe heart attack, but it quickly passed. Indeed, before they arrived at Bel-Air the old gentleman thanked her profusely and inquiring her name and address, had written it down upon a scrap of paper.

'We shall meet again one day, Madame, I hope. If not, I wish you to accept my heartfelt thanks for what you have done for me. I happen to have in my pocket a considerable sum of money, and in the hands of unscrupulous folk I might very easily have lost my money—and perhaps even my life!'

They shook hands after the old gentleman had told her that

Madame Humbert and the old gentleman in the train.

he was an American named Robert Henry Crawford, of Chicago, and assured her that he was quite well and able to continue his journey to the next station, which was Avenue de Vincennes. For two years she had forgotten all about the romantic meeting until one day she received a letter from a firm of lawyers in New York enclosing a copy of old Mr Crawford's will, by which she had been left £80,000. That was the original figure which Thérèse stated, but through gossip—no doubt started by His Excellency—the fortune was swiftly increased, first to a million pounds sterling, and then to four millions. This figure the Humbert family never questioned, and for nearly twenty years that followed all Paris believed that Thérèse Humbert was entitled to that sum—after certain divisions.

Whoever prepared the copy of the will, or whoever were the lawyers in New York—these things were never ascertained. It is sure, however, that the documents bore the stamp of authenticity, and were not questioned for the many years the imposture lasted.

The old man from Chicago died suddenly in Nice—the death certificate of a man named Crawford who lived in the Rue de France being produced—and by the conditions of the will his fortune was to be divided between Marie d'Aurignac, Thérèse's sister, who was then a child at school at Neuilly, and two nephews, Robert and Henry Crawford, while out of the fortune the three were to pay Thérèse Humbert fourteen thousand pounds a year.

Madame Humbert at once employed a very reputable firm of Paris lawyers to investigate, and according to their report it was found that the brothers Crawford who lived in America were both millionaires and that the legacy was of but little account to them.

Their American lawyers wrote to Madame's lawyers in Paris, expressing a wish that the money should remain in the Crawford family if possible, that it should remain intact in a safe in Madame Humbert's custody, except for the payment to her of fourteen thousand pounds annually, as the will provided. It was also suggested that as both brothers had seen a photograph of the schoolgirl, Marie d'Aurignac, one or the other of them should marry her when she left school. Then the safe should be opened and the fortune of four millions be divided.

Such was the curious, romancit story that went about Paris and which, coming, as it did, from the lips of the Minister of Justice, nobody dared to doubt. The invention, on the face of it, was ridiculous, though certainly there were letters from lawyers—forged, no doubt—to give it an appearance of fact, which set all Paris agog, and brought Thérèse Humbert fame and credit, so that from her humble home in a side street and her stream of creditors, she assumed the position of a wealthy *grande dame* and the guardian of her young sister's destinies until the marriage of convenience should take place.

Thus it was, in 1881, that the mythical story of the Crawford millions was launched with the connivance of Frederic Humbert and his wife's two brothers, Romain and Emile d'Aurignac—both ne'er-do-wells—and aided and abetted by His Excellency the Minister of Justice. A great white mansion was taken in the Avenue de la Grande Armée and luxuriously furnished as a fitting home for a woman of such great fortune, and in the downstairs room the largest fireproof safe procurable was set up for all to see—the sealed safe containing the four millions sterling, of which Robert Henry Crawford had died possessed.

Because the Minister of Justice himself was a relative and had testified to the truth of the romantic story, not a soul disbelieved it. Madame Humbert became the centre of smart society in Paris, and to be seen at her receptions, or to be a visitor at one or another of her famous country homes was a hall-mark of notoriety. As soon as she was firmly established in that magnificent house in the Avenue de la Grande Armée, the extravagances of the ex-washerwoman became astounding. The most famous people of both sexes in France scrambled for her invitations, and the state she kept up was almost regal. Her dresses and jewels were constantly being described in the Paris Press, for everyone became dazzled by the luxury with which she surrounded herself.

Whence did the money come to keep up that expensive establishment? I will explain.

In 1883, rumours were afloat that Madame had quarrelled with the Crawford brothers, but only after the publication in one of the minor newspapers of an article which threw doubt upon the whole story. An ingenious journalist had summoned courage to question the statement of the most powerful woman in France. As a matter of fact, the journalist in question had been born in Toulouse, had known old Aurignac and his story of nobility, and also of the Marcotte myth.

IV

In this article, Thérèse scented danger lest several people who had lent her money on the security of the safe and its millions should make secret investigations. Therefore she invented the quarrel between old Crawford's nephews and herself. It proved to be a pretty quarrel. The Crawford brothers first began to worry her over small matters of details, one of which was that the money should be removed to the Crédit Lyonnais for safer keeping. To this Madame objected. The matter came to Court, and after much bickering it was at last settled by Madame consenting to have three armed guards placed over the safe from sunset to sunrise each day. It seemed reasonable to suppose that the Crawfords were not imaginary, for non-existent persons do not embark upon expensive law-suits. Indeed, there started an amazing series of actions; some by the Crawfords, and others by Madame Humbert, which were fought out sometimes in the American Courts, and more often in Paris. And so the 'Humbert Millions' became a stock heading in the French newspapers, and the public began to follow the interminable lawsuits which were constantly cropping up.

Huge fees were paid to some of the most famous lawyers in France to defend Madame Humbert's rights, while similar fees were paid to other legal luminaries of equal distinction by the two American millionaires. In her defence, Thérèse was actively aided by her husband's father, the Minister of Justice, and so clever were her poses that everyone believed her to be in the right in resisting the unjust claims of old Crawford's nephews. Indeed, for nearly a generation, these constant law-suits were reappearing, together with occasional affidavits, sworn by either Robert or Henry Crawford, both of whom were in

America, and all sorts of information, evidence taken on commission in Chicago, and squabbles in the French Courts, until such a mass of judgments were obtained and appeals quashed that when the bubble burst nobody could make head or tail of what was the actual commencement of the great litigation upon which lawyers had fattened for years. Indeed, the most ludicrous part of it was that the lawyers themselves very often did not clearly know what they were actually fighting about! But the litigation achieved its purpose, for it seemed to show that the Crawford brothers did actually exist, and that they were endeavouring to obtain possession of the formidable-looking safe.

And all this time Marie d'Aurignac, Thérèse's sister, who had now left school, was the fiancée of Henry Crawford, whom she had, according to her story, met three times while he was on flying visits to Paris to see his French lawyers. During one of the trials in which Maître Waldeck-Rousseau was engaged, he referred to Mademoiselle Marie as 'the eternal fiancée,' a title which stuck to her until the eventual exposure of the swindle.

As was afterwards proved, she had been introduced to an American by her sister, Thérèse, at the Hôtel Continental. The man was represented to be Mr Crawford, and the girl, in her innocence, believed him to be the person whom she was destined to marry. The bogus Crawford was evidently of an engaging character, and good-looking, for Marie seems to have taken a liking to him, and to have met him on other occasions, and had, indeed, sung his praises to her friends. All of this went, of course, to bolster up the great fiction.

Meanwhile 'La Grande Thérèse' had become the most imposing figure in Parisian society. Her expenditure was lavish. Her accounts were investigated after the *débâcle*, and it was discovered that in the year 1897 she spent upon gowns £3780 at Doucet's and £1400 at Worth's, while her hats alone cost her over £850 in the Rue de la Paix. Truly the washerwoman turned adventuress was reckless in her expenditure, and further, such extravagance showed people how very wealthy she really was.

The public never dreamed that from the first moment that great mansion had been rented and furnished, Madame, who gave such expensive and exclusive parties, had existed always upon credit—or rather, upon the credulity of her dupes. That she found level-headed bankers, financiers and business men ready to advance large sums simply upon her assurance that the sealed safe contained four millions sterling in cash and securities was utterly amazing. If the story of Madame's clever duplicity had been written as a novel it would surely have been dismissed as fiction. But in this case we are faced with hard, yet astounding facts. Never in the history of crime had there been such an impudent and colossal fraud, and none so ingeniously conceived. The never-ending series of actions in the Courts between the Crawford brothers and herself established a confidence that the two sons of her late benefactor were alive, yet, as a matter of fact, they had no existence save in the imagination of the public. The whole proceedings, so complex that no lawyer has ever been able to unravel the tangle, was merely 'La Grande Thérèse' fighting herself. And she was paying for it all.

Imagine, then, how cleverly she hoodwinked the lawyers who appeared both for and against her, and how extremely careful she must have been in the preparation of every detail. In this she was assisted by her brothers, Emile and Romain d'Aurignac, who acted as her agents in many of her affairs. But, after all, it was her father's trick of the old oak chest being played again, but this time the harvest was not to be counted in single francs, but millions. Tempted by the promise of high rates of interest, hundreds of people lent Thérèse money in secret, all being assured that when the safe was opened at Marie's marriage they would receive back their loans with profit. The very lawyers who had appeared for her in the Courts became her agents for the borrowing of money, and to anyone who was sceptical, Madame, in great secrecy, would produce a bundle of letters purporting to be from the non-existent Crawfords—a trick which rarely failed to extract money. The time came, of course, when certain creditors desired their money, and became impatient to see the contents of the ponderous safe. But, no! The agreement with the Crawfords was that it was not to be opened until Marie's marriage, and she was not yet out of her teens. So, its creditors became unduly pressing, Madame paid the interest out of further loans from other people. And thus the game proceeded.

V

The first person of importance who seems to have had his suspicions seriously aroused was a banker from Lyons named Delatte, who had lent a considerable sum upon the strength of Madame's story and sight of the sealed safe. To several other creditors he declared that the whole affair was a fraud, but one and all disbelieved him. Madame's behaviour, her plausibility, her proof of the existence of the Crawfords, and her generosity in the matter of dinners and entertainments disarmed suspicion.

But Monsieur Delatte, pretending that he was reassured and satisfied, played a waiting game until one day, while guest of Madame Humbert at the Château de Vellexon, he quite innocently asked where Henry Crawford was. She declared that he was living in Boston. He could obtain no further information except that he had a house in Somerville, a suburb of Boston, but he acted as nobody else seems to have thought of acting, for, a week later, without telling anyone of his intentions, he left Havre for New York, and duly arrived in Somerville. Though he made every inquiry he could discover nobody of the name of Crawford, either in Somerville or in Boston itself. He engaged a well-known firm of private inquiry agents, but their search in Chicago also proved futile. To a friend in Paris he wrote declaring that the Crawford brothers did not exist, and that he was returning to expose the swindle. His friend awaited his return, but he never came. A month later, however, news was received in Lyons that the body of a man who, from papers found upon him, was identified as M. Delatte, had been found in the East River between New York and Brooklyn. Whether the unfortunate man met with an accident, was the victim of foul play or committed suicide has never been cleared up. In any case, had he returned to Paris, as was his intention, he could, no doubt, have made things very uncomfortable for Madame and her accomplices.

Within two months another of Madame's dupes came to an untimely end. In this case it was the manager of an important commercial house in Paris named Henri Vincendon, who, four years before, had lent Thérèse half a million francs. Since then he had been hard pressed for money, and had embezzled one hundred thousand francs belonging to the company which employed him. The books were, he knew, being examined, and soon his defalcations would be discovered, so he rushed to Madame and implored her to at least return him that sum. But he only received the same reply that all creditors' obtained, for Madame, without even expressing regret, told him that the safe could not be opened before the marriage of Marie, 'the eternal fiancée.' He pleaded with her, but although that very day she had obtained a further quarter of a million francs from a fresh victim, she would give him nothing. Therefore in despair the poor fellow went forth, and beneath a tree in the Bois he shot himself. Of almost similar cases there were several, though the actual cause of suicide never leaked out. It was only the ring of creditors themselves who knew.

A German journalist named Haberler, the Paris correspondent of a Berlin newspaper, having met Madame Humbert, considered that she behaved insultingly towards him, so in retaliation began to spread reports to the effect that the Crawford affair was a bogus one. At first nobody took any notice, but Madame's secret agents, her two brothers, came very soon afterwards and declared that the position was perilous, for many people were beginning to believe Haberler's statements. In consequence, Madame very quickly made peace with the journalist by paying him a very large sum, showing him the forged letters of the Crawford brothers, and inviting him to her parties, thus closing his mouth. To those who asked the reason of his change of opinion, the man replied that he had now seen proofs of the existence of the Crawfords, and he deeply regretted that he had defamed the much-criticised holder of the four millions sterling. This was not the only case in which Madame was blackmailed by those who thought they might obtain money by exhibiting animosity, for, of course, to sustain the fiction was vital to her schemes.

Marie d' Aurignac was exhibited everywhere, at Trouville, at Longchamps, at Monte Carlo, Aix, Pau and other places, for in company with her sister she went the usual round of watering-places, where the world gaped at the girl who was affianced to the American multi-millionaire, and at whose marriage the great safe would be opened and the stuffed-in four millions sterling would tumble out upon the floor. This was all a clever ruse on the part of Thérèse, who was nothing if not theatrical in her display. Besides, sight of the fiancée was calculated to attract further moths to the candle. It seems utterly incredible that any woman should carry on such a gigantic swindle against the shrewdest and most competent business men and financiers in France. But the fact was that Madame Humbert's two brothers—who were the forerunners of the modern press-agent—had boomed her to such an extent that, with her father-in-law as Minister of Justice, nobody dared doubt her word.

And so nightly those who were fortunate enough to receive invitations to the great white mansion in the Avenue de la Grande Armée—myself included—stared in awe at the safe containing the huge fortune.

No swindler, however clever he or she can be, can ever carry on the game for all time. A slip of the tongue must come some day, perhaps in a moment of confidence or perhaps after a post-prandial liqueur. Madame Humbert was no exception, despite her marvellous ingenuity and her grasp of complicated legal proceedings. It seems that late one night, while sitting with Jules Bizat in the great conservatory—which led out from the big panelled dining-room which, by the way, I well remember—she was guilty of a very grave indiscretion.

Bizat was a high official of the Banque de France, and though he had not lent Thérèse any money, he was a little inquisitive, because his father-in-law was deeply involved as one of Madame's creditors. Conversation turned upon the contents of the safe, as it so often did, and quite artlessly he asked:

'You, of course, saw what was placed in the safe by Henry Crawford. Of what did the securities mainly consist?'

To this she replied, 'French Rentes.'

That was the first indiscretion which eventually led to her undoing. Hitherto she had always remained silent, declaring complete ignorance. But this admission caused Monsieur Bizat to reflect. If French Rentes were sealed in that safe it would be necessary for her to cash French Rente coupons each year! So pretending ignorance, he at once instituted inquiries at the Banque de France and soon ascertained that no coupons had been cashed. Jules Bizat was a wise man. He held his tongue. But he was the first man to discover the actual fraud.

VI

Thérèse, however, at once discovered her mistake. She had put into the man's hands a weapon against herself. Further, creditors were pressing, and from day to day she did not know when the bubble might burst. For several weeks she existed in hourly anxiety, when once again her fertile brain evolved a further plan by which she might raise money from the public and thus pay the creditors now pressing on every hand for the formal opening of the sealed safe.

To Romain and Emile she disclosed her plans, as result of which another enormous fraud was launched upon the public under the name of the Rente Viagère. Romain d'Aurignac was put up as the figure-head of this new concern, though Thérèse, the ex-washerwoman, had worked out all the details. She had gauged the public of Paris very accurately, and she knew that ultra-luxurious offices would be one of her best assets. So, in the Boulevard des Cappucines, great offices were opened with departments so numerous as to be bewildering, while discreet uniformed attendants wearing white gloves directed clients hither and thither. The place was the biggest 'bluff' ever attempted in modern history.

Now inside those gorgeous offices, which only a genius of make-believe could have ever conceived, a wonderful business was in progress—a business to bolster up the clever manoeuvres of the ex-laundry-maid of His Excellency the Minister of Justice. The Rente Viagère was nothing else than a big bogus insurance company who promised you annuities without any capital to meet its liabilities. Thérèse had started this wonderful insurance company—with the backing of the well-known lawyers who were fighting for her against the inexorable Crawfords—with one object only. It was her master-stroke. She badly wanted money by which to be able to buy French

Rentes, cash the coupons and thus set aside any suspicions which had arisen in the mind of Jules Bizat. If he found that the coupons were cashed, he would surely remain satisfied then! There is no doubt that when 'La Grande Thérèse' started the Rente Viagère she had no idea of how rapidly the swindle would grow, or of the thousands of people who would invest their small savings in it. The prospectus, drawn up in consultation with her two brothers, was so alluring, and so full of unusual benefits, that thousands of people of the middle classes invested their hard-earned savings, purchased annuities and insured their lives in a concern which was absolutely bogus. The great offices, with their big staff and liveried porters, never had more than a thousand pounds' balance at the bank, though often they took over the counter four or even five thousand pounds a day.

The Rente Viagère was the pet secret scheme of 'La Grande Thérèse.' To those who came each evening to her *salon* she sang its praises as an aid to the poor of France to save and to benefit. But nobody knew of her connection with it. Her brother Romain was full of details as to what they were accomplishing for the benefit of La Belle France, while Gustave Humbert, Minister of Justice, when questioned, expressed the greatest admiration of the scheme.

So the name of Thérèse Humbert became—after the death of her husband Frederic—a name to conjure with. Her critics had been silenced by bribery, or by counter-blackmailing cleverly carried on by her shrewd brothers who were, after all, adventurers after her own heart, and sons of the old peasant who adventured with his battered old box to obtain a few francs from the credulous.

Business went well. Millions of francs poured into the ever-open palm of Thérèse—*alias* the Rent Viagère. Every person who entered the magnificent portals of those fine offices, after being interviewed by suave, black-coated 'directors' who in their gorgeous rooms exuded financial credit—came out the poorer. From every corner of France thrifty working folk invested money in the corporation, bought annuities or insured their lives. With the money thus falling into the lap of 'La Grande Thérèse' she bought French Rentes, the coupons of which she began to cash each quarter-day and thus allayed the suspicion aroused in the mind of M. Bizat. Thus she started a second fraud in order to bolster up the first, and for several years the two big swindles ran side by side. We know that in the first year of the existence of the Rente Viagère Madame paid, in two months, for gloves alone £32, and £220 for hats at shops in the Rue de la Paix, while her florist's bill in the same sixty days amounted to well over £1000.

No doubt the Rente Viagère was much more profitable to Thérèse and her brothers than the sealed safe, the truth of which might at any moment be exposed, even though the Courts had decided that it could not be opened before Marie's marriage. Some say that M. Gustave Humbert, being Minister of Justice and aware of the fraud, had contrived that the Court should make that decree and thus protect his daughter-in-law. There were, however, still people who, unable to get their money back, and seeing no prospect of it, had grown very angry and impatient, and even though the proceeds of the Rente Viagère swindle were being used to stave off such people, they were growing inadequate. Madame Humbert had borrowed three million pounds from unsuspecting people upon no other security than her well-told story of her meeting with old Crawford in the train, and it was becoming clear that the day of reckoning was fast approaching. Yet the creditors were always faced with the decree of the Supreme Court that the safe might not be opened. And at the same time 'the eternal fiancée' was going about Paris happy, smiling, and certainly in ignorance of the part she was playing in the big conspiracy which her sister had engineered so successfully.

In the Courts several persons adjudged bankrupt attributed their insolvency to loans made to Madame Humbert, until at last, early in 1901, a number of her creditors held a meeting, when it was agreed that they had been swindled. One of these pointed out that after Madame had upon borrowed money paid for the defence of those never-ending lawsuits which had gone on for nearly fifteen years, there could not be very much left even if the safe were opened and the money divided. And, after all, the Crawfords would have to have their share. So on the face of it, they argued, Madame had borrowed more than her share of the money, with the result that they, the creditors, would probably obtain nothing.

Unfortunately for Madame Humbert this argument was placed before the great lawyer, M. Waldeck-Rousseau, who had appeared against Madame Humbert many times in Court—though, in his ignorance, paid by 'La Grande Thérèse'—and who had not great liking for her. He had all along been suspicious, being one of the few notable men who would listen to a word said against her genuineness and honesty. In fact, he had for a long time past become convinced that the whole thing was a huge fabrication, and, moreover, he had learnt that in secret the brothers d'Aurignac were the moving spirits in the Rente Viagère, though they were never seen at the offices and their identity was carefully concealed from everyone concerned.

VII

After making a number of secret inquiries, M. Waldeck-Rousseau felt that the time was ripe to prick the bubble. His son-in-law, who had been badly 'bitten' by Madame, had died, leaving his wife in sore straits, and there were other friends of his who had been wickedly imposed upon. Besides, the great game had been in progress for nearly twenty years, and though some people had received interest at times, yet nobody had, in all that period, seen the shadow of the money advanced. Therefore he went to the *Matin* newspaper and placed all the facts he had collected before the Director, who promised to make, in a series of articles, a direct attack upon the myth of the sealed safe.

By some means Madame Humbert heard of this and went boldly to the editor of the *Matin* and threatened an action if he dared to publish anything calling her honesty into question. But the editor coolly replied that he should act as he thought best, and next morning there appeared an article inspired by M. Waldeck-Rousseau, demanding the immediate opening of the safe. For nine days these virulent articles continued, declaring that the story of the Crawford millions had not foundation in fact, until the creditors were practically forced by public opinion to unite and take an action against Madame Humbert for a reversion of the decision against the opening of the safe.

For some months the case was delayed by counsel who defended Madame, and in the meantime the investors in the Rente Viagère suddenly awakened to the fact that they had lost their money, though even at that time there was no suspicion that Madame Humbert had been implicated in the bogus concern.

M. Waldeck-Rousseau was actively assisted in his investigations by M. Emile Zola and an able *juge d'instruction* named Borsant. At length the hearing of the creditors' appeal could no longer be delayed, and the presiding judge who heard the case decided that the only way by which the truth, so long delayed, could be ascertained was to have the seals broken and the safe opened. Notwithstanding a vigorous defence on the part of two famous counsels retained by Madame, May 9th, 1902, was the date fixed for the opening of the mysterious safe, and Madame was ordered to give the key into the custody of the Court.

'La Grande Thérèse,' seeing that the game was up, remained at home until the day before the opening, when, with her two brothers and her young sister Marie, she quietly left the Avenue de la Grande Armée and disappeared.

Next morning four officials of the Court, with M. Waldeck-Rousseau, the editor of the *Matin*, M. Emile Zola, and creditors representing just over three millions sterling, assembled in the room, the seals were broken, the time-stained tapes torn away and the safe was opened!

It was not empty, yet its sole contents consisted of an English halfpenny and a brick—evidently in imitation of the old oak chest trick!

Instantly the news got abroad that the Humbert millions only existed in Madame's imagination. One half of the creditors were furious, the other half hung their heads in shame that they should have been so cleverly imposed upon, while Paris, which always enjoys a good joke, laughed at the unfortunate creditors' plight.

Warrants were issued that day for the arrest of the fugitives. It was known that they had fled to London, but, though three French detectives were sent over, Scotland Yard could discover no trace of them. M. Goron, at that time Chef de la Sureté, has told me of the world search he ordered for Madame and her brothers—her sister not being included in the charges—yet through seven months no trace of them could be found. In the middle of December, however, a cheque upon the Crédit Lyonnais, bearing the name of Romain d'Aurignac, came to Paris, and showed that it had been cashed in Malaga, in Spain. The Spanish police were at once informed, and on December 20th, 1902, 'La Grande Thérèse' and her two brothers were found living in rather poor circumstances in a back street in Madrid.

It seems that the house was surrounded by the police, as the brothers were known to carry firearms, and they first caught sight of Madame's pale, anxious face peering at them from behind a blind. A ring at the door-bell resulted in the appearance of Romain d'Aurignac, who, with a laugh, said: 'I know why you are here! You want me! Here I am!' and he gave himself up, evidently in the hope of allowing his brother and sister to escape. This ruse failed, and all three were promptly arrested, and, after the extradition formalities were concluded, were brought to Paris by six of M. Goron's agents, and eventually tried at the Assize Court of the Seine on February 6th, 1903.

VIII

All three prisoners preserved an amazing calm, while Paris still enjoyed the huge joke, and the creditors were furious. How much Madame Humbert really did borrow on the strength of her unsubstantiated story will never be known, for many creditors of high standing, bankers and others, dared not come forward and confess themselves victims of what was a variation of the old confidence trick. Hence they made no statement or claim. It is, however, estimated that in one way or another five million pounds passed through the ex-washerwoman's hands.

In the trial there were many delays and adjournments, as is usually the case in France, so it dragged on from February until August. To all questions 'La Grande Thérèse' remained mute. She would make no admission. The President of the Court asked her to say where the Château de Marcotte was situated, but she only smiled. And again she smiled when asked for the addresses of the Crawford brothers. Only once did he obtain a direct reply to a question. He asked: 'Who were the Crawfords?' In reply, Madame Humbert, with great dignity, answered: 'Monsieur le Président, I shall tell my secret in due course, when the Public Prosecutor has spoken his last word.'

This attitude amazed all Paris, and the story she told a week later was certainly most astounding. It was decidedly clever, and in telling it she evidently thought she would be believed because of French prejudices against the Germans. She confessed that old Crawford had never existed, but that the person who had bequeathed to her the four millions was none other than Marshal Bazaine, who had surrendered the fortress of Metz to the Germans, the money being the sum paid to him by the enemy as price of his treachery.

'For a long time I was not aware of this, Monsieur le Président,' she went on. 'But as soon as I knew the truth I felt that I could not retain the blood-money. I am a patriotic daughter of France, so I destroyed both the will and the bonds, and burned the many packets of bank-notes which were English, German and French. That, Monsieur, accounts for the emptiness of the safe'.

'Exactly, Madame,' was the judge's retort, 'but it does not account for the brick!'

At which the Court roared with laughter. Of course, not a soul believed her statement, and in the end the jury found her guilty of fraud and she was sentenced to five years' solitary confinement, but, strangely enough, the jury decided that her guilt was in 'extenuating circumstances.' Her brother Romain was also sent to solitary confinement for three years, and Emile for two years, while the celebrated safe was on view for a year or more in a second-hand shop in the Rue Blanche.

Thus ended a most colossal fraud which, engineered by a shrewd and resourceful woman, who must also have possessed great courage and a remarkably clear brain, ran its course for nearly twenty years before final exposure, and which will for ever remain one of the most amazing of all gigantic swindles.

*Julian Symons is one of the most distinguished figures in the
literature of crime, renowned both for his own fiction and for
his critical writings on the genre, especially* Bloody Murder, *his history of crime writing. He has also made several
notable contributions to the field of true-crime writing, and
his book* A Reasonable Doubt *considers a number of cases
where justice might have faltered. In* Unsolved! *I included
one of these pieces, his brilliant analysis of the mystery of Sir
Harry Oakes, and I am delighted to include another Symons
piece here: this time a departure from the desk to carry out his
own investigation...*

JULIAN SYMONS

The Invisible Man

THE PUZZLE

The car was standing at Elishaw Bridge crossroads, on the road from Jedburgh and the Scottish border, as Evelyn Foster drove up. She helped to run her father's taxi service at the village of Otterburn, a mile or two down the road, and was on her way home after taking a party to Rochester.

Now as she drove up, the stranger got out of the car and spoke to her. He said in an accent that she recognized as North Country, although it was not exactly Tyneside, that he wanted to get a bus to Newcastle. The people in the car had brought him this far from Jedburgh, but now they were taking the road south, to Hexham. Could she give him a lift?

He was a pleasantly spoken, dapper little man, neatly dressed in dark blue overcoat, dark tweed suit, and bowler hat. Evelyn Foster considered, told him that her Hudson car was for hire, and said that she would take him into Otterburn, where she wanted to refuel, and then see where he could catch a bus. The occupants of the other car, a man and a woman, did not get out. The stranger thanked them for their hospitality, and the car drove off down the road to Hexham. The stranger got into the Hudson and sat beside her. The time was nearing seven o'clock on a cold, hard January night.

Within a few minutes they were at the Foster garage, in Otterburn's single street. She had told him that the fare to Ponteland, a journey of twenty-odd miles over the Northumbrian moors, would be about £2, and he agreed to this. From Ponteland he could easily get a bus into Newcastle. In the meantime, he said, he would go along to the Percy Arms, just along the road, and have a drink. She could pick him up either there or just beyond, at Otterburn Bridge.

Evelyn left him, and went into the house. There she saw her mother.

'What does he look like?' Mrs Foster asked.

'Oh, very respectable. Gentleman-like—he looks a bit of a knut.'

'Where is the man now?'

'He's gone down to the Percy Arms for a drink.'

Her mother thought that £2 was rather too much to charge, and her father said that the fare should be £1 16s. Her sister Dorothy suggested that it was unwise to travel alone with a stranger over the lonely moor, and said she should take as companion George Phillipson, a joiner in the village with whom Evelyn was friendly.

'I'll call for him,' she agreed.

She borrowed her mother's torch, and she drove away. The time was twenty minutes past seven. She did not see George Phillipson in the village (although in fact he was there), and did not call for him. The stranger hailed her at the Bridge, got into the car, and they began the drive across the moors. While they drove the man in the bowler hat talked to her, and what he said took on some importance in view of what happened afterwards. He did not know much about Newcastle, he told her, but lived in the Midlands. He had a car of his own, he said, and he appeared to know a lot about cars.

So the time passed, pleasantly enough, until they reached Belsay, only six miles from Ponteland. Now he suddenly told her to turn back.

'Why do you want to go back, when we have come so far?'

'That's nothing to do with you,' he said, and now his manner had changed.

She turned the car. He crept along the seat towards her, and took hold of the steering wheel. 'Oh no,' she said. 'I will do the driving.'

He lifted his hand and struck her over the eye, so that she could hardly see out of it. He took the wheel, pushed her over to the side of the car so that she could not move, nipped her arms. Then he drove back most of the way to Otterburn and stopped on the hill at Wolf's Nick, beside the snow-covered Ottercaps.

Now, surprisingly, he offered her a cigarette. She refused it.

'Well, you are an independent young woman,' the stranger said.

Her impressions after this were confused, but terrible. He struck her, kicked her, knocked her into the back of the car. Then he assaulted her, despite her resistance. She became unconscious. Vaguely she was aware that he had taken a bottle or tin from his pocket, that he was pouring something over her, that the something had gone up in a blaze, that she was burning.

There was a bump, as though the car were passing over rough ground. The bump roused her, burning as she was, and she managed to open the car door and push her way out of it. She found herself on the frosty moor. She thought she heard a car draw up, she thought she heard a whistle, but she could not be sure. With agonizing slowness she began to crawl back across the moor towards the road, and help. . . .

At about ten o'clock that night Cecil Johnson, driver of one of Foster's buses, was passing Wolf's Nick, on the journey from Newcastle to Otterburn. He saw something smouldering on the moors and, with the conductor, got out to investigate.

'Why, it's the firm's new Hudson,' Johnson cried as they approached the car. The back of it was almost burned out. The roof was a sheet of glowing embers, fanned by the dry, frosty air. One back tyre was still burning, otherwise there were no flames. There was nobody inside the car. Then they heard groans.

A few yards away they found Evelyn Foster. She was lying face downwards, trying desperately to suck the ice on the moor. The flames had burnt her so that she was practically naked from the waist down.

'It was that awful man,' she said, as they knelt down by her side. 'Oh, that awful man. He has gone in a motor-car.'

Johnson wrapped her in his overcoat, and they took her home. The doctor was summoned and came to Otterburn from Bellingham, nine hilly miles away, but time was of little importance, for there was nothing to be done. Evelyn Foster died early the next morning, but before she died she was able to tell her story to her mother while the Otterburn constable, Andy Ferguson, sat near by taking it down. The account of it that has been written so far is the story that she told to Andy Ferguson in the hours before death. Although in great pain, Evelyn Foster was perfectly lucid while making her statement, and even apologized to the doctor for bringing him out on such a night. What she said about the assault was, in view of what happened afterwards particularly interesting.

'Did he interfere with you?' her mother asked.

'Yes.'

Now Mrs Foster broke down and wept, and Evelyn cried: 'Oh, mother, I couldn't help it. I was fighting for my life.'

Evelyn did not know, as everyone present agreed, that there was no hope for her, but a little while before she died at seven o'clock in the morning, she must have realized it.

'I have been murdered,' she cried. 'I have been murdered.' They were her last words.

It was a horrifying crime, but not, the Northumberland County Police must have thought, one which was likely to resist solution for long. There were a good many clues—the occupants of the car from Jedburgh, who would certainly be able to identify and fully describe the stranger; the barman in the Percy Arms, where he had been going for a drink; possibly the people in the car that had picked him up after the crime. Or if this car did not exist (for she had been vague about the car and the whistle), and the man had tried to escape on foot, he certainly would not get far without being noticed, on the frostbound and lonely moors.

And there were other, material clues, found on the scene of the crime. Near to the car a man's glove was found, and so also was Evelyn's scarf. There was a footprint near by, and a mould of this was taken. Her purse had come out of her pocket and lay on the moor, with the money in it untouched. Altogether, there seemed quite sufficient evidence to discover and identify the murderer, and Captain Fullarton James, the Chief Constable, expressed himself as confident that the case could be handled locally. Neither now, nor at any later time, was Scotland Yard called on for assistance.

But the clues that had seemed so substantial all led nowhere, and to no person. The stranger seemed to have been an invisible man—invisible, at least, to everyone but Evelyn Foster. Several motorists were traced who had been in the vicinity of Jedburgh that Tuesday afternoon and evening, and had taken the road to Hexham, but none had admitted meeting a man like the stranger. The man had told Evelyn that the people in the car had given him tea in Jedburgh, but no hotel or café in the town or near it remembered such a party coming in. Every farmhouse, public house, hotel and café for miles round was visited, and the most dramatic manhunt ever known in Northumberland was carried out on the moors. This search was without result.

There was, of course, the usual crop of false clues. There was a man who had behaved suspiciously and had asked for a lift to Darlington, a local shepherd had seen a stranger on the moors, there was a man in Newcastle who talked like an American and had spoken strangely of the crime, and another man who entered a house in Newcastle and told the occupants that there was a body in the back of his car. All these men were between twenty-five and thirty years of age, all were clean shaven, all wore bowler hats and dark overcoats. They served to confirm the vagueness of a description which applied to hundreds of men in the district.

In Otterburn village, too, the man had been invisible. He had said that he was going to the Percy Arms, but the barman there told the police that no stranger had come in on that Tuesday night. Nor, he added, had Evelyn Foster herself come in to ask for him. This was perhaps the first fact that caused the police to feel doubt about the truth of Evelyn Foster's whole story.

And once doubt was felt, there was plenty of confirmation for it. In one detail at least, Evelyn Foster's story was inaccurate. There were no marks of burning on the heather between the road and the point at which the car stopped. The car was found in gear, and a local motor engineer told the police that it had been driven slowly off the road, and set on fire after it had stopped. The fire had not originated in the front of the car, and there was every indication that petrol from a tin carried in a luggage box at the rear had been used. An empty petrol tin was found on the carrier platform at the back of the car, and the neck and cap were discovered near by.

There was the further point that her story of the man pushing her over in the seat and then driving back from Belsay to Wolf's Nick was very improbable. It is very difficult to drive in such a position, and the handbrake on this Hudson car was on the right. Surely she could have pulled it, or got her foot on to the foot brake, to stop the car?

The evidence which must have finally determined the police view of the case, however, was that of Professor Stuart MacDonald, professor of pathology at Durham University, who examined the body after death. Professor MacDonald found extensive burning, most severe on the middle part of the body and in the front. The distribution and severity of the burns suggested that some portions of her clothing had contained an inflammable substance. The burning had started in front, and was most severe on the upper and inner thighs. Its intensity diminished, both upwards and downwards. The distribution of the burns suggested that the girl had been sitting down during some period of the burning.

But the vital points brought out by Professor MacDonald were two. First, there was no sign whatever that Evelyn Foster had been raped. Second, there was no sign of any blow on the face or head sufficiently violent to have stunned her.

It was four weeks after Evelyn Foster died that the inquest, formally opened within three days of her death, was resumed. It was held in the little War Memorial Hall at Otterburn, next door to the Percy Arms. The Coroner's table was draped with a black cloth, and the jurors sat at the trestle table. They were all local men who had known Evelyn well, the vicar, the sub-postmaster, the proprietor of the Percy Arms, a farmer, mill workers. The hall was lighted by acetylene gas, and the light was needed, for the surrounding moors were now in the grip of winter. Some of the roads to Otterburn were impassable, and

Captain Fullarton James ran into a snowdrift while on the way to the inquest, and had to be dug out.

This jury of local men heard some thirty witnesses out of the two hundred from whom the police had taken statements. There is no doubt that they were expecting to have some account of strangers rumoured to be in the district, and of police investigations into their behaviour. One of the jurymen, indeed, had himself seen a stranger—although not one he could positively identify—near the Post Office at about seven o'clock.

Instead of this, they listened to a step-by-step account designed to show that Evelyn Foster had set fire to the car herself. They heard the engineer, they heard Professor MacDonald. They were warned by the Coroner that Evelyn Foster's statement was not to be taken as evidence of fact.

The Coroner showed clearly enough his own agreement with the police viewpoint, in the questions he asked Professor Mac-Donald:

> *Coroner:* Assuming that the car was standing where you saw it, Professor, and the door was open, and she threw some petrol into the back of the car, and then set fire to it—her left leg probably on the running board, her right on the edge of the step into the back of the car—could flames have come back and blinded her?
>
> *MacDonald:* I think it is possible.
>
> *Coroner:* Assuming she herself had upset some petrol over a portion of her clothing and then ignited the car, then that would have been a possible cause?
>
> *MacDonald:* Yes.
>
> *Coroner:* If she had taken the petrol tin and poured petrol over herself in that way, is it possible that she might have got two extra splashes on the top above the breast?
>
> *MacDonald:* It is possible.

Why should Evelyn Foster, a quiet, rather timid, unimpeachably respectable girl of twenty-eight, run her car on to the moors and attempt to burn it? The car had been bought by Evelyn herself out of her savings—she had some £500 in the Post Office when she died—and, to obtain a cheaper rate, had been insured in her father's name. It was suggested by the Coroner that she would have benefitted financially by burning the car—he apparently did not realize that the insurance company would not pay more than the car's current market value.

'On the other hand,' the Coroner added, generously providing another motive, 'you have cases where, for some inexplicable reason, either for notoriety or for the sake of doing something abnormal, a person would do a thing like this.'

The summing up was practically a direction to the jury to say that Evelyn Foster fired the car herself. They were out for just over two hours. When they returned the foreman, McDougal, who was head gardener at Otterburn Towers near by, stood up and read the piece of paper in his hand.

'The jury find a verdict of wilful murder against some person unknown.'

There was silence. Then the Coroner said: 'I suppose you mean that somebody deliberately poured petrol over her and then set her on fire.'

'Yes.'

The Coroner wrote it down. Then he rose. 'That concludes the hearing. Thank you, gentlemen.'

It was not, however, the last comment made on the case. On the day after the verdict Captain Fullarton James made a statement which aroused great indignation in Otterburn. He said:

'We are satisfied that the motor-car in which Miss Foster's supposed murderer is said to have travelled from Jedburgh does not exist.

We are also satisfied that the man she described does not exist.'

INVESTIGATION AND ANALYSIS

Did the man exist? This was the question that I set myself to answer on a visit to Otterburn in a fine week of September 1956, more than twenty years after Evelyn's death. Foster's Garage is still in the main street, but the family's original anger at the attitude of Coroner and police had faded with the years. They could add nothing new to what had appeared in the newspapers, and had no hope of a solution to the crime. I talked, however, to a large number of people in Otterburn, Newcastle and around about, who were more or less directly connected with the case. I also talked to senior officers of the Northumberland County Police at Morpeth.

These gentlemen received me with courtesy and friendliness, but the friendliness was blended with some reserve. There was more reason for this than the rash statement of Captain Fullarton James. At the outset of the case the police had committed a serious blunder. The burnt out car was discovered soon after ten o'clock on Tuesday night, and the police knew of it very shortly afterwards. They put no guard over it, however, until Wednesday morning.

In the meantime (as I learned from a newspaperman in Newcastle) an enterprising journalist had gone out to Wolf's Nick, examined the car thoroughly, lifted the bonnet, found Evelyn Foster's scarf on the ground and put it over the car headlamp, and—it was strongly suggested to me—made the footprint of which the police took a mould. No evidence about this footprint was offered at the inquest. No fingerprint evidence was offered. Nothing was said about the glove found on the scene—was this also perhaps dropped by the reporter?

I should add that this blunder is not officially admitted by the police. A local policeman, now retired, strongly denied that the car had been left unguarded; the police at Morpeth refused to comment on the point. That it is a fact, however, is proved by one small detail of the evidence at the inquest. The police constable who first found Evelyn Foster's scarf, late on Tuesday night, saw it lying on the ground and left it there. When Inspector Russell visited the scene, on Wednesday morning, the scarf was hanging over the car headlamp. If the car was guarded continuously, how had it got there?

This initial error does not, of course, invalidate the theory of arson, but it does suggest that acceptance of this theory would have been welcome to the police. In Otterburn village I found great bitterness about the case, and much criticism of the police. There were roadmenders, I was told, who had seen a car at Elishaw Bridge at the time Evelyn's car drew up; there was a local schoolmistress who had been stopped by a stranger at Otterburn Bridge, a man so unpleasant and strange in his manner that she quickly left him; there was another roadmender who had heard a car turn round outside his house near Belsay (it was suggested by the police that Evelyn Foster had never driven further than Wolf's Nick). None of them was called.

Everybody, police and locals, agreed that the Otterburn police constable, now long retired, was the man who could tell me more about the case and the people involved, than anybody else. When I found Andy Ferguson, living now at Seaton Burn near Newcastle, he refused quite positively to say anything at all. The glove, the scarf, Evelyn Foster's character? His lips were tightly closed.

My own conclusion from those days spent in Otterburn is a firm one: Evelyn Foster was murdered. And there are several points which tell us something positive about her murderer. But before coming to them, let me analyze what may be called the negative side—the case against Evelyn Foster, which was based on her dying statement.

There are four main points to be answered:

1 Her failure to enter the Percy Arms and ask for the stranger.

2 Her unlikely account of the way in which he drove back from Belsay.

3 Her story of being attacked and raped.

4 Her story of the car that approached afterwards, and the whistle.

Let us go through the points in order. She said that the man 'hailed her' at the Bridge, which is no more than a few yards beyond the Percy Arms. If she really meant that he hailed her—called to her—then she might have heard him and not stopped at the hotel. It must also be remembered that her story was told in a low voice and spasmodically, so that the constable taking notes could not always hear what she said.

The second point, like much else in the story, is really in her favour. If she had wished to do so, she could easily have invented so many much more probable incidents which would have involved a change of seats, and his taking the steering wheel.

She said that the man hit her, and this possibility was not denied by Professor MacDonald, who agreed that a light blow in the eye, or even a blow on the head, might well leave no trace. She did not say that the blows stunned her, but that she 'became unconscious,' possibly from shock or fright. The questions put by the Coroner were almost throughout phrased so that her story appeared in the most unfavourable possible light.

The point about the rape is the most interesting of all. When her mother first asked Evelyn what had happened, she replied: 'Oh, it's been that man. He hit me and burned me.' There was nothing here about rape. Later she agreed when her mother asked if the man had 'interfered with her,' but at first Mrs Foster did not necessarily put a sexual interpretation upon this reply. In fact she did so only at the suggestion of the police solicitor.

I should add that the possibility, which was at one time in my own mind, that Evelyn Foster might have been carrying on an affair with a local man, unknown to her family or other Otterburn inhabitants, was decisively disposed of. The police never found anything to support such a theory; and I was assured by more than one person in the village that the community was so closely knit that it would have been absolutely impossible for such a relationship to have existed without being known to people in the district. Professor MacDonald's opinion was that she had died a virgin, although the nature of the burns made it impossible for him to be quite sure.

And finally, a car did stop at Wolf's Nick, at about half past nine. The driver saw smoke and flames from the car on the moor, could see nobody moving out there, and drove on without stopping to investigate. His later movements were checked, and his story authenticated. This could have been the car that Evelyn Foster heard.

There is also what may be called the problem of the missing matches. Evelyn did not smoke, or carry matches. No matches were found in or near the car. She had no lighter. How, then, did she set fire to the car?

And there is another point. If, as was suggested, she meant to set fire to the car and claim that it had been an accident, what would she have said about the missing passenger? Certainly no insurance company would have paid up without verification from him.

Summing up, one may admit that Evelyn Foster's dying statement is not tidy, nor wholly satisfactory. Yet the contradictions involved in denying it are quite staggering. Accept it as a statement basically true (although inaccurate in some details) and we have a picture of the murderer.

He was a man with a criminal record, he probably lived or had lived in the North East, and he was a skillful car driver. It is quite likely that, just before the Otterburn murder, he had committed another crime.

Here is the reasoning behind these conclusions.

His criminal record. Once we accept Evelyn's story, and accept as a fact that there *was* a car at Elishaw Bridge, we must ask: why did not its occupants come forward? There can be only one good reason—that they were afraid of revealing themselves to the police. This would be natural enough if they were criminals, who had recently done a job up in Scotland, and had decided to split up temporarily. It would be interesting to know how far the police pushed this line of enquiry.

He probably lived in, the North East. Or at least he knew it very well. The road from Otterburn to Belsay has not greatly changed since 1931, although at Wolf's Nick the embankment has been built up. At that time, however, there was *practically no other spot along this road* where a car could have been driven onto the moor. The bank here was steep, the drop between 4 feet and 4 feet 6 inches, but it was not precipitous. The person who, on this dark night, knew exactly where he should stop to drive the car off the road, obviously had very considerable local knowledge.

He was a skillful driver. To drive the car down the bank was a tricky, and even dangerous, operation. There was no reason why Evelyn Foster should have risked it—or, incidentally, have tried to fire the car from the back rather than from the engine. On the other hand, there was every reason why her murderer should want to get the car off the road and on to the moor. It meant that he ran much less risk of immediate detection by a passing car, and thus helped to facilitate his escape.

There remain two questions. Why did he do it and how did he escape? We are in the region of what is no more than logical conjecture in suggesting that the man had a record not merely of crime, but of violent crime. There can be little doubt that when he first asked for a lift, he genuinely wanted to be driven to Ponteland. Something on the way changed his ·mind. Perhaps Evelyn Foster asked indiscreet questions, perhaps he suddenly felt himself in danger of discovery through her, perhaps his presence alone with her on the moors roused the urge to sadistic violence that is felt by many criminals. We do not know the reasons, only what happened.

Nor do we know how he escaped—whether he had an accomplice who picked him up, whether he managed somehow to get to Newcastle, or made his way to Hexham and there rejoined his companions, or found a hiding place on the moors. He walks out of the story, after killing Evelyn Foster, as abruptly as he had walked into it; but the memory of the invisible man, neat, gentlemanly, bowler-hatted, the man who was seen by nobody but Evelyn Foster but who surely existed, still haunts the people of Otterburn and the moors.

No name this time, alas — but do you get the feeling that perhaps it is only the law of libel that prevents it? Time will tell.

That no such consideration restrained Damon Runyon in the series of pieces that follow is a tribute, in part, to the greater freedom of the press that obtains in America, and there is no doubt at all that US newspapers have had a much greater impact on the cause of justice: witness Watergate, which simply could not have happened in Britain and many other countries, and the recent palaver about the publication of Spycatcher, still unresolved as this book goes to press.

The Snyder-Gray case was headline news all over the world as the story broke, and it still ranks as one fo the most celebrated murders of all time. As Damon Runyon says at the end of his reports, 'We have been three-sheeting Henry Judd and Ruth to good purpose.'

Ruth Snyder with her daughter Lorraine.

DAMON RUNYON

The 'Perfect' Crime that was Unspeakably Dumb

Long Island City, New York, April 19, 1927

A chilly looking blonde with frosty eyes and one of those marble, you-bet-you-will chins, and an inert, scare-drunk fellow that you couldn't miss among any hundred men as a dead set-up for a blonde, or the shell game, or maybe a gold brick.

Mrs Ruth Snyder and Henry Judd Gray are on trial in the huge weatherbeaten old court house of Queens County in Long Island City, just across the river from the roar of New York, for what might be called for want of a better name, The Dumbbell Murder. It was so dumb.

They are charged with the slaughter four weeks ago of Albert Snyder, art editor of the magazine, *Motor Boating*, the blonde's husband and father of her nine-year-old daughter, under circumstances that for sheer stupidity and brutality have seldom been equalled in the history of crime.

It was stupid beyond imagination, and so brutal that the thought of it probably makes many a peaceful, home-loving Long Islander of the Albert Snyder type shiver in his pajamas as he prepares for bed.

They killed Snyder as he slumbered, so they both admitted in confessions—Mrs Snyder has since repudiated hers—first whacking him on the head with a sash weight, then giving him a few whiffs of chloroform, and finally tightened a strand of picture wire around his throat so he wouldn't revive.

This matter disposed of, they went into an adjoining room and had a few drinks of whiskey used by some Long Islanders, which is very bad, and talked things over. They thought they had committed 'the perfect crime,' whatever that may be. It was probably the most imperfect crime on record. It was cruel, atrocious and unspeakably dumb.

They were red-hot lovers then, these two, but they are strangers now. They never exchanged a glance yesterday as they sat in the cavernous old court room while the citizenry of Long Island tramped in and out of the jury box, and the attorneys tried to get a jury of twelve men together without success.

Plumbers, clerks, electricians, merchants, bakers, butchers, barbers, painters, salesmen, machinists, delicatessen dealers, garage employers, realtors and gardeners from the cities and the hamlets of the County of Queens were in the procession that marched through the jury box answering questions as to their views on the death penalty, and their sympathies toward women, and other things.

Out of fifty men, old and young, married and single, bald and hairy, not one was found acceptable to both sides. Forty-three were excused, the State challenged one peremptorily, the attorneys for Mrs Snyder five, and the attorneys for Gray one. Each defendant is allowed thirty peremptory challenges, the State thirty against each defendant.

At this rate they may be able to get a jury before the Long Island corn is ripe. The State is asking that Mrs Snyder and her meek looking Lothario be given the well-known 'hot seat' in Sing Sing, more generally known as the electric chair, and a lot of the talesmen interrogated today seemed to have a prejudice against that form of punishment.

Others had opinions as to the guilt or innocence that they said they couldn't possibly change. A few citizens seemed kindly disposed toward jury service, possibly because they haven't anything at hand for the next few weeks, but they got short shrift from the lawyers. The jury box was quite empty at the close of the day's work.

Mrs Snyder, the woman who has been called a Jezebel, a lineal descendant of the Borgia outfit, and a lot of other names, came in for the morning session of court stepping along briskly in her patent-leather pumps, with little short steps.

She is not bad looking. I have seen much worse. She is

thirty-three and looks just about that, though you cannot tell much about blondes. She has a good figure, slim and trim, with narrow shoulders. She is of medium height and I thought she carried her clothes off rather smartly. She wore a black dress and a black silk coat with a collar of black fur. Some of the girl reporters said it was dyed ermine; others pronounced it rabbit.

They made derogatory remarks about her hat. It was a tight-fitting thing called, I believe, a beret. Wisps of her straw-colored hair straggled out from under it. Mrs Snyder wears her hair bobbed, the back of the bobbing rather ragged. She is of the Scandinavian type. Her parents are Norwegian and Swedish.

Her eyes are blue-green, and as chilly looking as an ice cream cone. If all that Henry Judd Gray says of her actions the night of the murder is true, her veins carry ice water. Gray says he dropped the sash weight after slugging the sleeping Snyder with it once and that Mrs Snyder picked it up and finished the job.

Gray's mother and sister, Mrs Margaret Gray, and Mrs Harold Logan, took seats in the court room just behind Mrs Snyder. At the afternoon session, Mrs Gray, a small, determined-looking woman of middle age, hitched her chair over so she was looking right into Mrs Snyder's face.

There was a rather grim expression in Mrs Gray's eyes. She wore a black hat and a black coat with a fur collar, a spray of artificial flowers was pinned to the collar. Her eyelids were red as if she had been weeping.

The sister, Mrs Logan, is plump and pleasant looking. Gray's wife has left him flat, in the midst of his troubles and gone to Norwalk, Conn., with their nine-year-old daughter. She never knew her husband was playing that Don Juan business when she thought he was out peddling corsets. That is she never knew it until the murder.

Gray, a spindly fellow in physical build, entered the court room with quick, jerky little steps behind an officer, and sat down between his attorneys, Samuel L. Miller and William L. Millard. His back was to Mrs Snyder who sat about ten feet distant. Her eyes were on a level with the back of his narrow head.

SOLVED

Gray was neatly dressed in a dark suit, with a white starched collar and subdued tie. He has always been a bit to the dressy side, it is said. He wears big, horn-rimmed spectacles and his eyes have a startled expression. You couldn't find a meeker, milder looking fellow in seven states, this man who is charged with one of the most horrible crimes in history.

He occasionally conferred with his attorneys as the examination of the talesmen was going forward, but not often. He sat in one position almost the entire day, half slumped down in his chair, a melancholy looking figure for a fellow who once thought of 'the perfect crime.'

Mrs Snyder and Gray have been 'hollering copper' on each other lately, as the boys say. That is, they have been telling. Gray's defense goes back to old Mr Adam, that the woman beguiled him, while Mrs Snyder says he is a 'jackal,' and a lot of other things besides that, and claims that he is hiding behind her skirts.

She will claim, it is said, that while she at first entered into the conspiracy to kill her husband, she later tried to dissuade Gray from going through with it, and tried to prevent the crime. The attorneys will undoubtedly try to picture their respective clients as the victims of each other.

Mrs Snyder didn't want to be tried with Gray, but Gray was very anxious to be tried with Mrs Snyder. It is said that no Queens County jury ever sent a woman to death, which is what the State will ask of this jury, if it ever gets one. The relations among the attorneys for the two defendants are evidently not on the theory of 'one for all and all for one.' Probably the attorneys for Gray do not care what happens to Mrs Snyder, and probably the attorneys for Mrs Snyder feel the same way about Gray.

Edgar Hazelton, a close-trimmed dapper looking man, with a jutting chin and with a pince-nez balanced on a hawk beak, who represents Mrs Snyder, did most of the questioning of the talesmen for the defense. His associate, Dana Wallace, is a former district attorney of Queens County, and the pair are said to be among the ablest lawyers on Long Island. It is related that they have defended eleven murder cases without a conviction going against them.

Damon Runyon at the time of the Snyder-Gray trail.

Supreme Court Justice Townsend Scudder is presiding over the court room, which has a towering ceiling with a stained glass skylight, and heavy dark oak furniture with high-backed pews for the spectators. Only no spectators were admitted today because the room was needed for the talesmen.

The court room is so huge it was difficult to hear what was going on at any distance from the bench. I believe it is the largest court room in the country. It was there that the trial scene in the picture *Manslaughter* was filmed.

In the court room on the floor below was held the trial of Mrs Nack in the famous Guldensuppe murder thirty years ago, when the reporters used carrier pigeons to take their copy across the river to Park Row.

Microphones have been posted on the tables, and amplifiers have been rigged up on the walls, probably the first time this was ever done in a murder trial, but the apparatus wasn't working any too well today, and one hundred and twenty newspaper writers scattered around the tables listened with their hands cupped behind their ears.

Here is another record, the number of writers covering the trial. We have novelists, preachers, playwrights, fiction writers, sports writers and journalists at the press benches. Also we have nobility in the persons of the Marquis of Queensbury and Mrs Marquis. The Marquis is a grandson of the gent whose name is attached to the rules governing the manly art of scrambling ears, but the young man wore a pair of fancy-topped shoes yesterday that surprised me. It isn't done you know, really!

The Reverend John Roach Straton was present wearing a Buster Brown necktie that was almost unclerical. A Catholic priest was on hand, but he carried no pad or pencil to deceive us. Some of the writers came attended by their secretaries, which shows you how far we have gone since the days of the carrier pigeons at the Guldensuppe trial.

There were quite a number of philosophers. I have been requested by my Broadway constituency to ascertain if possible what, if anything, philosophy suggests when a hotsy-totsy blonde with whom a guy is enamoured tells him to do thus and so. But then a philosopher probably never gets tangled up with blondes, or he wouldn't be a philosopher.

Mrs Snyder showed signs that might have been either nervousness or just sheer impatience during the day. Her fingers constantly toyed with a string of black beads at her throat. Her entire set-up suggested mourning. She has nice white hands, but they are not so small as Gray's. His hands are quite effeminate.

In fact, the alienists who examined Gray and pronounced him quite sane say he is effeminate in many ways. Gray showed no signs of nervousness or any particular animation whatever. He just sat there. It must be a strain on a man to sit for hours knowing the eyes of a woman who is trying to get him all burned up are beating against the back of his neck and not turn around and give her at least one good hot glare.

April 27, 1927

Some say Mrs Ruth Snyder 'wept silently' in court yesterday. It may be so. I could detect no sparkle of tears against the white marble mask, but it is conceivable that even the very gods were weeping silently as a gruff voice slowly recited the blond woman's own story of the murder of her husband by herself and Henry Judd Gray.

Let no one infer she is altogether without tenderness of heart, for when they were jotting down the confession that was read in the court room in Long Island City, Peter M. Daly, an assistant district attorney, asked her:

'Mrs Snyder, why did you kill your husband?'

He wanted to know.

'Don't put it that way,' she said, according to his testimony yesterday. 'It sounds so cruel.'

'Well, that is what you did, isn't it?' he asked, in some surprise.

'Yes,' he claims she answered, 'but I don't like that term.'

A not astonishing distaste, you must admit.

'Well, why did you kill him?' persisted the curious Daly.

'To get rid of him,' she answered, simply, according to Daly's testimony; and indeed that seems to have been her main idea throughout, if all the evidence the State has so far developed is true.

She afterward repudiated the confession that was presented yesterday, with her attorneys trying to bring out from the State's witnesses that she was sick and confused when she told her bloody yarn five weeks ago.

The woman, in her incongruous widow's weeds sat listening intently to the reading of her original confession to the jury, possibly the most horrible tale that ever fell from human lips, the tale of a crime unutterably brutal and cold-blooded and unspeakably dumb.

Her mouth opened occasionally as if framing words, and once she said no quite distinctly, an unconscious utterance, which may have been a denial of some utterance by the lawyer or perhaps an assurance to her soul that she was not alive and awake.

This is a strange woman, this Mrs Ruth Brown Snyder, a different woman to different men.

To the inert Henry Judd Gray, her partner in crime, sitting at the table just in front of her, as soggy looking as a dummy in his loose hanging clothes, she was a 'woman of great charm,' as he said in his confession which was outlined in court by a police officer yesterday.

To big, hale and hearty George P. McLaughlin, former police commissioner of New York City, who heard her original statement of the butchery, she was a 'woman of great calm,' as he said on the witness stand yesterday.

To the male reporters who have been following the trial she is all that, anyway, though they construe her calm as more the chill of the icy Northland, whence came her parents.

The attorneys for Mrs Snyder, the nimble Dana Wallace and Edgar Hazelton, indicated yesterday clearly that part of their line of defense, in this devil-take-the-hindmost scramble between Ruth and Henry Judd is to be an attempted impeachment of the confession, and Gray's attorneys showed the same thought.

Samuel L. Miller, representing Gray, charged that the confession of the corset salesman was secured while he was under duress and by intimidation and threats.

Gray sat with his chin in his hands, his eyes on the floor, scarcely moving a muscle as Mrs Snyder's confession, damning him in almost every word, was read. I have never seen him show much animation at best, but yesterday he seemed completely sunk. He occasionally conferred in whispers through his fingers with one of his attorneys, but with not the slightest show of interest.

It was Gray who slugged poor Albert Snyder with the five-pound sash weight as the art editor lay asleep in his bed, so Mrs Snyder's confession relates, while Mrs Snyder stood outside in the hall, seeing, by the dim light thrown into the chamber of horror by an arc in the street, the rise and fall of the paper-wrapped weight in Gray's hand.

What a scene that must have been!

Twice she heard her husband groan. Roused from an alcoholic stupor by the first thump on his head, he groaned. Then groaned again. Silence. Out came Henry Judd Gray, saying: 'Well, I guess that's it.'

But the confessions do not jibe here. The outline of Gray's confession, which will be read today, indicates Gray says he dropped the weight after whacking Snyder once, and that Ruth picked it up 'and belabored him.'

'Those were Gray's words—"belabored him,"' ex-Commissioner McLaughlin said yesterday.

District Attorney Newcombe overlooked an opportunity for the dramatic yesterday that old David Belasco, sitting back in the crowd, probably envied, in the reading of Ruth's confession. This was first identified by Peter M. Daly, the assistant mentioned above, after Ruth's attorneys had failed in a hot battle against its admission.

Newcombe stood before the jury with the typewritten sheets in one hand and talked off the words without elocutionary effort, the microphone carrying his voice out over the silent court room. The place was jammed. Women again. At the afternoon session they almost tore the buttons off the uniforms of the coppers on guard at the doors, trying to shove past them. The cops gallantly repulsed the charge.

The first paragraphs of the confession, made to Daly soon after the murder and under circumstances that the defense is attacking, were given over to a recital of Ruth's early life—born on Manhattan Island thirty-three years ago, a schoolgirl, an employee in the same magazine office with Snyder, then an artist when she married him.

The thing has been told so often before that I here go over it sketchily. Soon she was unhappy with her husband, fourteen years older than herself. He constantly belittled her. He threatened to blow out her brains. He was a good provider for herself and their nine-year-old daughter, but wouldn't take her out—so she took to stepping out, as they say. An old, old yarn—Friend Husband a non-stepper, Friend Wife full of go.

She met Henry Judd Gray, the corset salesman, in Henry's restaurant in the once-throbbing Thirties in New York, and the first thing anybody knew she and Henry were thicker than is meet and proper. She told Henry of her matrimonial woes, and Henry, himself a married man, with a young daughter, was duly sympathetic.

But let's get down to the murder.

She wrote Henry and told him how Albert Snyder had threatened her life. She wrote in a code they had rigged up for their own private use, and Henry answered, saying the only thing to do was to get rid of Albert. They had talked of ways and means, and Gray gave her the famous sash weight and went out to Queens Village one night to wipe Albert Snyder out.

They got cold feet that night and Albert lived. Then Snyder again threatened her, the confession said, and told her to get out of his house, so she wrote to Henry once more, and Henry wrote back, saying, 'We will deliver the goods Saturday.' That meant Saturday, March 19. They arranged all the details by correspondence.

Henry arranged his alibi in Syracuse and came to New York the night she and her husband and child were at the Fidgeons' party. She left a door unlocked so Henry could get in the room of her mother, Mrs Josephine Brown, who was away for the night. Ruth saw him there and talked with him a moment when she came back from the party with her husband and child.

Henry had the sash weight which she had left under the pillow in Mrs Brown's room for him. He had chloroform, some cheese-cloth and a blue cotton handkerchief. Also, she had hospitably left a quart of liquor for him of which he drank about half. She put her child to bed, then went into her husband's room and waited until he was asleep, then returned to the waiting Henry.

They talked briefly, and Henry kissed her and went into Albert Snyder's room. She stood in the hallway and saw Gray pummel the sleeping man with the sash weight as related. Then Gray tied Snyder's hands and feet, put the handkerchief, saturated with chloroform, over his face, besides stuffing his mouth and nostrils with the gauze, also soaked with chloroform. Then Henry turned Snyder over so the art editor's face would be buried in a pillow and rejoined Ruth.

Henry Judd wore rubber gloves at his sanguinary task, the confession said, and he went to the bathroom to wash his hands. He found blood on his shirt, so Ruth went into the room where the dead man lay, got one of Albert Snyder's shirts and gave it to Henry Judd. Then they went into the cellar and burned the bloody shirt and put the sash weight into a tool box after rubbing it with ashes.

Now, they returned to the sitting room, this pair, and Henry Judd suddenly thought of some picture wire he had brought alone, presumably to tie Snyder's hands and feet. At least, he had two pieces, Ruth said. One he had lost, so he took the other and went into the death chamber and wrapped the wire around Albert Snyder's throat tightening it with his fingers.

Then he went around and upset the premises generally, to bear out the robbery idea, then sat and gossiped, talking of this and that until daybreak, when Henry Judd tied his sweetheart's hands and feet and left to return to Syracuse. She first went out and got a wallet out of Albert Snyder's pocket and gave it to Henry Judd. She does not know how much it contained.

After Henry's departure, she rolled out of her mother's bed, whereon he had placed her, and aroused her little daughter, telling her to get a neighbor.

Such, in substance and briefly, was the story of that night in Queens Village.

There was a supplemental statement with reference to some letters, including one from Gray, sent from Syracuse after he had departed from New York to join hands with her in the slaughter. Peter M. Daly asked her, at a time when Gray had not yet been definitely hooked with the crime, how she reconciled the postmark with her statement of the murder and she said it was part of Henry's alibi.

Thus Ruth was 'hollering copper' on Henry, even before she knew Henry was 'hollering copper' on her. They didn't stand hitched a minute after the showdown came.

Wallace wanted to know if Mrs Snyder hadn't said she was confused and sick while making the statement, but Daly said no. He admitted Mrs Snyder had a crying spell and that a physician was called in. Wallace mentioned it as a fainting spell, but Daly wouldn't concede it was such. It seemed to be agreed it was some kind of a spell, however.

Daly said she asked if she could see Gray when he got to town. He said she seemed to know that Gray was on his way to New York. The defense devoted more time to Daly than to any other witness so far, Millard of Gray's counsel joining in the cross-examination.

Gray's attorneys had objected to some questions asked by Wallace and now Mrs Snyder's lawyers objected to Millard's questions.

This case has been presented from the beginning in rather a disordered manner, it seems to me, like one of those new-fangled plays that violate all the established rules from the theatre.

For instance, at the morning session, Millard started out cross-examining Lieutenant Dorschell, of the New York Police Department, relative to a drawing made by Gray of the hardware store in Kingston, where he bought the sash weight and the picture wire. This drawing was made at three o'clock in the morning of Gray's arrival in New York after his ride from Syracuse, where he was arrested. Millard inquired into the physical condition of Gray at the time he made the drawing and Dorschell said he seemed to be all right.

Millard then explained to Justice Scudder that he wanted to show under what conditions the drawing was made. He said he desired to present testimony showing that the drawing came after a long examination of Gray by the police, and to that end Justice Scudder gave him permission to call and cross-examine a witness who had not appeared before.

It is certainly somewhat unusual to bring in for cross-examination by the defense a witness who would ordinarily be one of the State's most important witnesses.

The witness was Michael S. McDermott, another lieutenant of New York Police, who brought Gray from Syracuse, and who told with infinite detail of Gray's confession. He said Gray took the thing as a joke at first, maintaining his complete innocence.

McDermott said Gray seemed to find the company he was in 'congenial' most of the journey, a statement that produced a light giggle in the court. He said that Gray at no time seemed to become serious until they told him they had the contents of his wastepaper basket, which included the Pullman stub.

' "Do you know, Judd, we have the Pullman ticket you used from Syracuse to New York?' Then he said, 'Well, gentlemen, I was at the Snyder home that night." '

McDermott said Gray voluntarily launched into a narrative of the bloody night in Queens Village. He told how Gray had subsequently given this same narrative to a stenographer and identified and initialed the various articles used in the commission of the crime.

Now the State proceeded to establish the purchase of the sash weight and picture wire by Gray in Kingston, March 4, last.

Margaret Hamilton, a buyer for a Kingston store, who knows Henry Judd, said she saw him there on that date. She is a stout lady, and wore a startlingly red hat and red scarf.

Arthur R. Bailey, a thin, gray, studious looking man, wearing glasses, a clerk in a Kingston hardware store, didn't seem to remember selling a five-pound sash weight on March 4, although he identified what you might call a bill of sale in his handwriting, taken from the records of the store. He said his store sold any number of sash weights, but he never recalled any transaction involving one sash weight. Mr Bailey obviously didn't care about being mixed up in this trial business, anyway.

John Sanford, a young Negro, testified most briefly to getting this sash weight from the warehouse.

It seemed a lot of bother about a sash weight that has lost some of its importance since the doctors testified that the wallops with it alone did not cause Snyder's death.

Reginald Rose, youthful, black-haired, black-browed and a bit to the sheikish side, a ticket seller for the New York Central, told of selling Gray a railroad ticket to Syracuse and a Pullman seat reservation to Albany on the night of March 19 for the following day, which was the day after the murder. Gray made the return reservation immediately upon his arrival in New York the night he ran down for the killing.

Millard became a bit curious over Rose's clear recollection of this particular sale of a ticket out of the many a ticket seller makes every day and it developed that Rose even remembered how Gray was dressed. He wore a fedora hat and an overcoat.

Rose said he remembered the sale because it wasn't commonplace to sell a railroad ticket to Syracuse and a seat to Albany.

Now came testimony about the party which Mr and Mrs Snyder and their small daughter, Lorraine, attended the night of the murder. It was at the home of Milton C. Fidgeon, and Mr Fidgeon himself took the stand, stout, smooth of face and prosperous-looking.

There had been liquor at the party said Mr Fidgeon. He served one drink, then someone asked if it was not time for another, so he went into the kitchen to produce the second shot.

Mrs Snyder came to him there and said she wasn't drinking, but to give her portion to her husband. The Snyders went home about two o'clock in a pleasant frame of mind, as Mr Fidgeon said on cross-examination by Wallace.

April 28, 1927

Right back to old Father Adam, the original, and perhaps the loudest 'squawker' among mankind against women, went Henry Judd Gray in telling how and why he lent his hand to the butchery of Albert Snyder.

She—she—she—she—she—she—she—she. That was the burden of the bloody song of the little corset salesman as read out in the packed court room in Long Island City yesterday.

She—she—she—she—she—she. 'Twas an echo from across the ages and an old familiar echo, at that. It was the same old 'squawk' of Brother Man whenever and wherever he is in a jam, that was first framed in the words:

'She gave me of the tree, and I did eat.'

It has been put in various forms since then, as Henry Judd Gray, for one notable instance close at hand, put it in the form of eleven long typewritten pages that were read yesterday, but in any form and in any language it remains a 'squawk.'

'She played me pretty hard.' . . . 'She said, "You're going to do it, aren't you?" ' . . . 'She kissed me.' . . . She did this . . . She did that . . . Always she—she—she—she—she ran the confession of Henry Judd.

And 'she'—the woman-accused, how did she take this most gruesome squawk?

Well, on the whole, better than you might expect.

You must remember it was the first time she had ever heard the confession of the man who once called her 'Momsie.' She probably had an inkling of it, but not its exact terms.

For a few minutes her greenish blue eyes roared with such fury that I would not have been surprised to see her leap up, grab the window sash weight that lay among the exhibits on the district attorney's table and perform the same offices on the shrinking Gray that he says she performed on her sleeping husband.

She 'belabored him,' Gray's confession reads, and I half expected her to belabor Gray.

Her thin lips curled to a distinct snarl at some passages in the statement. I thought of a wildcat and a female cat, at that, on a leash. Once or twice she smiled, but it was a smile of insensate rage, not amusement. She once emitted a push of breath in a loud 'phew,' as you have perhaps done yourself over some tall tale.

The marble mask was contorted by her emotions for a time, she often shook her head in silent denial of the astounding charges of Gray, then finally she settled back calmly, watchful, attentive, and with an expression of unutterable contempt as the story of she—she—she—she ran along.

Contempt for Henry Judd, no doubt. True, she herself

squawked on Henry Judd, at about the same time Henry Judd was squawking on her, but it is a woman's inalienable right to squawk.

As for Henry Judd, I still doubt he will last it out. He reminds me of a slowly collapsing lump of tallow. He sat huddled up in his baggy clothes, his eyes on the floor, his chin in hand, while the confession was being read. He seems to be folding up inch by inch every day.

He acts as if he is only semi-conscious. If he was a fighter and came back to his corner in his present condition, they would give him smelling salts.

The man is a wreck, a strange contrast to the alert blonde at the table behind him.

The room was packed with women yesterday, well-dressed, richly-befurred women from Park Avenue, and Broadway, and others not so well dressed from Long Island City, and the small towns farther down the Island. There were giggling young schoolgirls and staid-looking matrons, and my friends, what do you think? Their sympathy is for Henry Judd Gray!

I made a point of listening to their opinions as they packed the hallways and jammed the elevators of the old court house yesterday and canvassed some of them personally, and they are all sorry for Gray. Perhaps it is his forlorn looking aspect as he sits inert, numb, never raising his head, a sad spectacle of a man who admits he took part in one of the most atrocious murders in history.

There is no sympathy for Mrs Snyder among the women and very little among the men. They all say something drastic ought to be done to her.

How do you account for that—

But while Henry Judd's confession puts most of the blame on the woman, Mrs Snyder's attorneys, the pugnacious Edgar Hazelton and the sharp Dana Wallace, who remind me for all the world of a brace of restless terriers with their brick maneuvers, began making an effort yesterday that shows they intend trying to make Henry Judd the goat.

When District Attorney Newcombe stood up to read Gray's confession, a deep silence fell over the room, packed from wall to wall. Many of the spectators were standing. Mrs Snyder leaned forward on the table in front of her, but Gray never raised his eyes from the floor, then or thereafter.

You could hear little gasps as of horror or unbelief from some of the women spectators as Newcombe read on in a cold, passionless voice, especially when the confession got down to the actual murder.

It began with the story of their meeting in Henry's restaurant about two years ago. They were introduced by Harry Folsom of New Canaan, Conn., who had picked Mrs Snyder and another up in the restaurant, so ran the confession, rather giving the impression that the blonde was one of those women who can be 'picked up.' Gray said:

'She is a woman of great charm. I probably don't have to tell you that. I did like her very much, and she was good company and apparently a good pal to spend an evening with.'

I looked over at Mrs Snyder as this paragraph was read, and there was a shadow of a smile on the marble mask. The expression altered when the story began to tell an instant later of them starting intimate relations in August. Gray added:

'Prior to that she was just a woman I respected.'

Perhaps I should here explain that most of this confession was made by Gray on the train when he was being brought from Syracuse to New York after the murder and later elaborated in its details by him.

Well, they got very friendly, and soon she was calling him up and writing him. 'She played me pretty hard,' he said. He went out to her house for luncheon, and met her mother, although he did not think the mother knew anything of their relations.

Presently Mrs Snyder got to telling of her unhappiness with Albert. Gray told her, he says, that he himself was married and had a fine wife and was very happy at home, so there could never be anything between him and Mrs Snyder.

She told him of several attempts she had made on Albert Snyder's life, once giving him sleeping powders, and again bichloride of mercury, but Albert kept on living.

Finally, said Gray, 'She started to hound me on this plan to assist her.'

The plan for killing Snyder, presumably. But the little corset salesman added quite naively, 'I have always been a gentleman and I have always been on the level with everybody. I have a good many friends. If I ever have any after this I don't know.'

He said he absolutely refused to listen to the charmer's sanguinary wiles at first, then 'with some veiled threats and intents of love-making, she reached the point where she got me in such a whirl that I didn't know where I was at.'

Clarence A. Stewart, superintendent of the safety deposit vault of the Queens-Bellaire Bank of Queens Village, testified that Mrs Snyder rented two boxes, one under the name of Ruth M. Brown, the other under the name of Ruth M. Snyder. Stewart is a mild-looking man who kept his overcoat on while testifying. He stood up when asked to identify Mrs Snyder and peered at her through his specs.

Edward C. Kern, cashier of the same bank, heavy-set and bland, testified to the contents of these boxes. In the box taken in the name of Ruth M. Brown was $53,000 worth of insurance policies on Albert Snyder and receipts for the payment of the premiums. In the box under the name of Ruth M. Snyder were papers mainly of a family nature relating to the affairs of Ruth and her dead husband, such as fire and burglary insurance policies, receipts and the like.

There seemed to be plenty of fire insurance on the Snyder home. There was some Roxy Theatre stock among other things and papers representing small investments by the dead art editor.

Samuel Willis, a tall, spare, elderly resident of Queens Village, told of seeing Henry Judd Gray waiting for a bus at 5:50 on the morning of March 20, hard by a police booth at Hillside Avenue and Springfield Boulevard, in Queens Village. Police Officer Smith, on duty there, was indulging in a little pistol practice at bottles and Willis said Gray remarked after the officer finished:

'I'd hate to stand in front of him and have him shoot at me.'

The bailiffs had to rap for order. Cross-examined by Samuel L. Miller, the witness said his attention was attracted to Gray 'by that little dimple in his chin.' He said Gray took the bus with him and he saw no more of Henry Judd. This was just after

Gray had left the Snyder home to hurry back to Syracuse, you understand.

April 29, 1927

There was little breathing space left in the yellowish-walled old court room when the morning session opened.

In the jam I observed many ladies and gents with dark circles around their eyes which indicated loss of sleep, or bad livers. I identified them as of the great American stage, playwrights, producers, actors, and even actresses.

They were present, as I gathered, to acquire local color for their current, or future contributions to the thespian art, and the hour was a trifle early for them to be abroad in the land. They sat yesterday writing through the proceedings and perhaps inwardly criticizing the stage setting and thinking how unrealistic the trial is as compared to their own productions.

Among the other spectators comfortably chaired, or standing on tired feet, were ladies running from a couple of inches to three yards wide. They were from all parts of Long Island, and the other boroughs of the large and thriving City of New York, the inmates of which are supposed to be so very blasé but who certainly dearly love their murder cases.

A big crowd waited in the hallways and outside the court house. Tearful females implored the obdurate cops guarding the stairs and the court room doors, to ease them through somehow.

It was a strange gathering. Solid-looking citizens found a morning to waste. They would probably have felt greatly inconvenienced had they been requested to spend the same amount of time on a mission of mercy. Several preachers and some of our best known public 'pests' were scattered around the premises. What a fine commentary, my friends, on what someone has mentioned as our vaunted intelligence.

Peggy Hopkins, Countess Morner and what not, Joyce, the famous grass-widow, came again to dazzle all the beholders with the magnificence of her display. It was Peggy's second visit. Probably she didn't believe her eyes and ears on her first visit that a lady had seemed to have some difficulty in getting rid of her husband. Peggy never did, you can bet on that. She wore a suit of a distressing green and a red fox collar and arrived at the court house in a little old last year's Rolls-Royce.

Paul Mathis, a thin, dark youth, was the first witness. He remembered carting Henry Judd from the Jamaica Station on the subway on Fifty-eighth Street, March 20, the morning of the murder.

The fare was $8.55. Gray gave him a five cent tip. It is not likely Mathis will ever forget Henry Judd if the young man is like the average taxi jockey.

William L. Millard of Gray's counsel, verbally belted away at Mathis rather snappishly, trying to find out if the young man's memory of Henry Judd hadn't been encouraged by the district attorney's office. Millard has a cutting voice when he is cross-examining and is given to sharp asides. The Court has generally admonished him on several occasions.

Justice Scudder does not allow the lawyers to get far out of conversational bounds. My friend, Senator Alexander Simpson, of Hall-Mills fame, would probably feel his style was quite cramped in Justice Scudder's court.

Van Voorhees, a thin, middle-aged man, conductor of the train that carried Gray back to Syracuse from his murder errand, identified Gray. So did George Fullerton, a dusky porter.

'We concede the defendant was on the train,' said Millard, closing that line of testimony.

Now came Haddon Gray, of 207 Clark Street, Syracuse, the insurance man who unwittingly helped Judd Gray with his famous alibi. Haddon and Judd had been friends twenty years, but are not related. Gray is a young man of brisk manner and appearance, of medium height, with black hair parted in the middle and slicked down. He was neatly dressed and displayed a lodge emblem on his watch chain and another on his lapel. He spoke very distinctly.

Haddon Gray said Judd had enlisted his support in Syracuse in the keeping of a date in Albany with a woman Judd referred to as 'Momsie.' Judd had once shown him a photo of 'Momsie.' Haddon Gray said he now knew her as Mrs Snyder.

This obliging Haddon, thinking he was merely assisting an old pal in a little clandestine affair, hung a sign, 'Don't Disturb,' on Judd's door at the Onondaga Hotel, rumpled the bed, called the desk downstairs and left word he was ill and was not to be aroused before a certain hour, and finally mailed some letters that Judd had written. All this after Judd had left Syracuse for New York.

Judd told Haddon he was afraid his firm might check up on him, wherefore the arrangements set forth above. Haddon did not hear from Judd again until Sunday afternoon, March 20, when Judd, just back from his bloody errand to Queens Village, called him on the telephone. Haddon Gray and a friend named Harry Platt went to see Judd at the Onondaga and Judd said he had not kept the 'date' in Albany as a telegram from Momsie had reached him there summoning him on to New York. Then the witness said Judd told him a startling story.

He—Judd—said he had gone to the home of Momsie while she and her husband were out and entered by a side door. He was waiting in a bedroom when he heard Momsie and her husband returning. Then he heard a great commotion and looking out through the door of the room he saw Momsie slugged by a dark man.

Henry Judd told Haddon he hid in a closet, and two men came in and rummaged around in the closet over his head, looking for something. Then they went out and Henry Judd bolstered up his courage and looked about. He went into a bedroom and found Momsie's husband on the floor. He lifted the man onto the bed, and said in doing so he must have gotten blood on his vest and shirt as he bent over the man and listened if his heart was beating.

He showed Haddon Gray the shirt and said it was Snyder's shirt but the witness wasn't clear as to how Judd explained having it. Also Judd had a suitcase containing the suit of clothes he had worn to New York, also the bloody shirt and a briefcase, which Harry Platt took to get rid of at Judd's request. Platt took the suitcase to his office.

After relating this tale Judd went to Haddon's home and spent the evening playing with Haddon's children. Haddon came to New York after Judd's arrest, saw his old pal in jail and said:

'Judd, did you do this?'

'Yes, Haddon; I did.'

Henry Judd, inert, head down as usual, never glanced up as he heard his boyhood friend testify, and Haddon Gray proved in his testimony that he was about as good a friend as a man could hope to have.

Harry Platt, an insurance adjuster of Syracuse, very bald, rather florid, and with glasses, was next. There was a touch of the old beau to Harry's appearance. He repeated the tale of slugging told him and Haddon by Judd. He said he gave the suitcase to his stenographer to be destroyed.

Mrs Anna Boehm, of Syracuse, stenographer for Platt, a plump lady wearing glasses and obviously a bit nervous, told of receiving a package from Platt containing a suitcase. In the suitcase was a suit of clothes and a hat. She gave it to her husband. The husband, Anthony Boehm, corroborated that statement. He burned the package in a furnace.

At 12:27, Newcombe stood up and said:

The People Rest.

There was a sudden stir and the bailiffs rapped for order. All the attorneys gathered about Justice Scudder's bench in a conference with the Court.

When the State rested rather sooner than was generally expected, the attorneys for the defendants asked for time to prepare certain motions. They were given until four o'clock in the afternoon. These motions, all for dismissal on one ground or another, were probably presented more on the broad premise that they can't rule you off for trying, rather than the expectation they would be granted. Millard wanted the motions made in the absence of the jury, but Justice Scudder saw no necessity for that.

If the jurors didn't understand the motions any better than most of the laymen collected in the court room, Justice Scudder was quite right. The language was quite technical.

Now the woman and the crumpled little corset salesman, their once piping-hot passion colder than a dead man's toes, begin trying to save their respective skins from the singeing at Sing Sing, each trying to shove the other into the room with the little green door.

'What did Mrs Snyder say about the confession of Gray's—that squawk?' I asked her attorneys yesterday.

'Well, let's see, she said he—' began Dana Wallace, the buzzing, bustling little man who sits at Mrs Snyder's side in the court room when he isn't on his feet, which is seldom.

'She said—Well, wait now until I recall what she said,' put in Edgar Hazleton, the other attorney for the woman.

They seemed at a loss for words. I suggested: 'Did she say he is a rat?'

'Well I suppose it would amount to that in your language,' replied Wallace. (What did he mean 'my' language?) 'Only she didn't use that term.'

'No, no,' chimed in Hazleton, 'not rat.'

'She said, in substance, 'and to think I once loved that—that—' Well, I think she used a word that means something like coward,' Wallace concluded.

'Do you think she will keep her nerve on the stand?' I asked.

'Yes,' they both answered in unison.

I am inclined to think so, too.

Whatever else she may lack, which seems to be plenty, the woman appears to have nerve. Or maybe she hasn't any nerves. It is about the same thing.

In any event, she has never for a moment cowered like her once little pal of those loving days before the black early morning of March 20. She has been cold, calm, contemptuous, gusty, angry, but never shrinking, save perhaps in that little walk to and from the court between the recesses. She then passes before the hungry eyes of the spectators.

That seems to be her most severe ordeal. She grips her black corded-silk coat in front with both hands, and seems to hasten, her eyes straight ahead. However, we shall see about that nerve now.

We were, in a manner of speaking, in the chamber of horrors with Mrs Ruth Brown Snyder yesterday afternoon, mentally tip-toeing along, goggle-eyed and scared, behind her, when the blond woman suddenly gulped, and began weeping.

She had taken us, just before the tears came, step by step to a bedroom in her little home in Queens Village. We were standing there, you might say, all goose-pimply with the awfulness of the situation as we watched, through the medium of the story she told on the witness stand, the butchery of her husband by Henry Judd Gray.

Maybe the ghost of the dead art editor suddenly popped out on her as she got us into that room and was showing us the picture of the little corset salesman at his bloody work while she was trying to stay his murderous hand. Anyway, the tears came, welling up into the frosty eyes of the blonde and trickling down over that marble mask of a face.

Plump Mrs Irele Wolfe, the gray-haired matron of the Queens County jail, hurried to Mrs Snyder's side and put her arms around the weeping woman. A few sips from a glass of water, and Mrs Snyder was again composed sufficiently to go on with the fearful tale of the killing of her husband that she started early in the afternoon and by which she hopes to save herself from the electric chair.

She blamed it all on Gray, even as he will blame it all on her. The baggy little man sitting inertly, as always, in the chair just a few feet from her listened to the woman with only an occasional glance at her.

Yet it would be interesting to know his thoughts. This was his old Momsie. This was the woman he once thought he loved with a great consuming love—this woman who was trying to consign him to the electric juices. He seemed to stagger slightly as he walked out of the court room at the close of the session, whereas before he had tried to put a little snap into his tread.

This woman broke down twice while she was on the witness stand, once when she had us in that death chamber, with Henry Judd Gray pounding the life out of her husband, as she claims, and again when she mentioned the name of her nine-year-old daughter, Lorraine.

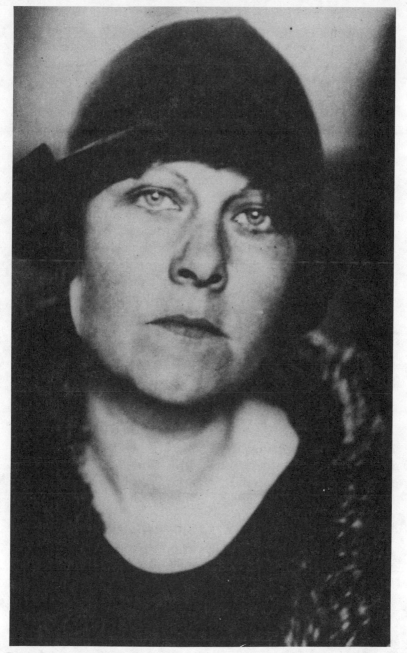

Ruth Snyder in a break during the trial.

But in the main she was as cold and calm sitting there with a thousand people staring at her as if she were at her dinner table discoursing to some guests. She kept her hands folded in her lap. She occasionally glanced at the jury, but mostly kept her eyes on Edgar Hazleton, one of her lawyers who examined her on direct-examination.

This examination was not concluded when Court took a recess at 4:30 until Monday morning. It is the custom of Queens County courts to skip Saturday.

Mrs Snyder wore the same black dress and black coat that has been her attire since the trial started. She made one change in hats since then, discarding a tight-fitting thing that made her chilly chin jut out like an iceberg. Someone probably told her that the hat was most unbecoming, so now she wears one with a brim that takes some of the ice out of the chin.

Her dress and coat are neither fashionable nor well cut, so I am informed by ladies who may be taken as authorities on the subject. Still, they make her look smaller than her weight of around 150 pounds would indicate. She wears black silk stockings and black pumps.

Her face was flushed a bit today, probably from excitement, but she uses no make-up. Slap a little rouge and powder on Mrs Snyder, give her a session with a hairdresser, and put some of Peggy Joyce's clothes on her, and she would be a snappy-looking young matron.

When her name was called by her attorney, Hazelton, soon after court opened this afternoon, she stood up quickly and advanced to the witness chair with a firm step. She had been twisting her hands and biting her nails just before that, however, indicating she felt nervous, which is not surprising, in view of the eyes turned on her.

It seems a great pity that old man Hogarth isn't living to depict the crowd scene in the court room yesterday. Tad* might do it, but Tad has too much sense to risk his life and limbs in any such jams.

Some strange-looking characters almost fought for a chance

---

*Tad was the penname of T.A. Dorgan, satiric artist whose drawings were a popular syndicated newspaper feature in the Twenties.

to leer at the principals in the trial. Apparently respectable men and women showed the court attendants cards, letters, badges, birth certificates and automobile licenses in an effort to impress the guardians of the portals with their importance and the necessity of their getting into the court room.

Dizzy-looking dolls said to represent the social strata of Park Avenue—the upper crust, as I understand—were there, not a little proud of their heroism in getting out so early. Some were escorted by silly-looking 'muggs' wearing canes and spats.

But also there were men who might be business men and women with something better to do, standing chin deep in the bloody scandal of this bloody trial and giving some offense to high heaven, it seems to me, by their very presence.

The aisles were jammed so tightly that even the smallest copy boys, carrying copy of the day as it ran red-hot from the fingers of the scribbling writers of the newspaper delegations, could scarcely wiggle through. The women outnumbered the men about three to one. They stood for hours on their tired feet, their eyes and mouths agape.

Justice Scudder peered over his glasses at a jammed court room and warned the crowd that at the first disturbance he would order the premises cleared.

Then he bowed slightly to the attorneys for the defense and Hazleton arose and stepped up to the table in front of the jury box.

He is a short, serious-looking man, with a hawk nose, and a harsh voice. A pince-nez straddled his beak. He wore a gray suit, and a white starched turned-down collar and a black tie yesterday morning. The collar flew loose from its neck and moorings early in Hazleton's discourse and one end scraped his ear.

He at first stood with his hands behind him, but presently he was gesticulating with his right, waggling a prehensile index-finger most forcibly. He perspired. He stood on his tiptoes. He was so close to Henry Judd that he almost stuck the index-finger in the defendant's eye when he pointed at Judd.

Occasionally a titter ran over the crowded court room at some remark made by Hazleton, who has an idiomatic manner of expression. That's what most of the crowd came for,

apparently—to laugh at something, even though it might be
human misery! The bailiffs would bawl 'Silence!' and glare
around furiously.

The purport of Hazleton's opening was about what had been
anticipated. He said he expected to show that Henry Judd Gray
was the arch criminal of the whole affair, and he depicted him
in the light of a crafty, designing fellow—

'Not the man you see sitting here,' yelled Hazleton, pointing
at the cowering Henry Judd, while the eyes of the jurors turned
and followed the finger. It was quite possible to believe that the
villain described by Hazleton was not the man sitting there.
Henry Judd looked anything but villainous.

Hazleton spoke about an hour, then Samuel L. Miller, of
Gray's counsel, stepped forward, dark, stout, well-groomed
and slick-haired—a New York type of professional young man
who is doing all right.

He laid a batch of manuscript on the table in front of the jury
and began to read his opening, rather an unusual proceeding.
His opening addresses partook more of the nature of closing
appeals. Miller had evidently given no little time and thought
to his address and had dug up a lot of resounding phrases, but
he was comparatively brief.

Harry Hyde, manager of the Jamaica branch of the Pruden-
tial Life Insurance Company, was the first witness called for
Mrs Snyder. He is a thin man with a Woodrow Wilson face
and glasses, and he kept his new spring topcoat on as he sat in
the witness chair. His testimony was what you might call
vague.

Hazleton tried to show by him that Mrs Snyder had called at
his office relative to cancelling the insurance on her late husband's life, but he didn't recognize Mrs Snyder as the woman
and didn't remember much of the conversation.

He did faintly recall some woman calling at his office,
however, and speaking of the Snyder policies. District Attorney
Newcombe moved to strike out the testimony, but the motion
was denied.

John Kaiser, Jr., another insurance man of Jamaica, a
heavy-set rotund man with a moustache and horn-rimmed
specs, testified on the subject of the insurance policies that are

said by the State to have been reasons for the murder of Albert Snyder.

He said he recalled Mrs Snyder coming to his offices and discussing the policies, but he couldn't recall the exact nature of the conversation.

Hazleton made a point of a clause in the policy that bore Snyder's signature, reserving the right to change the beneficiary.

Mrs Josephine Brown, mother of Mrs Snyder, was called.

Mrs Brown is a woman who must be around sixty. She speaks with a very slight accent. Mrs Brown is a Scandinavian. Her face is wrinkled and she wears gold-rimmed glasses. She was dressed in black but her black hat had a bright ornament. She gave her answers clearly and quickly.

She said her daughter had been operated on for appendicitis when she was a child and that the wound had to be reopened when she was eighteen. She lived with her daughter and son-in-law for six years and told of the visits to the Snyder home by Gray. On the third visit she told her daughter not to let Gray call again as 'it didn't look right.' Gray came no more.

On the occasions of his visit Mrs Brown said Gray talked mainly about the stock market.

Newcombe examined her closely as to her knowledge of Gray's relations with her daughter. She admitted she called him Judd and had never told Albert Snyder of his visits to the Snyder home. She was away on a professional visit the night Henry Judd hid in her room on murder bent.

So many daffy women and rattle-headed men outside, eager to see whatever they might see, rushed the court house corridors at one o'clock on a rumor that Mrs Snyder was on the stand, that the confusion took on the proportion of a riot. The halls and stairways were packed with struggling females. They pushed and shoved and pulled and hauled, and squealed and squawked. It was a sorry spectacle. The cops on duty at the court house were well nigh helpless against the onrush for a time.

Justice Scudder heard the tumult from his chambers and went out to take a look. Then he ordered the hallways cleared. In the meantime, the court room was jammed, and the spectators piled into the press section, grabbing all unoccupied seats. For half an hour the cops outside the court room would not recognize credentials of any kind until they could stem the human tide to some extent.

I doubt if there has ever been anything quite like it in connection with these trials, and I speak as a survivor of the Hall-Mills trial, and of the Browning trial, which wasn't a murder trial, except with relation to the King's English. The court room is said to be one of the largest in the country, but it could have been three times as large today and there wouldn't have been room for the crush.

A big crowd stood in the street outside all morning and afternoon, though they can see nothing there except the photographers at their sprinting exercises when a witness walks out of the court house.

When Mrs Snyder was sworn as a witness, Justice Scudder told her in a quiet voice that she was not required to testify as the law protected her but that on the stand she is subject to the same cross-examination as any other witness.

She turned in her chair and looked the judge in the face as he talked, and bowed slightly.

Her voice is a soprano, and very clear. It came out through the amplifiers much harsher than its natural tone, of course. The microphone on the desk in front of the witness stand was in the line of vision between Mrs Snyder and Hazleton, and she cocked her head to one side to get a clearer view of the lawyer.

She often emphasized some of her words, for instance, 'We were *not* happy,' when answering Hazleton's question about her married life with Albert Snyder. She never glanced at the staring crowd, though she often looked at the jury. As for the members of that solemn body, most of them watched her closely as she talked for a time, then their attention seemed to wander. Juror No 11 never looked at her at all, but then Juror No 11 never seems to be looking at anyone on the witness stand.

He has a faraway expression. Possibly he is wondering how business is going while he is away listening to all this murder stuff.

Mrs Snyder's first attack of tears came early in the examination, but was very short. The second time court suspended operations for several minutes while she wept. A dead silence reigned. It is well for men to remain silent when women weep, whatever the circumstances.

I asked a lot of men how she impressed them. They said they thought she made a good witness for herself. Then I asked some of the girls, who have been none too strong for Mrs Snyder, just as a general proposition. They, too, thought she had done very well.

You must bear in mind that this woman is talking for her life. If she is the cruel and cunning blond fury that Gray's story would cause you to believe, you would expect her to be calm. But if she is the wronged, home-loving, horror-stricken woman that her own tale would imply, her poise is most surprising.

She always referred to Albert Snyder as 'my husband,' and to her former paramour as 'Mr Gray'—'I tried to stop Mr Gray from hitting my husband and he pushed me to the floor. I fainted and when I came to I pulled the blanket off. . . .'—It was here that she was overcome by tears the second time.

She pictured Gray as the aggressor in the love-making of their early meetings. She wasn't happy at home, and she accepted the advances of the little corset salesman to intimacy. She said Gray was her only love adventure.

He borrowed her money and didn't pay it back, she said. He first suggested the idea of getting rid of her husband, and mentioned poisoning to her. Wherever Gray said 'she' in his confession, Mrs Snyder said 'he' in her testimony today. They have turned on each other with a vengeance, these two once-fervid lovers. There is no doubt they hate each other thoroughly.

It was difficult to tell just what effect Mrs Snyder's tale had on the jury, of course. In fact it would be unfair to make a guess until her tale is finished. It certainly had some elements of plausibility, despite the confession she now says was obtained under duress, and despite the motive of Albert Snyder's life insurance that is advanced by the prosecution.

Mrs Snyder's attorneys attempted to show today that she had tried to have the insurance reduced to cut down the premium, but their evidence on that point did not seem particularly strong. She insisted in her testimony that this had been the purpose.

She smiled just once with any semblance of joy, which was when Justice Scudder admitted, over the objections of the State, the bank books showing that Albert Snyder and Ruth had a joint account. It is by this account that the defense expects to show that Albert Snyder had full cognizance of his wife's payment of the premiums on the policies.

She says Gray always referred to Albert Snyder as 'the governor.' Once she accidentally tripped over a rubber gas tube in the house and pulled it off the jet. She went out and when she came back her husband was out of doors and said he had nearly been asphyxiated. She wrote Gray of the incident, and he wrote back:

'It was too damn bad the hose wasn't long enough to shove in his nose.'

When she testified in just that language there was something in her manner and way of speaking out the word that caused a distinct stiffening among the women in the court room.

'Brazen!' some of them whispered.

This gas jet incident, by the way, was alleged by the State to have been one of the times when Mrs Snyder tried to murder her husband.

She says Gray threatened to kill himself and her if she didn't do what he told her. She was afraid of Gray, she said, although the drooping little man in front of her didn't seem to be anything to be afraid of. She tried to break off with him, she said, and he threatened to expose her.

She said Gray sent her sleeping powers to give 'the governor' on the night of the party at Fidgeons', which was Albert Snyder's last night on earth. Moreover, Gray announced in the letter accompanying the powders, according to her testimony, that he was coming down Saturday to finish 'the governor.'

He came down all right.

'My husband was asleep. I went to my mother's room, where I met Mr Gray. We talked several minutes. He kissed me and I felt the rubber gloves on his hands. He was mad. He said, "If you don't let me go through with this I'll kill us both." He had taken my husband's revolver. I grabbed him by the hand and took him down to the living-room.

'I pleaded with him to stop when we got downstairs, then I

went to the bathroom. I said to Mr Gray, "I'll bring your hat and coat down to you." I heard a terrific thud. I rushed to my husband's room. I found Gray straddling my husband. I pulled the blankets down, grabbing him and then I fainted. I don't remember anything more.'

That's her story and I presume she will stick to it.

May 3, 1927

For five hours and a half yesterday questions went whistling past that marble chin of Mrs Ruth Brown Snyder's, but she kept on sticking it out defiantly from under the little brim of her black hat, like a fighter that can't be hurt.

At a pause just before recess in the old court room with the sickly yellow walls in Long Island City she reached out a steady hand, picked up a glass of water from the table in front of her, took a big swig, and looked at Charles F. Froessel, the assistant district attorney, who had been cross-examining her, as much as to say 'Well, come on.'

But Froessel seemed a bit fagged out, and mopped a steaming brow with a handkerchief as Justice Townsend Scudder granted a motion by one of Mrs Snyder's attorneys for a recess until tomorrow morning.

The dialogue between Froessel and Mrs Snyder toward the close of the day was taking on something of the aspect of a breakfast table argument between a husband and the little woman, who can't exactly explain certain matters that the old boy wants to know.

She is a magnificent liar, if she is lying. You must give her that. She stands out 'mid keen competition these days, if she is lying. And if a liar she is a game liar, one of those 'that's my story and I'll stick to it' liars, which is the mark of the able liar.

And I regret to report that she seems to impress many of her listeners in the light of a wonderful liar rather than as a poor widowed soul falsely accused. The men were rather softening up toward the blond woman at the close yesterday in sheer admiration of her as a possible liar, and even the women who leer at her all day long had stopped hating her. They seemed to be commencing to think that she was reflecting credit to femininity just as a prodigious liar.

Even Henry Judd Gray, the baggy-looking little corset salesman who was on trial with her for the murder, and who has
been sitting inert and completely befogged since the case
began, sat up yesterday as if they had suddenly puffed air into
him.

He had a fresh haircut and clean linen and looked all
sharpened up. He half started when she fairly shrilled 'no' at
Froessel when he was asking her about the life insurance on
Albert Snyder. Perhaps Gray had heard her say 'no' in that
same voice before.

It was about the life insurance for $53,000 on Snyder's life
that the assistant district attorney was most curious in his
cross-examination, and about which Mrs Ruth Brown Snyder
was the least convincing. It was to double in the event of her
husband's death by accident, and the State claims that Albert
Snyder didn't know his wife had taken it out.

It was a very bad session for her on that particular point. Her
answers were at times vague and evasive, but her voice never
lost its snap. She said the only motive Gray could have had for
killing her husband was to get the life insurance money, and
when it was suggested to her that she was the beneficiary, she
argued. 'Well, he knew he would get it away from me just as he
got money from me before.'

'Isn't it a fact, that you and Gray planned to spend that
insurance money together?' she was asked.

'No,' she said quickly.

Most of her answers were sharp yesses, or noes. In fact,
Froessel insisted on yes-or-no answers, though sometimes she
whipped in a few additional remarks to his great annoyance.

He hectored and badgered the blonde at times until her
counsel objected and the Court admonished him. Froessel, a
plump-built man of medium height, in the early forties, has a
harsh voice and a nagging manner in cross-examination. He
wears spectacles and is smooth-shaven and persistent, and
there is no doubt that Mrs Snyder at times wished she had a
sash weight handy.

She broke down once—that was when she was again leading
the way into the room where her husband was butchered, and

Henry Judd Gray: a newspaper photo during the trial.

where she claimed she saw Judd Gray astraddle of Albert Snyder in the bed. She repeated the story she told on her direct-examination.

'I grabbed Judd Gray and he pushed me to the floor and I fainted. When I came to I pulled the blankets off my husband and—'

Then the tears came. There was a microphone on the witness stand, and her sniffles came out through the amplifiers quite audibly. Mrs Irene Wolfe, the plump matron of the county jail, moved to her rescue with water, and presently Mrs Snyder went on.

'Watch her hands,' a woman advised me. 'You can always tell if a lady is nervous by her hands. If she presses them together she is under a strain. If they are relaxed, she isn't nervous.'

So I watched Mrs Snyder's hands as they lay together in her lap. They were limp, inert. Once or twice she raised one to adjust a strand of yellow hair that drifted out under the little black hat, or to apply a small handkerchief to her well-shaped nose.

Under a dim light, backgrounded by the old brown plush hangings behind the judge's bench, and seated on an elevated platform, the black-gowned figure stood out distinctly. Occasionally she fingered the black jet beads at her throat, and she always leaned forward slightly, the white chin pushed out belligerently. Her feet were still. She sometimes shook her head to emphasize a 'no.' Her voice, a little raspy through the 'mike,' has a musical quality.

Her speech is the speech of your average next door neighbor in the matter of grammar. I mean to say she is no better and no worse than millions of the rest of us. She says 'ain't' but I just read a long dissertation by some learned fellow who says 'ain't' will eventually be considered good grammar.

She displayed more boldness than adroitness in her denials when it was patent that she didn't care to go into details.

But she showed no disposition to hide anything about her affair with Henry Judd Gray.

May 4, 1927

That scared-rabbit looking little man, Henry Judd Gray, the corset salesman, is now engaged in what the cops would describe as 'putting the finger' on Mrs Ruth Brown Snyder, only such a short time back his ever-loving, red-hot Momsie.

He seems to be a fairly expert 'finger man,' so far. Perhaps his proficiency goes back to his early youth and much practice pointing the accusatory digit and saying, 'Teacher, he done it.'

He lugged us through many a rendezvous in many a different spot with Mrs Snyder yesterday afternoon, while the lady, who had done a little 'fingering' herself for three days, sat looking daggers at Henry Judd, and probably thinking arsenic, mercury tablets, chloroform, picture wire and sash weights.

This was after she had come out of a spell of weeping when her little daughter, Lorraine, was on the stand. That was a spectacle, my friends—the child in the court room—to make the angels shed tears, and men hide their faces in shame, that such things can be.

Henry Judd had scarcely gotten us out of the hotels which he and Mrs Ruth Brown Snyder infested in the days—ah, yes, and the nights—when their heat for each other was up around 102 Fahrenheit, when a recess was taken until this morning.

Everybody was weary of traipsing up and down hotel corridors and in and out of hotel rooms, but Henry Judd kept making a long story longer under the direct examination of Samuel L. Miller, the stout, sleek-looking young lawyer who is associated with William L. Millard in defending Gray.

Henry Judd hadn't gotten right down to brass tacks, which is after all the story of the butchery of Mrs Snyder's husband, Albert, and which Henry Judd will undoubtedly blame on the blond woman who has made him out the arch-sashweighter of the bloody business.

He had gone over his own early life before he met Mrs Snyder and was a happy little corset salesman, with a wife and child down in New Jersey. He wept when he spoke of that, but composed himself with a stiff jolt of water from the same glass that had but recently been pressed by the lips of his former sweetie.

It was a dull, dry recital, especially those numerous little excursions to hotel rooms. A trip to one hotel room might be made exciting, but when you start going through one of these modern hotels, room by room, the thing lacks zest.

Gray stepped to the stand with a quick tread, and an almost soldierly bearing, which was most surprising in view of the fact he has looked all folded-up like an old accordion since the trial started. He did not commence straightening up until Friday, when he found Mrs Snyder nudging him toward that warm chair at Sing Sing.

He raised his right hand with great gravity as the clerk of the court administered the usual oath. He did not sit down until told to do so by Justice Townsend Scudder, and he listened gravely while Justice Scudder told him he did not have to testify unless he wished. Gray bowed to the Court.

Sitting there was a scholarly-looking young fellow, such a chap as would cause you to remark, 'There's some rising young author,' or maybe a college professor. He wore a dark, double-breasted suit of clothes with a white linen collar and a tie that had an almost indecorous stripe. A white handkerchief peeped out of the breast pocket of the coat.

His dark hair, slightly kinky, made a tall pompadour. His horn-rimmed spectacles have yellowish lenses, which, added to the old jail-house tan he has acquired, gave him a sickly complexion under the stand lamp by the witness stand with its three lights like a pawnbroker's sign.

His hands rested quietly in his lap, but occasionally he raised one to his probably throbbing forehead. His voice is slow and steady, and rather deep-throated. A cleft in the middle of his chin is wide and deep. The psychologists and philosophers have noted it without knowing just what to make of it. He has a strange trick of talking without moving his upper lip. Or maybe there isn't anything strange about it.

He answered Miller's questions without hesitation and with great politeness. You might say with suavity, in fact.

'I did, sir,' he would say. Always the 'sir.' He would impress you as a well-educated, well-bre, WELL-MANNERED YOUNG CHAP. You can't see inside 'em, you know. He has a remarkably bad memory that will probably get him in trouble when the abrupt Froessel, of the district attorney's office, takes hold of him.

'My memory does not serve me well as to conversation,' he remarked on one occasion. He did not seem to be abashed by any of the very personal questions asked him, or rather read by Miller, who has a stack of typewritten notes in front of him. He is obviously frightened, however, which is not surprising when you consider he is facing the electric chair.

He invariably referred to the blond woman, who he says got him in all this mess, as 'Mrs Snyder,' his tale of their introduction in Henry's restaurant by one Harry Folsom not varying from hers. He said he did plenty of drinking when he was with her on those hotel trips, and on jaunts through the night life of New York. She told him of her domestic troubles and he said she talked of leaving her husband and putting their child in a convent. He told her, so he said, that he hated to see a home broken up, which sounded almost ironical coming from a gent with a wife and child himself.

They exchanged Christmas presents, and he bought one for her mother.

Gray's own mother cried bitterly when her son took the stand. Mrs Snyder talked much to him on insurance, Henry Judd said, and once he had induced her to pour out some arsenic which she had in the house to poison rodents, and one thing and another, as she explained to him.

But he hadn't reached sash weights and such matters when Justice Scudder declared the recess. It was a long day in court, with much happening before the defense for Mrs Snyder rested and the defense of Gray began with the immediate production of Henry Judd.

Out of the dark tangles of this bloody morass there stepped for a brief moment a wraith-like little figure all in black— Lorraine Snyder, the nine-year-old daughter of the blond woman and the dead art editor. She was, please God, such a fleeting little shadow that one had scarcely stopped gulping over her appearance before she was gone.

She was asked just three questions by Hazleton as she sat in the big witness chair, a wide-brimmed black hat shading her tiny face, her presence there, it seemed to me, a reproach to civilization.

Justice Scudder called the little girl to his side, and she stood looking bravely into his eyes, the saddest, the most tragic little figure, my friends, ever viewed by gods or men.

'You understand, don't you, that you have to tell the truth?' asked Justice Scudder kindly. I thought he was going to seize the child in his arms.

'Yes,' she said faintly.

'Then sit right down there and listen carefully,' said Justice Scudder. 'If you do not understand the question just say, "I do not understand." Lean back in the chair and be comfortable. The Court rules the child shall not be sworn.'

So she sat down and the jurors gazed at her and everybody in the room felt like bawling. Mrs Snyder gasped and shed tears when her child appeared—tears that probably came from her heart.

She hasn't seen Lorraine since her arrest. I doubt if Lorraine saw her mother across the big room or that the child fully comprehended where she was. Surely she could not know that all these strange-looking men gathered there were trying to kill her mother. It was a relief when Lorraine left the stand. Two minutes more and they would have been short one reporter in the press section.

'Lorraine,' said Hazleton, 'do you remember the morning your mother called you?'

'Yes, sir.'

'Was it daylight or dark?'

'Light.'

'And how long after she called you did you call the Mulhausers?'

'Right away,' piped the child.

'That's all,' said Hazleton.

'Not one question by the district attorney, Your Honor,' said Newcombe.

'No questions,' said Miller of Gray's counsel.

Thereafter while Gray was being examined, Mrs Snyder sat with her elbows on the table, her head bowed, a picture of dejection as great as that presented by Gray for some days. The child seemed to have touched her heart, and the defiant pride with which she has faced her accusers disappeared.

Finally the head came up again and the greenish blue eyes, a bit watery, were leveled on Gray, but it soon drooped once more. The woman seemed a picture of remorse. One-tenth the thoughts she was giving to Lorraine at that moment applied three months ago would have kept her out of that court room.

Mrs Snyder was on the stand three hours and a half yesterday. She quit the witness chair at 2:05 at the afternoon session and walked with slow step back to her seat at her attorneys' table followed by plump Mrs Wolfe, the jail matron.

She was 'all in.' She kept her head down as she passed in review before the leering eyes of the spectators. Her face was a dead, dull white. Her dearest girl friends, as Mrs Snyder calls them, couldn't have called her pretty without being arrested for perjury. She looked very badly indeed. She had no pep left but still I defy any other woman to produce any pep after so many hours of dodging.

The conclusions of some of the more nervous listeners at the close of Mrs Snyder's examination were that hereafter no blonde shall be permitted to purchase a window sash weight without a prescription and that all male suburbanites should cancel their life insurance forthwith and try all the doors before going to bed.

She left not one but two doors open for Henry Judd Gray, so Froessel dug out of her. I think the fact of these unlocked doors will weigh heavily against Mrs Snyder when the jury commences tossing the evidence into the scales of consideration. That, and the insurance that 'the governor' didn't know was loaded on his life. He was carrying plenty of weight along with this mortal coil, was 'the governor.' That was Henry Judd Gray's name for him. Imagine the gall of the little whippet who sneaked into Albert Snyder's home and had a jocular title for him!

Not much jocularity to Henry Judd Gray now as he shrinks in and out of the court room in Long Island City while the ponderous machinery of the law grinds the sausage of circumstance into links of evidence.

It is likely that the case will go to the jury by Friday. It has taken two weeks to try a mother that the citizens of Pueblo County, Colorado, could have settled in two minutes under any

cottonwood tree on the banks of the Arkansas, if all the State of
New York has developed is true. But the citizens of Pueblo
County are forehanded and forthright gents.

Spectators were permitted to remain in the court room during
the noon recess and the ladies brought their ham sandwiches
and tatting right along with them to while away the hour. They
gossiped jovially about the troubles of their sister, Ruth, and a
lovely time was apparently had by all. Strange it is, my friends,
that morbid impulses move the gals to bite and kick for a place
on the premises where a sad, distorted version of life is being
aired.

The reader may recall that yesterday I drew attention to the
blonde's magnificence as a liar, if she were lying, and today she
stepped right out and admitted her qualifications as a prevari-
cator. She claimed the belt, you might say, when the following
tête-à-tête came off between her and Assistant District Attorney Charles F. Froessel when the cross-examination was in
progress this morning. 'You lied to the neighbors?' 'Yes.' . . .
'You lied to the policemen?' 'Yes.' . . . 'You lied to the detectives?' 'Yes.' . . . 'You lied to Commissioner McLaughlin?' 'Yes
. . . 'You lied to the Assistant District Attorneys?' 'Yes.' . . .
'You lied to your mother?' 'Yes.' . . . 'You lied to your daughter?' 'Yes.' . . . 'You lied to everybody that spoke to you or with
you?' 'Yes.'

If that isn't lying it will do until some lying comes along.

Mrs Snyder came in for the morning session looking a bit
more marbley than usual. She seemed somewhat listless as
Froessel began 'madaming' her again. Her voice was tired.
Still, nearly six hours on a witness stand is not calculated to
enliven anyone.

Froessel started off in soft accents as if he wished to be a
gentleman no matter how painful, possibly in view of the fact
that some folks thought he was a little harsh with her Monday.
By about the third question, however, he was lifting his voice at
the witness. He desired brevity, yes or no, in her answers, since
she had a penchant for elucidation. Froessel didn't seem to
realize that a blonde loves to talk.

She sat all morning with her hands in her lap; listless, loose hands they were. The familiar black jet beads were missing from the throat in the morning, but she came back with them in the afternoon and toyed with them constantly. Nerves at last!

The greenish blue eyes looked at Froessel so coldly that once he shivered and glanced around to see whence came that draft.

The blond woman wasn't as self-possessed as she had been the day before and she got somewhat tangled up right off the reel as to what she had testified with reference to her knowledge of Gray's murderous intentions against 'the governor.' The poor old 'governor'! There were two strikes on him any time he walked under his own rooftree.

The ice in the blonde cracked up as Froessel kept picking at her, and her voice was petulant as she answered one question with: 'I tell you I don't remember what I did.'

She was sore at Froessel, that was apparent. It takes a bold man to deliberately make a blonde sore, even though she be a prisoner of old John Law. Froessel yelled at her with great violence, especially when she tried to go beyond his questions, and she gave him some very disquieting glares.

'May I explain that?' she asked a couple of times.

'You may not!' he said acidly, and the greenish blue eyes sizzled.

'Just answer questions, madam, and do not attempt to explain matters,' said Justice Scudder from the bench, peering down at her over his glasses.

'Well, yes or no covers so much, Judge, I can't answer,' she replied sulkily.

Froessel escorted the woman back to her home in Queens Village and to that bloody early morning of March 20. He went over her story on that occasion with her, word by word. He got a bit excited at her answers and hammered the table with great violence.

'No buts—no buts!' he yelled.

'I object to the attitude of the district attorney,' interposed Hazleton, and Justice Scudder chided Froessel, but requested Mrs Snyder to be more direct in her answers.

'And when you went into the room of your mother you saw

Henry Judd Gray was there again. . . . And the first thing he did was to kiss you?'

'Yes.'

'And you kissed him?'

'Yes.'

'Knowing, or believing, whatever you want to say, that he was there to kill your husband?'

'Yes.'

Just like that.

Three gentlemen contemplating marriage to blondes hastened to the telephone booths to cancel their troth, shivering in their boots as they went.

She said that the thud she heard while she was in the bathroom was the impact of the sash weight landing on the sleeping Albert Snyder. It must have sounded like Babe Ruth hitting a home run, judging from her description, though the doctors found no fracture of the skull.

Anyway, that was when she rushed to her husband's room to find Gray on the bed astraddle of Albert Snyder, where she grabbed at Gray, when he pushed her away, and when she fainted—as she told it.

Froessel was very curious about her actions after she came out of the faint. He wanted to know if she had tried to do anything for her husband in the way of kindly ministration. Any wifely aid? Any tender care?

'No,' she said, just like that. She hadn't done a thing, merely pulled back the blankets and took a quick look at him. She said she didn't see the wire around his throat or anything like that. She didn't even touch the body to see if it was cold.

Jim Conroy, another assistant district attorney, got out the suitcase that was checked at the Waldorf by Gray and which was recovered by the police after the murder.

'Whose pink pajamas are these?' asked Froessel, as Conroy, a young man, blushingly held up some filmy robes de nuit, as we say at the club.

'Mine,' she said.

'Whose blue pajamas are these?' asked Froessel, and Conroy gingerly exhibited more slumber suitings.

'Gray's,' she answered, grimly. No 'Mr Gray,' not even

'Judd Gray,' today. Just Gray-like.

'Whose toilet articles are in this box?' inquired Froessel.

'Both,' she said, laconically.

Hazelton objected to the district attorney 'parading for the forty-ninth time adultery before this jury—we are not trying that.' The spectators glared at Hazelton for interference with their just due for all the effort it cost to get into the court room.

Froessel picked up a copy of the confession she made immediately after the murder and read it line by line, asking after each line, 'Is that the truth?'

He finally got tired of asking that and requested her to say 'yes' or 'no' at proper intervals and save his breath.

She denied most of the statements attributed to her in the confession, especially with any reference to her part in the actual slaughter of her husband. She had more lingual vigor left at the finish than he did.

May 5, 1927

Bloody apparitions rising out of his memory of that dreadful night in Queens Village probably gibbered at the window of Henry Judd Gray's soul yesterday afternoon.

His voice kept lifting, and hurrying, as he sat on the witness stand, telling his version of the murder, until finally as he reached the climax of the tale, it came pouring out of the amplifiers with a rush, hard driven by a note of terror.

You wouldn't have been much surprised to see the little corset salesman suddenly leap up and go tearing out of the crowded court room with his hair on end. The red fingers of fear were clutching his heart as he said:

'I struck him on the head, as nearly as I could see, one blow. I think I hit him another blow, I think I hit him another blow because with the first blow he raised up in bed and started to holler. I went over on the bed on top of him, and tried to get the bedclothes over his mouth, so as to suppress his cries.' A distinct thud was heard and a commotion stirred the men and women packed like sardines in one part of the court. A couple of court attendants quickly picked up the limp form of Warren

Schneider,* brother of the dead man, and carried him from the
court room, beating the air with his hands and crying aloud,
'Albert, Albert.'

Few eyes turned to see. They were all watching the man on
the witness stand, up to this moment more like a baggy dummy,
popping out, through a mechanical mouth, words thrown in by
the ventriloquist's voice.

'He was apparently full of fight. He got me by the necktie. I
was getting the worst of it because I was being choked. I
hollered, "Momsie, Momsie, for God's sake help me." I had
dropped the sash weight. She came over and took the weight
and hit him on the head, and throwing the bottle of chloroform
and the handkerchief and the wire and everything onto the
pillow.'

Necks craned for a look at the woman who has been called
'The Bloody Blonde,' as she sat almost hidden from view
among her attorneys and guards, and the spectators crowded in
close around her on every side. The blond head, covered with a
little black hat was bent low. You could not see the marble
white face at that moment. It was between her hands. She was
crying. Her mother, Mrs Josephine Brown, was crying. So, too,
was the mother of Henry Judd Gray, a small woman in black.
She was sitting so close to Mrs Snyder she could have reached
out and snatched the black hat off the blond head.

The spectators gasped. For one brief moment, at least, Henry
Judd Gray, most of the days of his life a dull, drab sort of a
fellow, busied with a corset clientele, attained the proportions
of a dramatic figure.

He was gulping as he turned on the high light of his tale, and
frequently swigged water from the glass on the table in front of
him. His attorney, Samuel L. Miller, stepped to the bench at
4:30, the usual hour of the afternoon recess, and suggested the
recess to Justice Scudder.

'Oh, I can go on all night,' Gray spoke up, addressing his
remarks to the Court. 'There are some points that I want to
clear up.'

Justice Scudder nodded.

---

* Albert Snyder had modified the family name.

The little corset salesman started to backtrack in his story and Justice Scudder said, 'You told us that a moment ago.'

'Well, I'd like to go back if possible, Your Honor, because we went down into the cellar.'

'Very good, but don't repeat.'

'I see,' said Gray, picking up the crimson trend of his story, on down to where he said, his voice now lifting even above any previous note:

'I tied her feet. I tied her hands. I told her it might be two months, it might be a year, and it might be never, before she would see me again—and I left her lying on her mother's bed, and I went out.'

His voice broke. The eyes that show much white, like the eyes of a mean mule, glistened behind the yellowish glasses in the vague light of the old court room. Henry Judd Gray, but a few minutes before the stark figure of a dreadful tale of blood, was close to blubbering.

As the Court announced the recess, a bable of voices broke out in the court room, and men and women stared at one another and argued noisily.

'I say to you that if ever human lips uttered the truth, this was the time!' bawled Willard Mack, the playwright, one fist clutching a wad of paper, the other his hat, as he stared about him wild-eyed and excited. 'They'll never shake that fellow!'

'The man told a good story,' ruminated David Belasco, the famous dramatist and producer, who hasn't missed a day of the trial. 'I thought he would. A good story, indeed—indeed—but,' and he shook his gray head, 'weak in spots, weak in spots.'

Thus the opinions differed among the celebrities, and we had a fresh batch of them, including Olga Petrova, and Irving Berlin, and Ruth Hale, the Lucy Stoner, who would officially be Mrs Heywood Broun if her conscience permitted. Also Frankie Farnum, the hoofer, as well as all our good old standbys like the Marquis of Queensbury.

One thing is certain, Henry Judd Gray made a far stronger impression on the side of veracity than did the lady who is popularly referred to as his paramour. At times I thought Henry Judd was undergoing all the keen pleasure of a small boy telling a swell ghost story to his playmates such was his apparent joy, but along toward the finish my flesh was creeping, like everybody else's.

At first he seemed to have a certain air of bravado, perhaps a remnant of the same curious spirit that may have sent him into the murder in the first place—the desire of a weakling fellow to show off, you might say.

But gradually it became rather apparent it seemed to me, that here was a man who had something on his chest that he greatly desired to unload. He was making public confession, perhaps by way of easement to a sorely harassed conscience.

That is, if he was indeed telling the truth, the whole truth, and nothing but the truth, so help him God. He put all the blame on the woman, to be sure.

He said she egged him on to the murder, steadily, insistently, until he found himself sprawling on top of poor Albert Snyder that night in Queens Village. He said she plied him with liquor at all times. He made himself out pretty much of an 'A-No 1' fathead right from taw, a victim of an insidious blonde, though at no time yesterday did he mention any of his feelings for her, if any.

That will perhaps come today. He babbled all their indiscretions, though it was expected he would tell even more—and worse. In fact, it was rumored during the afternoon that Gray's counsel intended asking the court to bar the ladies from the court room, a canard that had several hundred females prepared to go to law for their rights as listeners.

If anyone retains an impression that Prohibition still prevails in the land, they should read Henry Judd Gray's testimony, although they may get a vicarious snootfull before they have gone very far, if they are susceptible to suggestion.

Henry Judd was quite a rumpot to hear him tell it, especially when he was with Mrs Snyder. He said she cared for gin, while he went in for Scotch. He inhaled all of a small bottle of whiskey left for him by Mrs Snyder and most of a quart that he found himself in the room the night he waited in the Snyder home on murder bent.

In fact, one gathered the murder was conceived in whiskey and executed in whiskey, as is not uncommon with many other forms of crime these days. They were in bed together in the

The body of Albert Snyder.

Waldorf, and she had come in 'so plastered up' that he had a lot of trouble getting her into the feathers, when she first suggested the murder to him.

It was born in that bed in the Waldorf, he said, about the third week in February of 1927. 'The plan that was later carried out,' as Henry Judd put it.

One way and another, Henry Judd gave Mrs Ruth Brown Snyder quite a bad reputation with the jurors, who sat listening open-mouthed to his tale, though it must be admitted he didn't spare himself. He pictured himself more as an able two-handed drinker than as a murderer, however. He gave the palm to Mrs Snyder in this respect.

'I had two or three drinks,' or 'I had four or five drinks,' or 'I drank plenty.'

This was the tenor of the early part of his discourse, tending to show no doubt that he was generally well tanked-up when he was with Mrs Snyder. In fact, he said he was usually in a fog. He must have been if he drank all he says, what with the quality of liquor these days.

Mrs Snyder's favorite pastime was trying to knock her husband off, as one gathered from Henry Judd's tale. She told Gray she had tried sleeping powders, gas, auto accidents, and bichloride of mercury, but had no luck. She put it just that way to Gray, he testified—'no luck.'

She gave him four mercury tablets when he had an attack of hiccoughs, so she informed Gray, and the corset salesman says he remarked, 'My God, don't you know that's deadly poison?'

'I thought so, too, but it only made him vomit.'

'It is a wonder it didn't kill him.'

'It is a wonder,' she agreed, 'but it only made him vomit fifteen or sixteen times that night.'

'What were the aftereffects of this?' Gray asked her, he said.

'It apparently cured the hiccoughs,' she replied.

'Well, that's a hell of a way to cure hiccoughs,' Gray said was his comment. There were no titters from the crowded court room. Somehow, the situation in which poor Albert Snyder moved, was commencing to dawn on the spectators. They gazed in wonder and awe at the blond woman who is all the Borgias rolled into one, if what Gray says is true.

She was despondent most of the day. The defiance with which she faced the world at first has faded. Only once or twice she sat up yesterday and glared at Gray. His recital of the ten-day trip that they took through New York State, told without the omission of any of the details, was probably shameful even to this woman who must be shameless, if what the man says is the truth.

He admitted he borrowed money from her, but he claimed he had paid it all back a little at a time, except $25, which he still owes her. Mrs Snyder will probably always have something coming to her. The impression you got from Gray's early recital was of a most despicable little tattle-tale, but you must bear in mind the man is fighting for his life, and men stoop to anything when life is at stake.

Gray's testimony, as drawn from him by Attorney Miller, was really not much different from the story set forth in his original confession made to the police and already read into the records of this case, save in detail, until he came to the murder.

You may remember Mrs Snyder says she was in the bathroom when she heard a thud, and looked into her husband's room to find Gray astride her husband on the bed. She said she tried to pull Gray away, that he pushed her, and that she fainted, and recalls nothing else.

It is for the twelve good men and true to say who is telling the truth. For the first week of the trial, the blond woman appeared to be the stronger character of the two, and with the little corset salesman an inert heap in his chair, she was apt to impress the casual observer.

Now the situation is just reversed. The woman seems to be completely sunk, and while I wouldn't say that Gray stands out as any Gibraltar, he at least shows some signs of life. But where she seemed defiant, he appears repentant in his attitude. He did not hate Albert Snyder—he had never met the man, he testified yesterday, though he may have seen him on one occasion with Mrs Snyder, whereas he claims the woman often expressed to him her dislike of her husband. Gray said:

'She asked me once if I would please help her out by shooting her husband. I said absolutely no. I had never shot a man in my life, and I wasn't going to start in by murder. She asked me if I knew of any other plan, and I said absolutely no, I could not help her out, and she must see the thing through alone.'

But she kept at him, he said. Blondes are persistent, as well as insidious. She kept at him. Drunk, or sober, he was always hearing the suggestion that he step out to Queens Village and slaughter Albert Snyder. You couldn't have seen the average man for heeldust after the first crack from the lady, but Henry Judd held on.

He suggested something of Mrs Snyder's regard for him by testifying she said she would rather have him at home at all times instead of traveling around with those corsets, though he were only a truck driver.

'I told her that was impossible, that I had a family and a home to maintain and that they must be taken care of—that I would not break up my home,' Henry Judd so declared, though it was quite apparent he didn't have any qualms about breaking up Albert Snyder's home.

He often cleared his throat as he talked, probably stalling a bit for time before his answers, though in the main he answered only too readily to suit attorneys for Mrs Snyder. Both Dana Wallace and Edgar Hazleton were on their feet several times objecting to the testimony.

Henry Judd said he didn't know much about life insurance, but testified Mrs Snyder had shown him one of her husband's policies and wanted to know how much she would get from it in case of his death. It would appear Mrs Snyder went to work on that murder thought with Henry Judd soon after they met in the often-mentioned Henry's restaurant.

He at first told her that she was crazy and advised her to have a doctor look at a bump on her blond head. But she kept at him.

She wrote him every day and bought him silk pajamas. She even bought a Christmas present for his little daughter, who is about the same age as Lorraine. This was when there was a general exchange of presents between Henry Judd and Mrs Snyder. She told him she enjoyed spending money on him.

The story of their ten-day trip to Kingston, Albany, Schenectady, Amsterdam, Gloversville, Booneville, Watertown and Syracuse was interesting only in its disclosures of the fact that you can get plenty of liquor in those spots. At least,

Henry Judd did. He took a few drinks about everywhere they stopped, and they both got loaded in Scranton, Pa. when the trip was coming to an end.

It was when they got back from that journey that Henry Judd commenced to be more reasonable when she talked of making a murderer of him. He finally told her he would buy some chloroform for her but wouldn't help her use it. In the end he fell for it.

She had spoken about some heavy instrument, such as a hammer as a good thing to use in tapping Albert Snyder while he slept before the chloroform was applied.

'I think I suggested the window weight,' remarked Gray, quietly. He bought one on a trip to Kingston, a little later, bought the chloroform, the colored handkerchief, and all else.

'I went to Albany and had a lot of drinks, and I got to thinking this thing over, and I thought how terrible it was and I—'

'One moment,' bawled Hazleton, and the Court said never mind what he thought, to Gray.

He said Mrs Snyder wrote him outlining what he should do, just as he related in the original confession, and he obeyed her instructions, he said. He didn't say why. That remains the most interesting thing that he has to tell—Why?

He told of going down to Mrs Snyder's March 7 with the idea of disposing of the murder matter then, but Mrs Snyder met him at the kitchen door and said the time wasn't ripe. He walked around Queens Village quite a bit before he went to the house, Gray said; the mention of his wanderings telling more of his mental trepidations than anything else could have done.

Then came the plans for the second attempt, which proved only too successful.

'My God,' Mrs Snyder said to him at a meeting before the murder, 'you're certainly nervous, aren't you?'

'I certainly am. I hardly know what I am doing.'

Henry Judd shed what we might accept as a sort of sidelight on the Mrs Snyder that was before she bogged down under the strain of the past two weeks, when he testified about the letters she wrote to him when he was on the road, and the murder plot was well afloat.

She asked about his health. About his business. She mentioned little Lorraine. Then she told him to drop down by her home Saturday night and bring the things he carried, which were the murder things. She concluded:

'I hope you aren't as nervous as you were.'

May 6, 1927

Mankind at last has a clue, developed by the Snyder-Gray trial, as to the approximate moment when a blonde becomes very, very dangerous.

Gentlemen, if she asks you to try out a few sleeping powders, that is the instant you are to snatch up the old chapeau and take the air.

Henry Judd Gray gave this valuable tip to his fellow citizens from the witness stand yesterday, when he was under cross-examination.

He said that not until Mrs Ruth Brown Snyder induced him to serve as a sort of guinea pig of experimentation with sleeping powders, which she purposed using on her husband, did he realize he was completely under the spell of her magnetism that caused him to later join hands with her in the slaughter of her husband, Albert Snyder.

It was in May a year ago, that he inhaled the powders for her so she might see how they would work. He had knocked around with her quite a bit up to that time, but it seemed the old spell hadn't got down to business. After that, he said, he knew he would do anything she wanted.

He was in her power. Narrowly did I escape writing it powder. It wasn't fear, he said; no, not fear. She had never threatened him. It was more magnetism than anything else.

'And this magnetic force drew you on even without her presence and was so great it overcame all thoughts of your family—of your wife and child?'

So asked Dana Wallace, one of Mrs Snyder's attorneys, who was cross-examining for her side. There was a note of curiosity in the lawyer's voice.

'Yes,' said Henry Judd Gray, and the spectators turned from

him to peer at Mrs Snyder, the blond magnet. She looked about as magnetical as a potato yesterday. She sat crouched at her attorney's table with her black hat between her hands most of the time, though now and then she lifted her face to glare at Henry Judd.

One side of the marble mask is now red from the pressure of her hand against it as she listens to the man who claims she magnetized him into a murderer. He was surprisingly steady under Wallace's hammering at his story of the crime.

Someone remarked it may be because he is telling the truth. It is always rather difficult to rattle a man who sticks to the truth, a bright and highly original thought for the editorial writers.

Wallace is trying in his cross-examination to make it appear that Henry Judd's was the master mind of the murder, and, while Henry Judd is not dodging a lot of activity in the matter, he is harking back to the original defense of man, the same being woman. I wonder if Eve was a blonde?

Early in cross-examination, Wallace had Henry Judd standing up in the witness chair with the sash weight that figured to such an extent in the butchery held in his hands, showing the pop-eyed jurors just how he slugged the sleeping art editor on the early morning of March 20.

Henry Judd has a sash-weight stance much like the batting form of Waner, of the Pittsburgh Pirates. He first removed his big horn-rimmed glasses at Wallace's request.

'Show us how you struck.'

'I used both hands, like this.'

So explained the corset salesman, lifting the sash weight, which weighs five pounds, and looks like an old-fashioned coupling pin over his right shoulder. He 'cocked it,' as the ball players would say, pretty well back of his right ear. He is a right-hand hitter.

The tags tied to the sash weight to identify it as evidence dangled from the heavy bar below Gray's hands. The jurors and the spectators stared at the weird presentation. Gray did not seem at all abashed or nervous. Wallace asked, 'How hard did you strike?'

'Well, I could not strike very hard.'

He said Mrs Snyder had done a little practicing with the sash weight first—perhaps a bit of fungo hitting—and found that the weight was too heavy for her, and asked him to pinch hit for her when the time came.

'Did you practice with her?' demanded Wallace.

'Well—ultimately,' remarked Gray.

It was a gruesomely humorous reply, though I doubt if Henry Judd intended it that way.

You may recall that he said on direct examination that after he whacked Snyder one or two blows—he is not sure of the number—he dropped the sash weight to pile on top of the struggling art editor, and that Mrs Snyder picked up the weight and beaned her husband.

Wallace picked on Gray on that point no little and in the course of the dialogue the corset salesman uttered one tremendous truism.

'You testified you thought you hit him another blow because at the first blow he raised up in bed and started to holler,' said Wallace. 'Didn't you hear Dr Neail testify here that any of the three blows that struck Snyder would by itself have rendered him unconscious?'

Gray gazed owlishly at the lawyer through his thick yellowish lenses, and said, 'I was there, Mr Wallace, and Dr Neail wasn't.'

One thing Wallace did manage to do was to make it rather clear in his cross-examination that Gray did a lot of able, if murderous thinking, in going about the crime, especially for a man who was as soaked with booze as Gray claims he was. He had already drunk enough in his story to sink the battleship *Mississippi*.

He started out with the inevitable 'I had a few drinks' with which he prefaces most of his answers, and Wallace interrupted.

'Is there any day you know of in connection with this case that you didn't take a lot of drinks?' he demanded.

'Not since I've known Mrs Snyder,' replied Gray with surprising promptness.

When closely pressed, he was almost defiant, and sometimes a trifle stubborn. Wallace kept asking him about the chloroform—whose thought was that?

'Wasn't it your idea?' Wallace asked.

'Well, let it be my idea,' replied Gray.

He admitted he picked up a piece of Italian newspaper on the train en route to New York to kill Snyder and that it was after the murder he had suggested the mention of two foreigners by Mrs Snyder, whereas in the original plan for the crime, a colored man had been in their minds as the fictitious object of suspicion.

It developed, too, from his cross-examination that the murder was finally planned in a chop suey place in Jamaica. He admitted he took the wire from his office with which Snyder's throat was bound. He said she had told him to get rope, but he didn't get the rope because 'his mind was on his work' and he didn't think of it until he was leaving his office.

'Well, was Mrs Snyder's presence or spirit around you in the atmosphere dominating and controlling you when you picked up the wire?' demanded Wallace.

'It might have been,' said Gray.

'Do you believe in such things?' queried Wallace, eyeing the man carefully.

'I might,' answered Gray.

It seems that Henry Judd has some sense of shame left anyway, and probably a lot of remorse. Wallace got to questioning him on his testimony that he and Mrs Snyder occupied Lorraine Snyder's room for their intimacies whenever he went to the Snyder home.

'In spite of the fact that you had a little girl of your own, you did that?' asked Wallace.

'I'm ashamed to say I did,' replied Gray.

'You forgot your own flesh and blood?'

'I'm ashamed to say I did.'

Mrs Snyder raised her head and looked at him. Then she shook her head and dropped her face in her hands again. Gray said that, with only one or two exceptions, they always used the child's room as their trysting place, if that is what you call it.

Wallace referred to the plot for the murder formulated in the chop suey joint as 'the Chinese plan,' and Millard asked, 'Is that facetious, Your Honor?'

'The Court is quite ignorant,' replied Justice Scudder, wearily. 'The Court could not say. Proceed, gentlemen.'

Gray said, rather surprisingly, that he was not thinking of murder when he prepared his Syracuse alibi. He didn't know why he had picked up the waste in the street in Rochester that was used to give Albert Snyder chloroform. At times he didn't remember, too.

Hazleton darted to Wallace's side at intervals and coached his partner on some questions. Gray held himself in such a collected manner that both Miller and Millard, his counsel, were grinning gleefully.

He admitted he had felt the hands of the dead man, Snyder, though later he said it might have been the foot, and 'announced to the widow,' as Wallace casually put it, he thought the art editor was defunct. He said Mrs Snyder was standing at his side at the moment.

But he claimed he never saw the wire around Snyder's neck. He pressed a pistol into Snyder's hand though he couldn't exactly explain why. He denied Wallace's suggestion it was to show Snyder's fingerprints on the gun.

He admitted removing his glasses before entering the bedroom, and said the reason he took them off, he thought, was in case of anything in the way of a fight.

'So your mind was so attuned to the situation, that although you were drinking, you were preparing yourself for a combat?' asked Wallace. 'Not necessarily—no,' replied Gray.

That was where he was weak—on his explanation of his apparently well-planned actions leading up to them.

'And you remember that occasion very well when you struck Snyder, don't you?' asked Wallace.

'I do not remember very well now,' answered Gray.

He claimed he was in a haze from the time of the murder until he had passed Albany on his way back to Syracuse, yet he admitted sweeping up the cellar to hide his footprints and arranging to have the sash weight covered with ashes to make it appear it hadn't been touched. He said he did these things 'automatically.'

'You mean your mind was working to protect yourself?'

'Not necessarily—no.'

'Well, what did you do it for?'

'I don't know.'

Court then recessed until ten o'clock this morning.

Our line-up of celebrities was fairly strong again yesterday taking the field as follows:

Marquis of Queensbury, L.F.

Dave Belasco, R.F.

Olga Petrova, 1 b.

Francine Larrimore, 2 b.

Thurston, 3 b.

Willard Mack, ss.

Clare Briggs, c.f.

Lois Meredith, c.

One-eyed Connolly, p.

Mr Brick Terrett, one of the gentlemanly inmates of the press section, circulated a petition among his brethren that Thurston, the magician, be requested to conjure up a few additional seats from his hat for the newspaper folks.

It was a swell idea.

This remains the best show in town, if I do say so, as I shouldn't. Business couldn't be better. In fact, there is some talk of sending out a No. 2 company and 8,000,000 different blondes are being considered for the leading female role. No one has yet been picked for Henry Judd Gray's part but that will be easy. Almost any citizen will do with a little rehearsal.

May 7, 1927

The Snyder-Gray murder trial—you instinctively put the woman first in this instance–is about over, and the twelve good men and true, who have been stolidly listening to the horrible tale for two weeks will decide soon what shall be done with this precious pair, the cheaters who tried to cheat the laws of God and man and wound up trying to cheat each other.

At about three o'clock yesterday afternoon, all hands rested as they say when they have dug up all the testimony they think will do any good, or any harm, either. If the Sabbath peace and quiet of any neighborhood is offended by loud stentorian voices, that will be the lawyers warming up for a lot of hollering Monday.

Court has taken a recess until then. Dana Wallace will open in defense of Mrs Snyder. William L. Millard will follow Wallace, in an effort to talk Gray out of the chair.

Richard S. Newcombe, the grave district attorney of Queens County, will do most of the arguing for the State of New York.

And what, think you, do the blond woman and the little corset salesman expect from the twelve good men and true?

Gray—nothing. Gray's attorneys say he now has a clean conscience, since relieving it of the details of the butchery of Albert Snyder, and he thinks the jury will believe his story of how the woman wound her insidious blond coils about his life until he couldn't help doing anything she desired.

I gather from the statement that he expects no clemency. Blessed be he who expects nothing, for mayhap he will not be disappointed. I suppose that deep down Gray is hoping for mercy.

And the blonde? You can always look for a blonde to say something unique. Mrs Ruth Brown Snyder says, through her attorneys, Dana Wallace and Edgar Hazleton, that she doesn't see how 'any red-blooded men' can believe Gray's story—that hers was the heavy hand in the hammering and chloroforming and wiring to death of her husband.

He seemed to be red-blooded himself, this Albert Snyder, whose ghostly figure has stalked in the background of this horrible screen presentation of human life and death for two weeks. Much of that red blood is still on a pillow on which his head rested when Gray first beat down upon it with the sash weight, and which was still lying on the district attorney's table along with the other horrible exhibits of the crime after Court took a recess yesterday afternoon.

Two hundred men and women gathered about the table, pushing and struggling with each other for a mere peek at the exhibits. Several hundred others had gone into the street outside to pull and haul for a view of Olga Petrova, as she stood beside her Rolls-Royce, being photographed, and of Leon Errol, the comedian, and other celebrities who honoured us with their presence yesterday.

That scene in the court was one that should give the philosophers and psychologists pause. The women were far more interested in the bloody pillow than they would have been in a baby buggy. It was the last thrill left to them after Gray and Mrs Snyder walked out of the court, the woman passing rows of the leering eyes of her sisters with her head down, but with a dangerous gleam in the greenish blue eyes.

Henry Judd started off the day with a good big jolt of water from the glass on the table in front of the witness stand. He imbibed water while he was on the stand at the same rate at which he used to drink whiskey, if he was the two-handed whiskey-wrestler that his story would indicate.

Wallace touched briefly on Gray's whiskey drinking again as he went into the corset salesman's finances. He wanted to know if Henry Judd always paid for the drinks. Henry said he did, a statement which interested all the bootleggers present. They wondered how he could do so much elbow-bending on his income.

That was about $5500 a year, out of which Gray gave his family $3500 a year. He had around $2000 left for himself. Wallace asked:

'And you visited night clubs and went to parties and did your drinking and clothed yourself on $2000 a year?'

'That is correct.'

And then the philosophers and psychologists really had something to think about. Also the domestic economists then and there present.

Wallace seemed to be trying to connect Gray's purchase of some shares of stock in the corset concern for which he worked with some possible interest in the death of Albert Snyder, for financial reasons.

Q. May I ask you, with your mind in the condition it was under Mrs Snyder's dominance, and being fully aware of your own home conditions and business affairs, what did you expect to gain by aiding and bringing about the death of Albert Snyder? What was your idea, your personal idea, of what you would gain?

A. That is what I would like to know.

Q. What's that?

A. That is what I would like to know.

Q. And without any reason for it that you know of, a man of

your intelligence, you struck a man over the head with a sash
weight and did the things you say you did?

A. I did.

Q. And you want to tell this jury you do not know why you
did it?

A. I am telling.

Q. What did you intend to do after it was all over?

A. I didn't intend to do anything. I was through.

Henry Judd fell into a slightly philosophical strain as he
proceeded. He may have been qualifying to cover the next
murder case for some newspaper. Also his attitude toward
Wallace became gently chiding. He remarked, 'One sometimes
does things under the influence of liquor that one does automatically.'

It sounds quite true.

Wallace whipped many a question at Gray and then
shouted, 'I withdraw it' before Gray could answer. He could
not keep the little corset salesman from going beyond the
question at times. Henry Judd was inclined to be verbose while
Wallace tried to keep him pinned down to yes and no.

'Are you answering my questions that way because in one
form it involves her and in another form it involves you?'

'I am already involved.'

May 9, 1927

If you are asking a medium-boiled reporter of murder trials, I
couldn't condemn a woman to death no matter what she had
done, and I say this with all due consideration of the future
hazards to long-suffering man from sash weights that any lesser
verdict than murder in the first degree in the Snyder-Gray case
may produce.

It is all very well for the rest of us to say what *ought* to be done
to the blond throwback to the jungle cat that they call Mrs Ruth
Brown Snyder, but when you get in the jury room and start
thinking about going home to tell the neighbors that you have
voted to burn a woman—even a blond woman—I imagine the
situation has a different aspect. The most astonishing verdict
that could be rendered in this case, of course, would be first

degree for the woman and something else for the man. I doubt that result. I am inclined to think that the verdict, whatever it may be, will run against both alike—death or life imprisonment.

Henry Judd Gray said he expects to go to the chair, and adds that he is not afraid of death, an enviable frame of mind, indeed. He says that since he told his story to the world from the witness stand he has found tranquility, though his tale may have also condemned his blond partner in blood. But perhaps that's the very reason Henry Judd finds tranquility.

He sat in his cell in the county jail over in Long Island yesterday, and read from one of the epistles of John.

'Marvel not, my brethren, if the world hates you. We know that we have passed from death unto life, because we love the brethren. He that loveth not his brother abideth in death. Whosoever hateth his brother is a murderer: and ye know that no murderer hath eternal life abiding in him.'

A thought for the second Sunday after Pentecost.

In another cell, the blond woman was very mad at everybody because she couldn't get a marcel for her bobbed locks, one hair of which was once stronger with Henry Judd Gray than the Atlantic Cable.

Also she desired a manicure, but the cruel authorities would not permit the selected one to attend the lady.

Thus Mrs Snyder will have to go into court today with hangnails, and just those offices that she can give her bobbed bean herself. I fear that this injustice will prove another argument of sinister persecution when the folks start declaiming against burning the lady, if such should chance to be the verdict of the jury.

However, with all her troubles about her fingernails and the marcel, Mrs Snyder did not forget Mother's Day. She is herself a mother as you may remember, though the fact seemed to skip her mind at times when she was all agog over Henry Judd. Also she has a mother, who spent the Sabbath very quietly in that house of horror in Queens Village with Mrs Snyder's little daughter, Lorraine.

From the old jail Mrs Snyder sent her mother this:

Mother's Day Greeting—I have many blessings and I want you to know

how thankful I am for all that you have done for me. Love to you and kiss
Lorraine for me.   RUTH

Henry Judd Gray, although calm yesterday, declined his
breakfast. Moreover, he scarcely touched his lunch. Mrs Snyder, on the other hand, is reported to have breakfasted well and
was longing for some of the good Signor Roberto Minotti's
spaghetti and roasted chicken at noon.

They both attended divine services at the jail in the afternoon. Mrs Snyder seems quite calm, though at similar services
last week she was all broken up. As between the two, the blonde
seems to be rallying for the last round better than her former
sweet daddy of the days before the murder.

Judge Scudder, the tall, courtly, dignified man, who has
impressed all beholders of this proceeding as one of the ablest
jurists that ever wrapped a black robe around himself, will
charge the jury at some length because he must outline what
consists of four different degrees of homicide. He will undoubtedly devote much time to the conspiracy charge in the
indictment.

The jurors are men of what you might call average intelligence, I mean to say there are no intellectual giants in the box.
They are fellows you might meet in any club or cigar store, or
speakeasy. A good jury, I call it. I doubt if they will be
influenced by any psychological or philosophical twists that the
lawyers may attempt to offer them, if any.

May 10, 1927

Mighty short shrift was made of Mrs Ruth Brown Snyder and
Henry Judd Gray by that jury of Long Islanders—the verdict
being murder in the first degree for both, the penalty death in
the electric chair.

The twelve men went out at 5:20 yesterday afternoon and
were back in the box ready to deliver their verdict at 6:57, an
hour and thirty-seven minutes. They took off their coats as they
entered the jury room, hoisted the windows for a breath of air,
and took two ballots.

The first was ten to two for first degree murder, so I

understand, the second was unanimous. Justice moved on the gallop against the murderers once the jury got hold of the case.

Mrs Snyder, standing up to hear the verdict, dropped in her chair and covered her face with her hands. Henry Judd Gray, standing not far from her, held himself stiffly erect for a moment, but more like a man who had been shot and was swaying ever so slightly for a fall. Then he sat down, pulled a prayer book out of his pocket and began reading it.

He kept on reading even while the lawyers were up at Justice Scudder's bench arguing with the Court against immediate sentence. Mrs Snyder sat with her face buried between her hands. Justice Scudder finally fixed the time of sentence for Monday morning at ten o'clock.

Gray finally put the prayer book back in his pocket and sat looking straight ahead of him, as if he had found some comforting passage in the word of the Lord. He said to his guard on his way to his cell, 'I told the truth and my conscience is clear. My mother is glad I told the truth and God Almighty knows I told the truth.'

'Oh, I thought they'd believe me—I thought they'd believe me,' moaned Mrs Snyder to Father Patrick Murphy when she met him in the hallway going back to the jail. But before she left the court room there was a flash of the old defiance that marked her demeanor until the late stages of the trial.

'I haven't lost my nerve. My attorneys know that I have not had a fair trial, and we will fight this verdict with every ounce of strength.'

They have a curious custom in New York State of taking the prisoners before the clerk of the court after a verdict is returned and setting down their 'pedigree'—age, occupation, habits and the like. John Moran, the clerk of the Queens County Court, sits in a little enclosed booth like a bank teller's cage, just in front of the judge's bench, and Mrs Snyder was asked to step up there. Mrs Irene Wolfe, the matron of the county jail, and a guard supported her, the man putting his arm around the blond woman as if he was afraid the black-gowned figure would crumble and fall.

The law is a harsh institution. It would have seemed more merciful to take the woman away at once to some quiet place, where she could allow the tears she was choking back with difficulty to fall as they might.

But they stood her up there and asked her a lot of questions that seemed fatuous in view of what is already known of her, and she answered in a low voice—Ruth Brown Snyder, thirty-two years old, born in New York and all that sort of thing. Married? A widow. The tears began trickling down the marble-white cheeks.

Then they finally took her out of the court room by the same path she had trod so often the last couple of weeks. She was pretty thoroughly licked at that moment, and small wonder, for she had just heard twelve men tell her she must die.

Gray stood up before Moran, still holding himself stiffly, but did not weep. In answer to one of the set questions as to whether he is temperate or otherwise he said temperate, which sounded somewhat ironical in view of Gray's testimony during the trial as to the prodigious amounts of liquor he consumed.

He, too, was finally taken away, still walking as if he had put a ramrod down the back of his coat to hold himself so. Henry Judd Gray had said he expected such a sentence, and he was not disappointed.

The pair probably knew they were gone when they received word to make ready to return to the court room in such a short time after the jury retired. Rumor had tossed the verdict pretty well around Long Island City and the court room when the announcement came that the jury was ready to report, and the verdict was a foregone conclusion.

A few hours' delay might have produced hope for one or the other of the man and woman that fate tossed together with such horrible results. It was still daylight over Long Island City, although the yellowish-walled old court room was vaguely lighted by electric lamps, which shed less illumination than any lights I ever saw.

There was a painful stage wait, and in came Mrs Snyder and Gray, the former between two matrons, Mrs Wolfe and another, and Gray between two guards. Attorney Edgar Hazleton came in with her. He had evidently gone out to steel her for the verdict. He knew what it was, no doubt of that. She walked in with her little quick, short steps, but her face was gray—not white-gray, a dull, sickening gray.

The man walked firmly, too, but you could see by the expression in his eyes he felt what was coming. He seemed to be holding himself together with a strong effort.

Now a stir told of the coming of Justice Scudder, a lean, stooping figure in his black robe, bobbing his head to the right and left with little short bows like an archbishop. The crowd always rises at the entrance of the judge, then sits down again in some confusion, but this time everyone seemed to adjust himself in his seat again noiselessly.

Justice Scudder peered around from under the green-shaded stand lamp on his desk with an inquiring expression, and, as the roll of the jurors was called, they answered in very low voices. Only one said 'here' rather loudly, almost defiantly, it seemed.

The clerk of the court motioned the jurors to stand and then Mrs Snyder and Henry Judd Gray were also told to rise. They stood there, Mrs Snyder just behind Gray, leaning against the table. Gray had no support. They could not see each other.

Ten women fainted in the court room in the course of the day, such was the pulling and hauling and the general excitement of the occasion, but Mrs Ruth Brown Snyder remained as cool as the well-known old cucumber, even when she heard herself termed enough different kinds of animals to populate the zoo.

She was mentioned as a serpent by William L. Millard. Also as a tigress. Still, Millard gave her a back-handed boost, at that, when he called her a sinister, fascinating woman. Perhaps Mrs Snyder would have been just as well pleased if he had left off the sinister.

Cruel, calculating and cunning, he said she was. She kept her eyes closed while Millard was berating her, supporting her head on her right hand, an elbow leaned on the table. Her left hand was across her breast. Once she dabbed her eyes with a little kerchief, as if she might be mopping away a few tears.

But all that Millard said about Mrs Snyder was just a few sweet nothings compared to what Dana Wallace said about Gray. He was 'human filth,' 'diabolical fiend,' 'weak-minded,' 'despicable creature,' 'falsifier,' and finally a 'human anaconda,' which is interesting if true, and ought to get Harry Judd a job in any side show.

The little corset salesman just stared straight ahead while Wallace was blasting him. However, he was upright and alert and heard everything Wallace said, probably figuring it sounded libelous. His mother and his sister sat near by and comforted him.

There was much talk of the Deity on all sides. Both Millard and Wallace appealed to Him, and so, too, did the district attorney, when he came to summing up for the State. Newcombe was brief, and omitted brickbats for the defendants. He did compare Mrs Snyder with a jungle cat, possibly just to make sure that no animals had been left out.

The district attorney was in what you may call a soft spot, anyway, with the defendants at loggerheads, and each trying to push the other into the electric chair. However, from the beginning Newcombe has conducted this case with singular simplicity of method, and without any attempt at red fire.

Millard's argument for Gray was as expected, that Henry Judd was a poor fool, a dupe, and a lot of other things that mean a chump, who was beguiled by the woman.

However, he astonished the populace by advancing the theory that Mrs Snyder slipped Henry Judd a dose of poison the night of the murder, expecting her little playmate in blood would fold up and die also after he had assisted in dispatching Snyder. The poison didn't work, Millard said.

Furthermore, Millard made the first open suggestion of abnormality in Mrs Snyder. I heard hints that Gray's attorneys intended trying to show that the lady wasn't altogether normal, during the trial, but all that junk was kept out—by agreement, as I understand it—and only in his argument yesterday did Millard mention the abnormality.

For Mrs Snyder, the defense was she was the victim of Henry Judd, 'the human anaconda,' and he was but 'hiding behind the woman's skirts.' This caused Lieutenant McDermott, of the Police Department, to suggest mildly to me that it was a great phrase and true, in the old days, but now a woman's skirts are nothing to hide behind if a gent wishes to be really concealed.

Both Millard and Wallace were in favor of their clients being

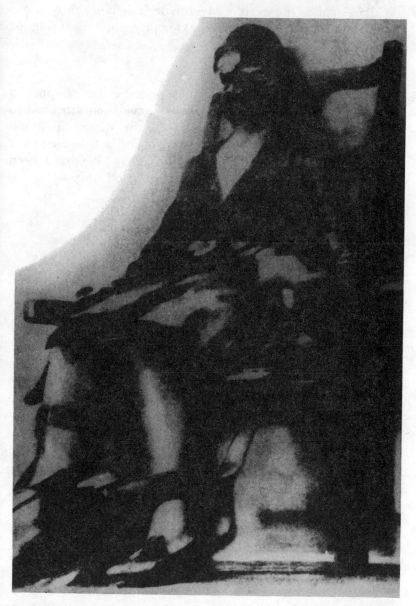

Ruth Snyder's final moment in the electric chair.

acquitted. Millard's was something of an appeal for pity, but
Wallace said, in the spirit of Mrs Snyder's defiance throughout
this trial, that she was not asking for pity, she was asking for
justice.

In some ways it was a disheartening spectacle, if one happened
to think how many spectators would have been attracted to
Long Island City to hear a few pleas for the Mississippi Flood
sufferers. In another, it was something of a tribute to the power
of good old publicity. It pays to advertise. We have been
three-sheeting Henry Judd and Ruth to good purpose.

F. TENNYSON JESSE

The Trial of Madeleine Smith

The case of Madeleine Smith has a perennial interest for what may be termed mystery fanciers, or, in more modern slang, murder-fans.

And yet, although Madeleine Smith, an old, old woman, died a few years ago in the United States, and one is now, therefore, at liberty to assert the inescapable conviction of all students of the trial that she was guilty, a certain mystery will always hang around this famous trial of 1857. But it is not a mystery of action, but of that strange thing, the human heart.

It was not Madeleine's heart which held mystery. That merely tried to hold its secrets, a very different matter. It is L'Angelier, the victim, who remains an enigma to this day.

I am aware that this statement may bring upon me the wrath of other students of this great trial, but I leave the reader who comes to this article with an open mind to judge for himself.

Madeleine Smith was the eldest daughter of a well-known Glasgow architect. Near her in age came a brother, Jack, and a sister, Bessie. There was a younger boy called James, and a little girl of twelve called Janet.

Only Janet, called by the defence, gave evidence at the trial, although Bessie was with Madeleine when L'Angelier was first introduced to her, and although Jack fetched her back from her father's country house, whither she fled after L'Angelier's death. In fact, the Smith family was protected in every way. Mr and Mrs Smith seemed to have taken to their bed and remained there.

L'Angelier was a penniless young clerk from Jersey, a Frenchman and a foreigner to Scottish eyes. It has always been an interesting question what the result of the trial might have

been had Madeleine Smith been the friendless foreigner and
the dead man the son of a wealthy and respected local family.

Yet Scottish justice is, as a rule, impartial and as good as can
be found in this rough-and-ready world, and I think the answer
to the undoubted bias in favour of the accused is to be found not
so much in the influence of the Smith family as in the fact that
L'Angelier had, after seducing Madeleine, proceeded to blackmail her and make her life a misery.

In fact, the verdict of Not Proven might be summed up as
meaning: 'We'll let you off this once, but don't do it again.'

Madeleine Smith was born out of due time. She was beautiful
in a handsome, defiant way that was not feminine enough for
the period in which she lived. She was a girl of strong physical
passion at a time when no woman was supposed to possess such
a thing.

She was talented and capable; but arranging the flowers in
her parents' home, and, if she were married, being a good
housekeeper in her husband's house, was all the mental effort
deemed suitable for a woman. In the late war, Madeleine Smith
would have driven an ambulance or filled some organising post
most admirably.

Pierre Emile L'Angelier, a peculiarly nasty little ladykiller,
earning about a pound a week, may have been, and probably
was, attracted by Madeleine's bright beauty as she passed
about the grey Glasgow streets.

But he also knew that she came of a wealthy family and he
pressed a mutual friend, a youth called Robert Baird, to
introduce them. Baird asked his mother whether he might
bring L'Angelier home one evening when Miss Smith was
visiting the house.

But Mrs Baird evidently thought such an acquaintance
unsuitable and declined permission, and the introduction took
place in the street. A clandestine acquaintance ripened between Madeleine and L'Angelier, but it was discovered by the
girl's father, and Madeleine attempted to end the acquaintance
in the same month that it had begun.

L'Angelier, however, was not to be shaken off, although
Madeleine made another attempt to get free of him in July of
1855. Her heart was not in the business of dismissal, however,

and the acquaintance continued, growing more and more intimate.

To Madeleine, L'Angelier's foreign origin, his poverty, his flowing whiskers, and his skilful love-making made of him a figure of romance. L'Angelier's mind was set from the first on marriage with this daughter of a wealthy family, and his seduction of her, if seduction it can be called when her passionate nature was more than ready to submit to him, was merely a step in his campaign.

In June of the following year Madeleine became L'Angelier's mistress. The lovers met sometimes in the woods outside her father's country house, sometimes in the house in Blythswood Square to which she used to admit him after the family were all asleep.

And during all this time a series of passionate love-letters went back and forth. He kept all of hers. She kept but one or two of his. Hers were supposed to show a shocking lack of decency, though nowadays they do not seem strange letters for a woman to have written to her lover whom she thought to marry. His show him as the unpleasing mixture of a sensualist and a preacher that he was.

The raptures of the early months began to fade for Madeleine. Her common sense told her that her father (and Mr Smith seems to have been the very personification of the terrible Jove-like Victorian papa) would never consent to a marriage with L'Angelier.

A Mr Minnoch, a middle-aged man of good standing and a friend of the Smith family, fell in love with her and asked for her hand. The solid comforts of Mr Minnoch's establishment, the charm of being its mistress and a young matron, began to appeal to Madeleine, and her letters to L'Angelier grew perceptibly colder.

He took fright and began to importune her. She definitely tried to break with him, only to find that he refused to let her go, that he even threatened to show her letters—those letters which would damn her for ever in the eyes of her contemporaries—to her father.

Madeleine Smith is not a lovable character, but it is possible to sympathise with the agonies of fear, with the remorse and

Madeleine Smith (top) and Pierre Emile l'Angelier: engravings from
a contemporary report of the trial.

disgust which must have taken hold of her. She had accepted Mr Minnoch's proposal in January, 1857, and she still could not get free of L'Angelier.

In February she told him candidly that she no longer loved him, but she could not pique him into returning her letters. She wrote to him imploringly, but to implore a blackmailer's mercy is a singularly useless proceeding.

She then asked the page boy to go to a chemist to buy her a bottle of prussic acid, saying she wanted it to whiten her hands. The chemist, very sensibly, refused to comply with her request.

She next began to write to Emile in the old strain of affection. While writing these loving epistles, making appointments for him to meet her, she was also employed in buying arsenic. She made three purchases in all, giving the usual well-worn reasons—one, the improvement of her complexion by using the drug as a face wash, and the other the even more hackneyed one of wishing to destroy rats.

Her first purchase, as far as is known, was made on February 21, and there is no doubt that L'Angelier's first bad attack of sickness was in the morning of the 19th. This was a strong argument in favour of her innocence.

But L'Angelier had thrice before been seized with sickness of the same description in the houses of his friends, and it may be that his illness of the 19th was not due to arsenic poisoning. But she was in possession of arsenic on the 21st, and L'Angelier was taken extremely ill on the 22nd. Madeleine bought arsenic again on March 6 and March 18.

Madeleine tried to get him to go away to the Isle of Wight for a holiday, but he refused to go further than Bridge of Allan. Now she began to write to him asking him to come and see her, using the most ardent phrases.

The prosecution maintained that she handed him poisoned cocoa from the window of her basement bedroom where he came there by appointment on the evening of March 22.

But the prosecution was never able to prove this meeting. Had they been able to do so, nothing could have saved Madeleine Smith. L'Angelier, recalled from Bridge of Allan by a letter—from whom the letter came could not be proved—left his lodgings that evening in better health, but at half-past two on Monday morning he was ringing the bell of his lodging-house violently.

His landlady helped him to his room, and there he vomited for about two hours. At five o'clock a doctor was sent for, but refused to come, merely suggesting twenty-five drops of laudanum and a mustard plaster.

The landlady continued to attend him, and he became so ill that she insisted on the doctor coming at about seven o'clock. The doctor gave him a little morphia and applied a poultice, making the sapient remark that time and quietness were required. By eleven o'clock L'Angelier was quiet enough, for he was dead.

Now the curious thing about L'Angelier's final agonies is this—although he seems to have known that he was dying, he never accused Madeleine Smith, or, indeed, mentioned her name. He did ask his landlady to send for a Miss Perry, a sentimental maiden lady, who had played the part of go-between for him and Madeleine, but by the time Miss Perry arrived he was dead.

Whether he had been going to accuse Madeleine to her we shall never know. According to Miss Perry's evidence at the trial he had said to her after his illness on February 19: 'I can't think why I was so ill after taking that coffee and chocolate from her.' Miss Perry understood her to mean Miss Smith.

He had added: 'It is a perfect fascination, my attachment to that girl. If she were to poison me I should forgive her.'

L'Angelier was an eminently practical person, and there is little doubt that he would not knowingly have taken poison from the hands of Madeleine or anyone else. And so we can be almost certain that in those last hours of agony on the morning of March 23 he realised for the first time that at least one previous attack of sickness may have been due to Madeleine's cocoa, and that the present one must have been caused by her.

If, when dying, he realised what Madeleine had done and yet refrained from naming that girl he had bullied and black-mailed, so much may, at least, be allowed to him for righteousness.

But why did this contemptible little lady-killer show such magnanimity? It was suggested, of course, by the defence that he might have taken the poison accidentally, or that some other person, not Madeleine, had murdered him, or that he had committed suicide. The last suggestion is the only one not outside of the region of possibility.

However, if he killed himself by repeated doses of that extremely painful poison, arsenic, he remains unique as a suicide. Also, it is far more in keeping with his character to blackmail Madeleine, or to go to her father and demand from him money for keeping silent.

It is, therefore, not only possible, but perhaps even probable, that a certain remorse entered his heart as he lay dying, for there seems no doubt that he knew that he was dying.

He said to his landlady: 'I'm far worse than the doctor thinks.' His pain and weakness must have been so intense, his knowledge that some lethal substance had been administered to him so certain, that he can have had but little hope, although he murmured: 'Oh, if I could get five minutes' sleep I think I would get better.'

Madeleine's name never passed his lips, nor would he give any hint as to the cause of his illness. This reticence and generosity in a man who had hitherto been completely ruthless is the most mysterious thing in the case.

There is no answer to the riddle, although it may be permitted to hope that the solution is to be found in the theory—which must always remain a theory—that regret touched his scheming little heart in his last hours.

L'Angelier's death seemed so inexplicable that an autopsy was held and more than sufficient arsenic to destroy life was found in the body. L'Angelier's effects were examined and Madeleine's letters were found.

She fled blindly and futilely to her father's country house, but came back unprotestingly with Mr Minnoch and her brother, Jack. All thought of marriage with the respectable Mr Minnoch was, of course, over for good; and, indeed, when that unfortunate man, who seems to have felt the discovery of her previous passion very acutely, had to give evidence against her at her trial, it is said he never looked towards her.

Yet Madeleine was worth looking at, in her full, sweeping, dark silk dress and her bonnet, which, shaped like a halo, showed the front of her sleek, dark head so that her cameo-like profile and beautiful complexion stood out unshadowed.

Rumour has it that one of the judges was peculiarly susceptible to the charms of a pretty foot and ankle, and that Madeleine sat slightly sideways in the dock, her skirt pulled up a little to display this charm, so exciting to the Victorians.

The trial was chiefly noticeable for the magnificent speeches by the Lord Advocate, for the prosecution, and the Dean of Faculty, for the defence. The latter, Lord Inglis, who was to become Lord Justice-General of Scotland, made a closing speech which has remained a model to this day.

The strength, the passion, with which he fought every inch of the ground, the brilliance of his arguments and the closeness of his reasoning, remain untouched by time. And if some of his oratory seems a trifle lush and old-fashioned, the same can be said of that of the late Marshall Hall, and still more so of the sentimental periods of Mr Clarence Darrow, most noted defence counsel in the United States.

Three of the Dean of Faculty's strongest points were:

1 That the prosecution could not show that Madeleine possessed any arsenic before February 21.

2 That there was no proof that L'Angelier had met Madeleine before his attacks of sickness on February 22 and March 22.

3 That it might reasonably be argued that L'Angelier's death placed Madeleine in a very awkward position, as her letters would be bound to be discovered.

There is not, perhaps, much force in the third argument. Madeleine could hardly be in a worse position than if L'Angelier fulfilled his threat of showing her letters to her father, and she may have hoped that if her lover's death passed off without comment the letters would be destroyed. They were, in any case, nearly all signed Mimi, or sometimes even Mimi L'Angelier. But the Dean of Faculty would not have found himself in nearly such a strong position when he argued that there was no meeting between the two on the crucial dates, if a little diary of

L'Angelier's had been allowed to be put into evidence.

The entry for February 19 ran: 'Saw Mimi a few moments. Was very ill during the night.' While that for February 22 read: 'Saw Mimi in drawing-room, promised me French Bible, taken very ill.'

It was ruled, however, that this diary was inadmissible as evidence of a fact against the accused.

The summing up was admirably fair, but certainly it gave the prisoner the benefit of every doubt and it was, probably, a very relieved jury that returned a verdict of Not Proven.

Madeleine Smith, who had remained the calmest and most unmoved person in court throughout the trial, wrote in a letter to the matron of the prison, that she was not at all pleased with the verdict! In the same latter she complained that the feeling of the people towards her round her home was not as kindly as that of 'the good people of Edinburgh' had been.

Apparently she expected to be found Not Guilty and received with acclamation. Even her excellent nervous system, however, found it impossible to bear home life after all the revelations that had been made, and she went to London alone, became a Socialist, and married, the first two steps being rare for a girl of those days, and the third something of an achievement, considering her past.

It is said, with what truth I do not know, that she made an excellent wife, and that her husband was very devoted to her, but that he never allowed her to do any cooking.

There would have been little risk, however, of Madeleine Smith attempting to kill for a second time. She was not a congenital killer, she was merely a woman who knew what she wanted and who, much rarer, knew when she had ceased to want it.

And her resolution was such that she was determined to have her way in both these matters. She was, in short, a woman born at the very worst time in the world's history for such as she; a time when women were not supposed to want much, but were also supposed to want that little long.

'I shall ever remain true to you,' Madeleine had written to L'Angelier. 'I think a woman who can be untrue should be banished from society.'

She had the courage of her change of conviction.

Frederick Seddon.

EDGAR WALLACE

The Trial of the Seddons

Seddon was essentially a business man, shrewd, neat, a little unimaginative. He was the type sometimes met with in the train on the way to the City: a man of dogmatic opinions, a little overbearing, wholly intolerant of other people's opinions. You could imagine Seddon holding rigid political views, and regarding all who did not share them as being outside the pale.

Generally he was accounted, by those who knew him best, as a very excellent manager; a man who gave nothing away, and who was credited with considerable possessions, which his thrift and his gift for driving a hard bargain had accumulated for him.

Seddon lived in a good-sized house at Tollington Park, North London, with his wife and five children. It was a fairly large house and his own property (as he often boasted), and here he carried on his profession of insurance agent, being superintendent of that district and having under his charge a number of collectors, who were kept very busy by their energetic taskmaster. Seddon was certainly a man bound to get on. In the interests of his business he worked day and night; he was indefatigable in his search for new 'lives,' yet found time to indulge in certain social amenities, and was an officer of a very honourable society, where he was considerably respected.

That Seddon was a true Freemason in the real sense of the word can be doubted. Men of his intelligence too often adopt Masonry as a means to an end, believing that fellowship with so many of the best intellects in a district gives them advantages in business. Nevertheless, it was his ambition to rise to the supreme heights of Masonry, and all his spare time was given to the assiduous study of the craft and to fitting himself for higher office than that which he at present held.

A mean, hectoring man, bombastic of speech, loud of voice, that crushed all opposition, his business grew rapidly, but not so fast as he could wish. The dominant passion of Seddon's life was money. Not every miser is a recluse, who hides his bags of gold in inaccessible places and shrinks from the society of his fellow-men. There are some, who are to be met with in every sphere of commercial activity, well-groomed misers who are not to be suspected of their vice, and Seddon was one of these. He worshipped money for money's sake. He never spent a farthing that he could avoid. His household accounts were most minutely examined day by day, and the money he doled out for household expenses was the smallest sum he could in decency offer to his unfortunate wife.

Seddon's dreams had a golden hue. The rich were very wonderful in his eyes, and he would find his recreation in relating to his friends his surprising knowledge of the wealth which was possessed by the great figures of the financial world.

He had saved penny by penny, pound by pound, gradually piling up his assets painfully and slowly. Never once had a large amount come to him in one sum, and one of his bitterest complaints was that he had no rich relations who were likely to die and leave him a fortune. Not the least interesting item of the newspapers was the paragraph which appears every day under the heading 'Latest Wills,' and he would pore over this in the evenings. Sometimes he would learn of a rich man or woman who had died intestate, the money going to the Crown, and this would throw him into a fury.

'All that money wasted! Thrown into the gutter! It is criminal! Why don't people have more common sense?'

I

There was in London, though of her existence Seddon was ignorant for some time, a middle-aged woman who shared Seddon's peculiar passion for money. She, however, had never had to scrape and strive. She had been left a small fortune in the shape of house property—at least it was a small fortune to her—which brought her in £5 or £6 a week. She was as mean as

Seddon, parting with every penny with the greatest reluctance, and worshipping money, even as he did, for money's sake.

It follows that she was a difficult tenant to any landlady who gave her accommodation, and she shifted her lodgings very frequently, taking with her the small boy whom she had adopted, Ernie Grant.

In his restless search for people whom he could persuade to take out insurance policies, Seddon came into contact with this middle-aged spinster, Miss Eliza Barrow, and these two sharp-minded beings recognised in one another kindred souls. Seddon's immediate interest in the woman was a purely business one, but he had ever an eye to the main chance, and it had been his practice to leave no avenue to fortune unexplored.

'Friends should pay dividends,' was one of his mottoes; and there is little doubt, after he had discovered that Miss Barrow was not a likely subject for insurance, that he turned over in his mind a way by which this new acquaintance should 'pay dividends.' Miss Barrow's complaint against landladies was perennial. Her interest in life was confined by the walls of the lodgings she had, and it may be imagined that they had not long met before she was telling him of her various landladies' enormities, the high cost of living, the peculations of lodging-house servants, and the difficulty of finding a home where these causes for distress would be more or less non-existent.

Seddon was a quick thinker. He had a big house in Tollington Park, and several of the upper rooms were unoccupied. This woman could pay dividends in the shape of rent, and in many other ways was a desirable tenant, for he had learnt of her house property and her steady income, and there was no fear that she would come to him on a Monday morning and bring excuses instead of money. So Seddon patted the little boy on the head with easy benevolence, and remembered his empty rooms.

'I think my rooms would suit you very well,' he said. 'We live very quietly; you will be in the house of a successful business man who may be able to help you from time to time in the matter of advice, and I'll arrange it so that you live more cheaply with me than you have been living heretofore.'

The arrangement was most welcome to the woman, who was

in the throes of one of her periodical fits of resentment against her landlady. She had lived in many homes. Once she had stayed with her cousin, Mr Frank Ernest Vonderahe, but that arrangement had not been satisfactory, and she had wandered off with her boy to yet another lodging.

Life at Tollington Park was entirely to Miss Barrow's satisfaction. She had the opportunity of talking business with Seddon; he admitted her to his confidence, allowed her to be present when he was handling the large sums of money which came in from the collectors—a sight very precious to Miss Barrow, who, in spite of her possessions, had probably not seen so much gold before. And the knowledge that he was trusted with such huge sums increased her confidence in him; so that she brought her own financial difficulties to him (the cost of repairs, tenants' demands and the like), and accepted his advice on all matters concerning her estate.

The friendship grew to a stage probably beyond her anticipations. Her confidence came to be a blind trust in his integrity and prescience. It developed, as was subsequently discovered, in her taking the rash step of purchasing an annuity upon his advice.

It is certain that Frederick Henry Seddon saw in Eliza Barrow a greater profit than the meagre sums he obtained by giving her lodging. There was about him the additional flavour of deep religious principles. Seddon had a reputation as a lay preacher and public orator. He was fluent of speech, better educated than most men of his class, and he could be, in his lighter moments, a most entertaining and charming man. He charmed Eliza Barrow to this end, that one day he induced her to sell her Indian stock for £1600, to get rid of her house property and to trust him with the money. She was obviously confident, from his manner to her adopted child, that the boy would lose nothing from being left in Seddon's charge, for she made no provision whatever for his future until a few days before her death.

Seddon had gone to work deliberately, with a set plan, and the first part of his scheme having been brought to a successful issue, nothing remained but to perpetrate the dreadful deed which he may have contemplated from the very moment he had

Eliza Mary Barrow: murdered for a pittance.

obtained Miss Barrow's confidence.

Since no poisoner has ever confessed his method, it is only possible to reconstruct the story of such a murder by an understanding of the murderer's mentality, and by piecing together such scraps of evidence as are available.

Seddon probably purchased a small quantity of arsenic in some part of London in which he was unknown. But he was shrewd enough to prepare, at the same time, a defence for himself. He purchased a number of fly-papers—paper impregnated with arsenic, which, when placed in a wet saucer, destroys any fly who lights upon it—and several of these he placed in Miss Barrow's bedroom.

He knew, for he had made a study of poison trials, that one of the questions which decides the guilt or innocence of any person accused of poisoning, is the accessibility of the poison: in other words, whether it is possible, through accident or design, for poison to be self-administered. The only way that arsenic could be self-administered by a demented or careless woman was to have strong solutions of arsenic in her bedroom. He did not apparently realise that, in ninety-nine cases out of a hundred where a person is found poisoned, the police look for a motive, and find one in a case where a person who had the opportunity of administering the poison directly benefits by the death.

'Seddon always thinks of everything,' said an admiring colleague. 'That is why he has been so successful.'

Undoubtedly Seddon thought of most of the possibilities, but never dreamt that his cunning plan would be exposed.

In many ways Miss Barrow was most favourably placed from his point of view. She had quarrelled with her relations, and those very distant relations. She had no personal friends, and beyond the Vonderahes, who came occasionally to see her, and were received with marked coldness, no interfering individual who would inquire too closely into her sudden demise.

II

The Seddon's family were on very good terms with their lodger. Maggie Seddon and her mother did the cooking for her. Seddon himself was seldom in her room. When she became ill, only on one occasion did Seddon give Miss Barrow her medicine. A doctor was called in, saw nothing suspicious, identified Miss Barrow's symptoms with a natural derangement; and if he was surprised when one day he was summoned to find the unfortunate lady *in extremis*, it was one of those surprises which are the normal experience of every medical practitioner, and he did not hesitate to give a certificate stating that her death was due to natural causes.

Three days before her death, Seddon persuaded Miss Barrow to make a will leaving all that she possessed to Ernest and Hilda Grant, appointing Seddon the sole executor. Again we see the cleverness of the move; for now Seddon had so arranged matters that suspicion would be even more remote from himself. He had no possible interest in her death (unless the secretly-arranged sale of the annuity came to light), and such sums of money and property which had been Miss Barrow's as would be left he might use until the children came of age.

Miss Barrow died on the Thursday, and no sooner was the breath out of her body than Seddon bustled off to interview an undertaker, and arranged for the cheapest possible funeral. Not only did he do this, but he made a gruesome bargain with the man which gives us an interesting insight into his mastering desire to save money at every opportunity. Seddon told the undertaker that an old lady had died in his house, and it would have to be an inexpensive funeral. He had found four pounds ten in the room, he said, and that would not only have to defray the funeral expenses, but find the fees due to the doctor. Thereupon the undertaker bargained to carry out the funeral at an inclusive price of three pounds seven and sixpence and allowed Seddon a small commission on the transaction. Seddon had memorial cards printed, with an appropriate verse of sorrow; he bought a quantity of black-edged envelopes and paper, and wrote a number of letters, which, however, were never delivered or posted.

No man could have taken greater precautions than did Seddon to clear himself of any suspicion that he was implicated in the death of this wretched lady. Miss Barrow died on the Thursday, and on the Saturday was buried in a common grave, although there was a family vault, about which Seddon could not have been ignorant. He was, however, anxious to get the body underground with the least possible delay, for, once buried, he knew that there would be considerable difficulty in getting an exhumation.

Although not on specially good terms, Miss Barrow had been in the habit of calling on the Vonderahes, and the fact that she had not appeared, and that they had seen nothing either of her or the boy, was remarked upon by Mrs Vonderahe.

'I can't understand why we have not seen Miss Barrow for so long,' she said to her husband. 'Why don't you walk round to Tollington Park and see how she is getting on?'

Ernest Vonderahe, who was not particularly interested in his cousin, was nevertheless a dutiful relative, and on the Wednesday evening strolled over to Tollington Park. The door was opened by Seddon's general servant, Mary Chater, who stared at him blankly.

'I've come to see how Miss Barrow is getting on. Is she well?'

The girl gasped.

'Haven't you heard?' she demanded in amazement. 'Miss Barrow is dead and buried—didn't you know?'

Vonderahe could only stare at her.

'Dead and buried?' he said incredulously. 'When did she die?'

'Last Thursday.'

'But this is only Wednesday!'

'She was buried on Saturday,' said the maid.

'Can I see Mr Seddon?'

The girl shook her head.

'He's out, and won't be back for an hour,' she said.

Staggered by this startling news, Vonderahe went back and saw his wife. At his suggestion, she dressed, and they went back again to Tollington Park, arriving about nine o'clock in the evening. This time they saw Maggie Seddon, the daughter, but Seddon was not visible.

'Father has gone to the Finsbury Park Empire and won't be back till very late,' she said, and could give them little or no information about Miss Barrow's illness, nor did they think it worth while to question the child.

The Vonderahes went home and a family council was summoned, consisting of Vonderahe and his brother, with their wives, and they discussed the mysterious suddenness of Miss Barrow's illness until far into the night, arriving at the decision that the two women should interview Seddon the next morning and discover more about the circumstances of the woman's death.

Accordingly, the next morning the two wives went to Tollington Park, and the door was again opened by Maggie Seddon. Apparently they were expected, for they were shown immediately into the dining-room. The visitors were kept for some time before the insurance superintendent and his wife made their appearance. He was his usual self, calm, confident, neatly dressed and in every respect self-possessed. But his wife displayed the greatest nervousness, and, throughout the interview which followed, was on the point of breaking down.

Seddon strode into the apartment, pulled out a watch (which proved to be the property of the late Miss Barrow), looked at it significantly and remarked in a loud tone that he hadn't much time to spare and he hoped that they would be brief. And then, when his wife began to speak, he silenced her firmly but kindly.

'Now,' said Seddon briskly, 'just tell me who you are, and things,' he said, and explained that his wife had been greatly shocked by the death of the lodger and had not yet recovered. 'You sit there and don't upset yourself. I can tell these ladies all they wish to know.'

Mrs Seddon may have had a suspicion that all was not well. The manner of Miss Barrow's death, the haste of the funeral, may have seemed to her suspicious things.

'Now,' said Seddon briskly, 'just tell me who you are, and what relation you are to the deceased Miss Barrow.' And, when he was told, he handed them a copy of a letter written to Vonderahe, which the latter had not received.

The letter was brief and to the effect that Miss Barrow was dead. It invited them to the funeral which had taken place on the previous Saturday. It added that, a few days before her death, Miss Barrow had left a will in which she gave 'what she died possessed of' to Hilda and Ernest Grant, and appointed Seddon as sole executor.

Apparently Seddon had everything prepared: the copy of the will and a large blank envelope into which he put these documents and handed them to one of the ladies present.

So far, in spite of the brusqueness of the man—his callous indifference to the feelings of Miss Barrow's relatives and the scarcely veiled antagonism he showed to these inquirers—there was nothing suspicious beyond his manner; and it is probable that, had Seddon been more conciliatory, expressed a little more sorrow and stage-managed that interview a little more deftly, he might have escaped the consequence of his villainy.

As it was, he again looked at his watch pointedly, and when one of the ladies asked if he would see Mr Ernest Vonderahe he shrugged his shoulders.

'I am a business man, and I think I've wasted quite enough time on this matter,' he said. 'I really can't be bothered answering questions put by inquisitive people.'

These two ladies had gone to Tollington Park with the misguided idea that, because of their relationship, they would be asked to take possession of Miss Barrow's effects. If the will were genuine, and her death had occurred under normal circumstances, they could not, of course, touch a single article without permission from the executor; and legally, Seddon's position was unassailable.

But in their ignorance of the law, they expected to be given certain of Miss Barrow's goods. Their real suspicions began when they found that, justifiably, Seddon meant to retain in his possession all the property the administration of which had been specifically left to him. It was only when they found that they were being sent empty-handed away from Tollington Park that they began to regard Seddon's behaviour as suspicious; and his ignorance of their psychology was responsible for his undoing.

It was not till some weeks later, on October 9th, after many family councils, that Mr Ernest Vonderahe saw Seddon. The insurance agent had gone to Southend for a holiday, feeling, he said, 'a little under the weather.' And that period gave Ernest Vonderahe an opportunity of making closer inquiries into the possessions of Miss Barrow when she died. He discovered something about her investments; she was the landlady of a

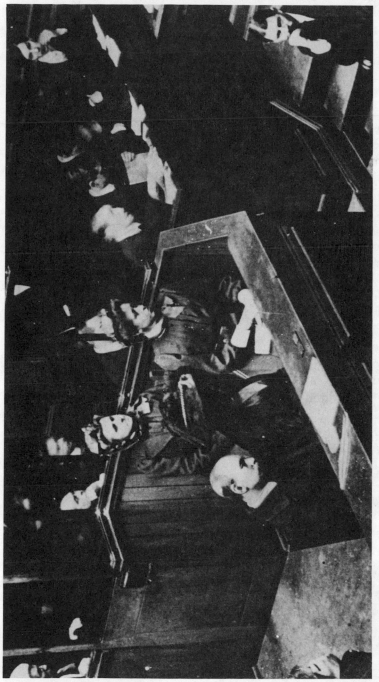

Frederick Seddon: tried for the most miserly murder.

public-house called the 'Buck's Head,' and the proprietress of a barber's shop adjoining the public-house; had a considerable sum of money in the bank, and at the time of her death had quite a large sum in ready cash.

Whether the relatives of Miss Barrow were chiefly concerned with the manner of her death, or whether they suffered under an indignant sense of being robbed of that which was rightfully theirs, we need not inquire. All the investigations which went on were in the direction of ascertaining the exact amount of benefit Seddon might have received from the woman's disappearance. It was a very proper and natural line of investigation, to which no exception could be taken. It is perfectly certain that, supposing the will to be genuine—and this was not disputed—whatever might be the result of their inquiries, they themselves could not be benefited by a single penny through the exposure of Seddon as a murderer.

The Vonderahes saw something of one of the 'beneficiaries' under the will. Little Ernie Grant came to see them, but was invariably accompanied by one of Seddon's children, either the girl or the boy, and the suspicions of the Vonderahes were deepened, because they saw, in this chaperonage, an attempt to prevent them questioning the child as to the manner of Miss Barrow's death.

On Seddon's return from Southend, Vonderahe decided to call upon him, and sent him a message to that effect. And the visitor was accompanied by a friend 'as witness.' Seddon had no illusions as to the antagonism of the deceased woman's cousin. He had heard something more than the subterranean rumbling which was to precede the cataclysm, and his line of preparation—to meet the unspoken charges which he knew Vonderahe would have in mind—took the shape of adopting towards his inquisitor a lofty and high-handed manner, which had served him so successfully in dealing with other disagreeable people in his business.

Like all poisoners, Seddon was completely satisfied of his own invincibility. And he could even challenge still greater antagonism by attempting to cow his inquisitive visitors into submission to his point of view. Vonderahe and his friend were in the parlour, cooling their heels, for twenty minutes before

Seddon and his wife came into the room.

.

III

'Mr Frank Ernest Vonderahe?' asked Seddon, and when the relative had answered in the affirmative, Seddon spoke to the second of the men, under the impression that Vonderahe's companion was his brother.

Seddon was smoking a large cigar, and motioned his visitors to chairs with a lordly air.

'Now what is all this about?' he asked. 'You are under the impression that some money is due to you from the estate of Miss Barrow? The will is perfectly clear, and I don't see why I should give you any further information. If your solicitor cares to see my solicitor, all very well and good.'

In spite of this high-handed proceeding, Ernest Vonderahe began to question the man.

'Who is now the owner of the "Buck's Head"?' he asked, referring to one of the properties which had been Miss Barrow's.

'I am,' said Seddon quickly, 'and the barber's shop next door is also mine. I've bought the property—in fact, I am always open to buy property if it shows any chance of a reasonable return. This house is mine, and I have a number of other properties. That is my private business: I buy and sell whenever a bargain is offered.'

The propriety of Seddon's purchasing properties of which he was the executor for his own benefit did not seem to have occurred to either of the two men, and Ernest Vonderahe shifted his inquiries to a complaint that his relative had been buried in a common grave, when there was a handsome family vault at Highgate available.

Seddon replied that he thought the vault was full up, though this excuse might have been invented on the spur of the moment. The 'Buck's Head' and the barber's shop had, he declared, been bought in the open market. It was his business to dispose of the property, and as his bids were higher than any others, there was nothing remarkable about it being knocked down to him. When they pressed their inquiries, Seddon said (I am quoting the statement of Ernest Vonderahe):

'That is for the proper authorities to find out. I am perfectly willing to meet any solicitor. I am prepared to spend a thousand pounds to prove that all I have done in regard to Miss Barrow is perfectly in order.'

Until this interview, according to the evidence which was subsequently offered at the trial of Seddon, the inquiries and the suspicions had been confined to the narrow circle of the Vonderahes and their intimate friends. But after this point-blank refusal of Seddon to discuss the affairs of the dead woman, and when it seemed that no useful purpose would be served by further interviews, the Vonderahes did what they should have done in the first place—communicated their suspicions to the police.

Such communications are not rare at Scotland Yard, and the police authorities act with the greatest circumspection before they take any drastic action to confirm the suspicions of relatives. There are probably twenty complaints to every exhumation; possibly the number is much larger. But the police, in this case, had something else to work upon than the bald suspicions of the Vonderahes. There was, in the first place, the hasty burial, and, in the second, the fact that, as executor or direct beneficiary, Seddon had obtained a number of effects which were the property of the deceased woman and which were now under his control. The doctor was interviewed by the police and, strengthened by his evidence, the Home Office made an order for the exhumation of the body.

These forces were at work all unknown to Seddon, who went about his daily business, satisfied in his mind that, if he had not allayed the doubts in the mind of Ernest Vonderahe, he had at least so baffled him, by his bold challenge to put the matter into his solicitor's hands, that no further trouble need be anticipated.

Removed to the cemetery mortuary, the body was examined by Drs Wilcox and Spilsbury, now Sir William Wilcox and Sir Bernard Spilsbury, the Home Office pathologists. Certain organs were removed and forwarded for analysis, and the body was reinterred.

It was a grim coincidence that Seddon's business took him to

St Mary's Hospital at the time when Miss Barrow's remains were undergoing chemical examination, and that he was shown over a portion of the laboratory whilst that examination was in progress!

The chemist's report to the Home Office was emphatic: a very large quantity of arsenic had been found in the remains, and on this report the Home Office ordered an inquest.

Seddon was working at his accounts one night when his daughter came to tell him that a policeman wanted to see him.

'A policeman?' said Seddon. 'What does he want? Ask him to come in.'

The officer walked into the room, helmet in hand, and handed him a paper.

'I am the coroner's officer,' he said, 'and this is a summons for you to attend an inquest on the body of Eliza Barrow, which will be held to-morrow.'

Not a muscle of Seddon's face moved. Eliza Barrow! Until that moment he had not known that an exhumation order had been made. This was his first intimation that the net was closing round him.

When the officer had departed, Seddon swept aside the work on which he had been engaged, and sat down, coolly and calmly, to work throughout the night, packing his wife and children off to bed, whilst he prepared answers to such questions as might be put to him.

The grey dawn of a November day found him haggard and drawn, his table littered with papers covered with his clerkly writing. He had prepared for every possible contingency; had an answer for every question which might possibly be put to him; had checked and compared answer with answer, so that his story should be logical and convincing.

The inquest lasted for the greater part of a fortnight. And now suspicion became certainty. Seddon's conduct, tested and probed, did not react, as he had hoped, to his advantage. On December 4th he was arrested on the charge of murdering Eliza Barrow.

For more than a month, while he was under arrest, his wife was allowed her freedom. But as the law officers examined more closely the evidence available, it was obvious that

Seddon's wife was also under suspicion; and, to the amazement and indignation of the murderer, she was arrested on January 15th, 1912.

Seddon plied the detectives with questions as to the nature of the poison, and as to whether it might not have been self-administered. 'It was not carbolic acid, was it?' he asked. 'There was some in her room. Have you found arsenic in the body?'

All Seddon's transactions with the deceased woman now came into the light of day, and, incidentally, the motive for the murder. Miss Barrow had converted a considerable amount of her shares, of which she possessed some £1600 worth, into cash, and purchased from Seddon an annuity of some £155 per annum. Whilst she lived, he had to pay her £3,5s. a week, and it was to save this paltry sum, in the belief that she would live many years, that Seddon had murdered her. The transaction in itself was not unusual. Seddon, as an insurance superintendent, dealt in annuities, but this time the transaction was carried out for his own benefit. The will, therefore, leaving everything she possessed to Ernie and Hilda Grant, was a hollow document which meant nothing, since her only possessions at the time of her death were the cash she had at her bank and her own personal possessions.

The trial, which began at the Old Bailey in March 1912, before Mr Justice Bucknill, excited general interest. The Attorney-General, Sir Rufus Isaacs, now Viceroy of India, appeared for the prosecution; Sir Marshall Hall, then Mr Marshall Hall, defended the man; whilst Mr Rentoul, now Judge Rentoul, defended Mrs Seddon.

Throughout the trial, Seddon kept up that unemotional, detached attitude which he had shown from the very moment of his arrest. Mrs Seddon, on the other hand, was a sad and dejected figure. She could indulge in none of the breezy exchanges which Seddon had with his counsel, nor could she regard with equanimity a visit to the witness-box, which Seddon welcomed rather than otherwise.

Seddon depended upon the fact that no person had seen him administer poison to the deceased woman. And this, as has already been pointed out, is the basis of confidence in the case of every man or woman charged with murder by poison. It was as though he put into words the attitude of such men:

'I am willing to admit that the woman died of poison. I admit that I benefited considerably by her death, but you cannot prove that I gave her the poison. I may have brought food to her, and unless the prosecution can, beyond all possible doubt, prove that poison was in that food, and placed there by me, you must return a verdict of Not Guilty.' Never in the history of criminal jurisprudence has there been a case where a convicted prisoner has been detected in the act of administering poison, either in food or otherwise. The poisoner banks upon suspicion being equally attached to other persons than himself, and thus securing the benefit of the doubt. Seddon's confidence was fated to receive a terrible shock. After an hour's deliberation the jury returned with a verdict of 'Guilty' against Seddon, and 'Not Guilty' against Mrs Seddon. Seddon bent over and kissed his wife; in another minute they were separated, never to see one another again except through the intervening bars.

The Clerk of Arraigns put the usual question: 'What have you to say that the Court should not give you judgment to die according to law?'

And then occurred the most dramatic and, to many people in the court, the most painful incident of the trial. Seddon stood stiffly erect and began a long speech which declared his innocence. He ended by making a Masonic sign which was unmistakable to Mr Justice Bucknill, himself a Freemason: 'I declare before the Great Architect of the Universe that I am not guilty, my lord.' The judge was visibly distressed, but, recovering himself instantly, passed sentence of death, and Seddon paid the penalty for his crime at Pentonville Gaol on April 18th, 1912.

Freeman Wills Crofts was trained as an engineer but suffered, in middle life, a serious illness that required a long and tedious convalescence. He filled the time by writing a detective story, The Cask, *that was subsequently published and later acclaimed as a classic of its kind. He wrote a mystery novel each year afterwards until his death in 1957, many featuring his series detective Inspector French. He wrote very little on true crimes, and so the short piece which follows is — like those by F. Tennyson Jesse and Edgar Wallace — something of a rarity.*

FREEMAN WILLS CROFTS

The Gorse Hall Mystery

At the beginning of November, 1909, Mr George Henry Storrs was murdered at his home, near Stalybridge, under circumstances which have never been cleared up.

Mr Storrs was a wealthy builder and mill-owner, and lived with his wife and his wife's niece, Miss Lindley, in a large house named Gorse Hall. There were three servants—a cook and housemaid resident in the building, and a coachman living with his wife over the stables.

Mr Storrs was a kindly and popular man, a good employer, and had no known enemies. He and his wife were a devoted couple, and both were on affectionate terms with Miss Lindley. The household may, indeed, be called a happy one.

Its peace, however, was destined to be rudely broken. About 9:30 on the night of September 10, 1909, when the family were sitting in the dining-room, a shot was suddenly fired through the window.

Seeing that no one had been hit Mr Storrs rushed to the window and pulled aside the blind. He could just see a dark figure disappearing into the shrubbery. When the ladies asked if he knew the man he replied, after a slight hesitation, that he did not.

Mrs Storrs was more alarmed than her husband, and next day she insisted on the police being informed and asked to keep a special watch on the house. She also had a large alarm bell put on the roof, and it was agreed that if this were sounded the police should instantly hurry over. It was suggested that the man was a homicidal maniac, and she was afraid that he might return.

Nothing unusual happened, however, for some seven weeks,

and then, on the last Saturday of October, Mr Storrs called on the police and asked them to be particularly vigilant in their watch. He said he had no special reason for making the request, but that he 'wanted to be sure.'

That night about midnight the alarm bell sounded and the police hurried to the house. But nothing was wrong. Mr Storrs said apologetically that he had wished to be sure that the alarm was really efficient, and had rung it as a test.

Sunday and Monday passed uneventfully, but on Monday evening tragedy really did visit the house. Some time after dinner the housemaid had to pass the scullery door, when she saw that the gas was alight. She looked in and found that the window had been broken open, but before she could investigate further a man jumped out from behind the door and seized her wrist. He had a revolver in his hand and he swore that if she made a sound he would shoot her.

Instinctively she twisted away from him, running screaming through the house. He did not fire, but followed her till they reached the hall. There Mr Storrs, attracted by the noise, rushed out of the dining-room. As soon as the man saw him he cried: 'I've got you at last!' Again he did not fire, but as Mr Storrs ran forward he closed with him and a terrible fight began.

In the meantime Mrs Storrs and Miss Lindley had also rushed out. For a moment they tried to join in the struggle. Mrs Storrs actually succeeding in tearing away the man's revolver. Then they saw him draw a knife. But Mr Storrs gasped out: 'The bell! Give the alarm!' and Mrs Storrs rushed off to ring it, while Miss Lindley fled down the drive to summon help from the Stalybridge Central Club, which was close by.

When assistance came the murderer had disappeared and Mr Storrs was at the point of death. He had received fifteen terrible knife wounds, and died without making a statement.

While neither the ladies nor the servants were able to give a detailed description of the murderer, declaring that there was nothing distinctive about him, they agreed that he was young-ish and poorly dressed, with a slight moustache and long fair hair. The revolver was of a cheap type, and yielded no clue.

A young man called Howard was arrested and charged with

the murder. He was a cousin of Mr Storrs, though he was personally unknown to the ladies. The evidence against him seemed purely circumstantial, but the police had a stronger case than was anticipated. When at the trial Mrs Storrs and Miss Lindley were asked if they could identify the murderer, they pointed dramatically to the prisoner, and swore he was the man.

No possible question of their bona fides arises; at the same time it became evident during the course of the trial that they were mistaken, Howard's innocence being proved beyond question. The verdict of Not Guilty was received with applause, and Howard left the court a popular hero.

Months afterwards a second man named Wilde was charged with the crime, stood his trial at Chester Assizes, and was also acquitted.

Since then the Gorse Hall Tragedy has remained a complete mystery, and no trace of the real murderer has ever been found.

In attempting to reconstruct what may have taken place in this strange tragedy, certain facts at once stand out as significant.

First, the murderer, whom for want of a better name I shall call John, had a definite grievance, real or imaginary, against Mr Storrs. This is proved by the facts that he said: 'I've got you at last,' and that he did not gain materially through his crime.

Second, Mr Storrs knew of this grievance and of his own danger. From his manner on the occasion of the attempt on September 9, it is almost certain that he recognised the man, and when he went to the police on the last Saturday in October, he evidently expected a further attack. Moreover, when he saw his assailant in the hall on the night of his death, he gave no exclamation of surprise, but grappled at once as with a known foe.

Third, Mr Storrs obviously wished to keep the affair secret. If he knew his own danger, as I have suggested he did, the fact that he made no statement on the subject proves this. But it is supported by his other actions. He did not inform the police of the first attack until the assailant had had time to get away. I will suggest presently that a second attack was made on the

Saturday night on which the alarm was sounded, and that on this occasion Mr Storrs suppressed any mention of John's presence for the same reason: to give him time to escape.

Fourth, owing to Mr Storr's upright character and kindly disposition, the secret was nothing with which he could reproach himself.

Fifthly, certain of John's actions seem to indicate an unbalanced mind. He entered the house on the night of the murder by smashing a window, and then committed the folly of turning on the gas. When he was discovered by the housemaid he followed her through the house, though he must have known her screams would attract attention. Again, to strike as many as fifteen times with his knife shows a fury quite abnormal.

With these salient points in mind, can we suggest any circumstances which might meet the facts?

I think we can.

At first sight it might seem as if the crime were committed by some epileptic or homicidal maniac, subject to recurrent fits of illness. But this theory would not account for the facts that Mr Storrs undoubtedly recognised his assailant and yet kept his identity secret. If he had not had some definite and personal reason for silence, he would surely have told the police who the man was.

Let us then try to fit a theory on to the facts we know. Let us begin by assuming that John is like Howard in personal appearance, and of an extremely unbalanced and excitable temperament. Let us further assume that he nurses a bitter hatred against Mr Storrs.

The cause of this hatred—that is, the motive for the crime—we do not know. There is not the slightest indication as to its nature in the evidence. All that we really know is that John had some overwhelming but mistaken sense of grievance against Mr Storrs.

We are probably on firmer ground when we picture John brooding over his fancied wrongs until his desire for revenge grows first into an obsession and then into actual mania.

On going to see Mr Storrs John blurts out his grievance and threatens vengeance. Mr Storrs, however, has no ill-feeling towards his visitor; in fact, he is sorry for him.

His kindly disposition makes him regret the young man's sense of injury, and he is willing to discuss the affair. But John, half insane, will not listen to reason, and Mr Storrs in self-defence is obliged to summon help.

John, seeing his chance gone, hurries away, determined to succeed at the next opportunity. The person who was called does not realise what he has prevented, and Mr Storrs, finding the whole matter painful, does not discuss it.

This reconstruction is still speculative and unsupported by direct evidence. But it is clear that John and Mr Storrs must have had some interview of the kind, in order to account for what follows. This interview, further, was probably not at Gorse Hall, as John was not seen by the inmates.

On September 10, John, who has bought a revolver, goes to Gorse Hall to make his attempt. He reaches the house, creeps up to the only lighted window, finds the blind does not exactly fit and that he can see Mr Storrs, and fires at him through the window. He sees that he has missed, and noticing that there are other people in the room, realises that if he remains for a further attempt he may be identified. So he hurries off.

Mr Storrs realises he is in danger, and asks the police to be specially vigilant. That night John makes his third attempt, but Mr Storrs sees him and rings the alarm. John again finds that if he remains, he will be caught. Mr Storrs, full of pity for the misguided youth, and hoping eventually to bring him to reason, tells the police he was only making a test, in order to give the young fellow time to escape.

It is obvious that there must have been some special circumstances about this attempt which enabled Mr Storrs to ring the alarm before being attacked. Perhaps, for example, he may have discovered John in the act of swarming up a balcony pillar or a waterpipe, or in such other position that the young man could not use his weapon.

On Monday, John again goes to Gorse Hall. Determined this time to make an end of the matter, he breaks in and commits the murder. He escapes from the country and is therefore not found by the police.

The above reconstruction, indicates the lines along which I believe the explanation of this mysterious crime must lie.

In the introduction to this book I have said something about
Erle Stanley Gardner and his Court of Last Resort, and in
the piece which follows the author tells very entertainingly
how it came into being, prompted by a three-part article about
him by Alva Johnston. 'A person who hasn't had the actual
experience can never visualize what happens when many
millions of people see something in print,' he said later. 'All I
know for sure is that many, many millions of people read that
I was the champion of the underdog. I was therefore literally
deluged with underdogs who needed championing.'

For the next decade the Court took up something like
eighty percent of Gardner's time, and it was undoubtedly the
most important thing in his whole life: a tremendous success,
something pioneering and hugely important. It's eventual
falling-part was a tragedy, and came about for the most
wretched reasons: Argosy magazine had come to depend very
heavily on the Court features for its huge circulation, but since
it was independent and beyond their ultimate control the
Editors felt uncomfortable, which led to tensions that grew
and grew, and finally exploded in a welter of resignations,
Gardner's included.

It did revive, and Gardner returned to it and Argosy, but
the workload proved too much, the articles became thinner
and thinner, and eventually the Court died. He continued to
be involved in police-work until his death, and wrote other
books on real crime, but there was never again anything to
rival the Courth of Last Resort, where he could be Perry
Mason...

ERLE STANLEY GARDNER

The Court of Last Resort

Man in general doesn't appreciate what he has until he is deprived of it. Then he starts to miss it. He takes good health for granted until sickness comes along. He takes three meals a day for granted until some unusual circumstance makes him go hungry. Liberty is only a term until he is deprived of it, and then he begins to realize what it means to have freedom of motion and freedom of choice.

Strange as it may seem, a diametrically opposite situation led to the origin of the Court of Last Resort.

I learned to value liberty not by having it taken away but by having such a marvelous demonstration of the advantages of freedom that I began to think what it must mean to be deprived of freedom.

In order to understand this somewhat paradoxical situation it is going to be necessary to touch on a most unusual murder case and give a bit of personal history.

The murder case is that of William Marvin Lindley, described in newspapers and magazines as 'The Red-Headed Killer'; the personal history relates to a biographical sketch written by the late Alva Johnston which ran several installments in *The Saturday Evening Post*. This biographical sketch was entitled 'The Case of Erle Stanley Gardner,' and included some of the spectacular and unorthodox methods which I used in connection with the trial of cases when I was a practicing attorney.

I have always claimed that an attorney is not necessarily bound to confine his cross-examination of a hostile witness to questions and answers on the witness stand. If a witness is certain of an identification, he should be absolutely certain of it.

He may testify under oath with all the positive sincerity in the world that the defendant is the man he saw running away from the scene of the crime two years ago, but if an attorney can get him to point to one of the assistant prosecutors by making the witness feel that the man at whom he is pointing is actually the defendant in the case, the witness's actions speak louder than words.

Of course, courts resent attempts to mislead a witness, so an attorney may well find himself in a position where the procedure, by which he might demonstrate that a witness is mistaken on a matter of identification, may be frowned upon by the court.

Therefore the problem of getting a witness to belie his words by actions, without violating the ethics of the profession or the rules of court is, at times, a rather tricky business.

During the days when I first engaged in the practice of law, legal ethics were not as sharply defined nor as rigidly enforced as they now are, and, with the singular optimism of youth, I was more confident of my own interpretation of what was proper.

I mention these matters because the early portion of my legal career, during which I was trying to build up a law practice in a city where I was virtually without friends or friendly contacts, was punctuated with spectacular incidents which made colorful copy for a biographer. As I expressed it at the time in a letter to my father, 'I have built up a law practice in which I am dealing with large numbers of clients of all classes—except the upper and middle class.'

Eventually my courtroom tactics attracted sufficient attention so that my practice became confined exclusively to clients of the upper and middle class, but Alva Johnston found the earlier chapters of my legal escapades much more interesting and therefore emphasized them in considerable detail.

Johnston also emphasized a quixotic streak which has always been part of my nature: to champion the cause of the underdog, particularly if he is without friends, without money, and his cause seems to be utterly hopeless.

By the time Johnston had finished stringing colorful incidents into his biographical sketch, his audience might well have received the impression that I made a habit of entering the lists on behalf of penniless defendants who were in hopeless predicaments, and by legal legerdemain could cause the doors of prison to swing wide open. The result was that just about every hopeless case in the United States was dumped in my lap in a deluge of fan mail.

Among these cases was that of William Marvin Lindley. This case was sent to me by Al Matthews, Jr., a Los Angeles attorney at law who has since become affiliated with the Public Defender's Office, but who, at that time, was a freelance. He had interested himself on behalf of Lindley after Lindley's conviction.

Lindley was at the time in the condemned row at San Quentin awaiting execution. He had been convicted of a brutal sex murder. The evidence against him was so overwhelming that until Al Matthews came along no one had extended the slightest sympathy or had bothered to give the case very much detailed study.

Al Matthews wrote me that he felt absolutely convinced Lindley was innocent, that he had been the victim of a bizarre combination of circumstances, and begged me to study the case.

At the time it seemed to me that every mail was bringing in a dozen similar pleas, but there was something about Al Matthews' letter, a certain sincerity that attracted my attention. I studied the outline Matthews sent down.

The murder had occurred during the aftermath of the great depression, and the characters who were involved in the crime were, for the most part, people who lived in more or less temporary camps along the banks of the Yuba River in California. One gathered the impression that these were persons of limited funds, limited education, and, in some instances, limited intelligence.

Some young girls, around the age of adolescence, had gone in swimming in the Yuba River. As a bathing suit, the victim of the crime wore simply a cotton dress.

William Marvin Lindley, a redhead, was at the time operating a boathouse on the banks of the river.

The victim of the crime had finished her swimming, changed

SOLVED

her clothes, gone into the house where her folks were living, made some remarks to her father, then had gone out again.

Some twenty minutes or half an hour later she was found in a dying condition. She had evidently been attacked after putting up a terrific struggle. She was able to sob out to her father the statement that it was 'that old red-headed liar in the boathouse, the old red-headed liar.' Some time later, and without ever clarifying this statement, she died.

A sheepherder, a young boy whose intelligence was not keen, to say the least, was herding sheep on the other side of the Yuba River, a distance of some two hundred yards. This sheepherder had sat under a tree, watching the girls while they were swimming. They left the water and entered the boathouse. Later on he noticed one of the girls go toward home and another girl went down to the water to wash her feet.

Prior to this time, a man, whom the sheepherder identified as Lindley, had been standing in the willows. He, also, was watching the girls swimming. After the victim had started back toward the levee, the sheepherder stated he had seen her struggling with 'Red,' the man who had been standing in the bushes watching her. They 'went down behind the willows.'

The sheepherder identified the man as 'Red' Lindley, the defendant. He based his identification in part upon the color of clothes that Lindley was wearing that afternoon.

At the time of the trial (and it should be noted that Lindley was not represented at this trial by Al Matthews, who didn't enter the case until after conviction) Lindley tried to produce an alibi. It was a nice alibi except that it broke down for the very period when the crime was being committed.

Apparently none of the persons connected with the case carried a watch, and it was necessary to work out time by depending upon the best estimates of the witnesses, starting from an event which had been pretty well established in the day's schedule.

All in all, Lindley's case seemed hopeless, merely another drab sex crime in which the culprit had become so inflamed at the sight of the adolescent girls bathing in the river that he lost all self-control, and despite the fact that there were witnesses who watched him and who could identify him, proceeded to go completely mad with lust.

Al Matthews had taken over, conducted an investigation and had filed a writ of *habeas corpus* in the State Supreme Court, also an application for a writ of error *Coram Nobis*, and a writ of *Coram Vobis*. Inasmuch as the Supreme Court had already considered the case on appeal and affirmed the conviction and sentence of death, it was necessary for the attorneys to resort to these last named, little used, hardly understood writs in order to have even a leg to stand on.

Enough of a showing had been made so that the Supreme Court had appointed a referee to take testimony, and then peculiar things began to develop. For one thing it turned out that the sheepherder was color-blind; and while he had stated that he had recognized the defendant by the tan-colored khaki clothes he had been wearing, it appeared by the time of the *habeas corpus* hearing that this witness was prone to describe virtually every color as tan. Not only was he color-blind but it developed that he had barely enough intelligence to enable him to testify. At one time he had told the referee that he did not know what it meant to testify under oath. He had identified a brown and white dress, worn by one of the women who was attending the referee's hearing, as black. He had then been asked to identify colored cards at a distance approximately equal to that at which he had seen the murderer, and he had identified a yellow card as being white, a gold one as being brown, an orange one as red, and a gray one as blue. At another time he had said that green was blue, gold was white, light brown was white, and pink was red.

The Supreme Court carefully reviewed the facts in the case as brought out in the hearing before the referee, co-ordinated those facts with the evidence in the case, and decided that Lindley had been properly convicted and must go to the gas chamber.

The date of execution was finally set. (There had been one or two reprieves while the various legal matters were pending, but now the date had been set, and Governor Earl Warren, who had been forced to leave the state temporarily on business, had pointed out to the lieutenant governor who would be in charge during Governor Warren's absence that he wanted no further reprieves in the Lindley case. The execution was to go ahead as scheduled.)

That execution date was but a short distance away. As I remember it, a matter of a week or ten days.

In any event, I telephoned Al Matthews, told him I would study the case, and he sent his wife down to see me, bringing with her the trial transcript and a few facts which would enable me to understand something of the nature of the case.

It was a long and involved transcript, and I labored through it, trying to become familiar with the case from the testimony of the witnesses and the study of the records.

There was one significant thing which Al Matthews had uncovered. There had been *another* red-headed hop picker in the vicinity on the day of the crime. That hop picker had not been working on the day of the murder. He had shown up later with marks on his face which could well have been made by a girl's fingernails. He had reportedly, in a drunken brawl that night, stated that he had been the one who had committed the murder, and he had mysteriously disappeared the next morning without even calling for his pay check. Some of those facts could be verified positively.

That was the case in a nutshell, and William Marvin Lindley was to die.

I carefully studied the evidence submitted by Lindley in support of his defense, and there was no question but what his alibi broke down at the very time the crime was being committed. The attorneys for the prosecution had made the most of that.

So then, having completed a study of the transcript, I decided to tackle the case from another angle.

Strange as it may seem, apparently it had never occurred to anyone to examine Lindley's alibi with reference to the movements of the murderer, whoever that murderer might have been, on the day in question.

I decided to do this and so found it necessary to work out a diagram of the scene of the crime according to distances, and to start co-ordinating the activities of the various people in relation to their contact with other people, forming a species of time schedule that was dependent entirely upon events rather than upon guesswork as to the hour, or the position of clock hands.

Once that was done, a very startling fact became manifest.

At the exact time witnesses had seen the murderer standing in the willows, watching the girls swimming, the defendant, William Marvin Lindley, had been riding in an automobile with the father of the murdered girl.

Again and again I went over this schedule and there simply couldn't be any other possible answer. The evidence given by the father himself, the evidence given by other witnesses, showed that this must be true. There wasn't any escape from it.

At that time there was no opportunity to do anything by strictly legal methods. Lindley's execution was almost a matter of hours. There was no time to make a formal appearance, no time to set in motion any type of legal proceedings even if it had been possible to conceive of any type of legal proceedings which had not been previously tried. The defendant had had the benefit of all the writs that the most adroit and ingenious attorney could possibly have conjured up.

There was only one thing to do.

I sent a letter to each justice of the State Supreme Court; I sent copies of those letters to the State's attorney general; I sent letters to the office of the Governor, pointing out page by page in the transcript the manner in which this synthetic schedule had been built up, making all due allowances for the greatest margin of time-elapse possible. Under this schedule there was no question that at the very moment several witnesses had seen this mysterious man standing in the willows, the man who was positively identified as being the murderer of the victim, the defendant, William Marvin Lindley, had been riding in the automobile with the girl's father some miles from the scene of the crime.

Afterward, and entirely off the record, I learned something of the scene of hectic activity which followed the receipt of these various letters. Still off the record, as I understand it, members of the California Supreme Court unanimously requested Lieutenant Governor Fred Howser, who was in charge at the time, not to permit the execution to take place until there could be a further investigation, and another stay of execution was granted.

The case began to attract quite a bit of attention. The press picked up the fact that I had written a letter in connection with it and set forth some of my contentions.

It will be noted that I am commenting in detail on the Lindley case because of its repercussions. The Lindley case standing by itself, however, is well worth serious study by anyone who is at all interested in the administration of criminal law.

Simply consider the facts of the case at the time Al Matthews, Jr., had taken an interest in it:

The girl had been found in a dying condition. She had made a statement which certainly pointed to the defendant Lindley as the perpetrator of the crime. The police had investigated and found an eyewitness who positively identified Lindley as the man who had been waiting in the bushes, watching the girls swimming, who had subsequently grabbed one of the girls, and, after a terrific struggle, had dropped down out of sight behind the bushes.

Lindley had claimed an alibi, trying to prove that he wasn't there at the time of the commission of the crime. That attempted alibi seemed to have broken down for the exact period that the crime was taking place. Lindley was without funds. An attorney had been appointed by the court to defend him, and the jury, evidently considering Lindley a murderer and a liar, had promptly brought in a verdict finding him guilty of first-degree murder, with no recommendation, thereby automatically making it mandatory that a death sentence be imposed.

I will never know what peculiar hunch attracted Matthews to the case, because a cursory study of the evidence would certainly indicate that the defendant was guilty, but when Matthews began to dig he uncovered new evidence showing that the eyewitness, who had identified Lindley largely because of the color of his clothes, was color-blind; and that another red-headed man, who had been in the vicinity of the crime, had scratch marks on his face, and, in a drunken condition the very night of the crime, had admitted that he was the perpetrator of the offense.

When I interceded on behalf of the defendant the wire services sent out 'copy' which was published in various newspapers throughout the country.

At that time, my friend Raymond Schindler, the famous private detective (with whom I collaborated again on later cases) was an advisory editor of a factual detective magazine, working in connection with Horace Bailey Brown, who was editor in chief. Brown, himself a veteran article writer, with considerable editorial experience, was eagerly looking for new angles on crime stories so that he could get away from the usual hackneyed approach and turn out a magazine that would attract the interests of the reading public.

When Schindler and Brown read the notice in the press stating that I had entered the Lindley case, they wired asking me if I would care to write something about it for the magazine in question.

Nothing could have suited me better.

I was for the moment at an impasse. There was certainly no legal remedy left to the defendant. The lieutenant governor had granted a temporary stay of execution, but Governor Warren's attitude in the matter was quite well known, and now that Governor Warren had returned to the state there was no further authority left in the hands of the lieutenant governor to act in the matter.

So, feeling that nothing remained to be done from a legal standpoint, I decided it would be interesting to see what would happen if the people generally were given some first-hand knowledge of the peculiar situation disclosed by the transcript in the Lindley case.

So I wrote an open letter to Governor Warren, which I sent to the magazine and which was published.

I have been told that the Governor's office received a deluge of mail as a result of this letter. Governor Warren, despite any previous statements he may have made, did the right thing and he did it in a decent manner. He promptly commuted the sentence of the defendant to life imprisonment so that there would be an opportunity for a further investigation.

Lindley—never a robust man emotionally—had been living in the shadow of death for months. He had been figuratively dragged into the death chamber and then hauled out again, only to be once more dragged in and then jerked out. As a result, his mind had become unsettled. The man was, in the opinion of many, hopelessly insane. In fact I understand that some of the members of the Supreme Court had made definite recommendations that because of this insanity alone the execution should not be permitted.

In any event, Lindley was declared insane, and his sentence commuted to life imprisonment. There the case stands to this day.

There is very persuasive evidence that another red-headed man may have committed the crime. An extensive search was made for this mysterious red-headed hop picker who had what may have been fingernail scratches on his face, who had certainly been in a state of extreme nervousness, and who had vanished so mysteriously on the day following the murder of the girl. That search was made far too late. It was made by private parties who did not have the facilities available to the police. The search was fruitless. The man has never been found.

The Lindley case is perhaps as good an example as we can conjure up at the moment of the necessity of making a scientific, careful investigation of all of the facts in a case while those facts are still available.

Because of the identification made by the dying girl (an identification which was, of course, not as definite as should have been the case if Lindley had actually committed the crime), the so-called eyewitness identification by the young sheepherder, the police became convinced that Lindley was the murderer. They diligently searched for any evidence that would enable the prosecutor to build up a good case against Lindley in court, and they brushed aside any evidence which might have pointed to developments that would have been in Lindley's favor.

As a result, this other red-headed suspect, who certainly should have been apprehended and interrogated, was permitted to leave the community without an attempt made to find him or question him. The itinerant witnesses vanished to the four winds, and Lindley was left with a sentence of life imprisonment.

The Lindley case, however, was destined to have far-reaching developments.

Harry Steeger, head of Popular Publications Inc., which publishes *Argosy* Magazine, and for many years a warm personal friend, had been corresponding with me about undertaking an adventure of sorts.

The year before I had taken an expedition down the entire length of the peninsula of Baja California, starting at Tijuana, and, after several weeks of wild adventure over twelve hundred miles of mountain and desert, reaching the very southern tip of the peninsula at Cape San Lucas.

I had written a book about that trip, and since, despite months of careful planning, the whole trip had almost been abandoned because of developments in the Lindley case, I had mentioned briefly the fact that only the commutation of sentence in this case had left us free to make the trip. The point was important in the book because the Lindley matter so materially shortened the time available for preparation that we had no alternative but to throw things into the car helter-skelter, and try to unscramble them on the road.

This book, *The Land of Shorter Shadows,* had fascinated both Harry Steeger and his wife, Shirley, a member of the New York Botanical Gardens, and a tireless and enthusiastic worker.

The upshot of it was that Harry and Shirley Steeger, two of my secretaries, Sam Hicks of Wyoming, and I started once more down the long twelve-hundred-mile route. We had plenty of shorthand notebooks, quantities of film, a veritable battery of cameras, and this time were determined to see that the peninsula was fully covered.

Even with the very best in the line of modern equipment, including jeeps and a 'power wagon' equipped with power winches, four-wheel drive, oversized tires, etc., this trip down the peninsula of Baja California is a long, hard, and at times a dangerous grind. There are days when forty miles is a full day's journey, and several times we went for two days in succession without meeting a single car on the road.

Since this expedition started late in February, the days were short and the nights were long. It was necessary to make camp during the last of the daylight hours, and then after supper, when the dishes were done, the sleeping bags spread on the ground, air mattresses inflated, there would be an hour or two for just sitting around the campfire.

The peninsula of Baja California is distinctly and individually different. The elephant trees are almost exclusively indigenous to that terrain, and, as I understand it, the *cirio* trees are not found in any other spot on earth. The nights were nearly always cool and cloudless. The days were, for the most part, hot with the dry heat of the desert. The air was a tonic and a benediction rolled into one. At night the steady, unwinking stars marched tirelessly across the heavens.

All about us was the immensity of a wild country. The firelight was the only reassuring memento of man's ability to master his environment. It would throw a fitful circle of illumination for some thirty or forty feet and reflect back in a rosy glow from the weird *cardon* trees pushing their cactus-like limbs high into the air. Lower down, on the floor of the desert the flames would illuminate prickly pear, *cholla* cactus, ladyfinger cactus, and, perhaps in the background, a sweet *pitahaya* or organ-pipe cactus.

Beyond the circle of campfire, darkness filled an unknown terrain with a mystery which the human mind instinctively translated into terms of danger. . . . A sudden screaming howl from the encircling darkness caused us to give an involuntary start before we recognized the familiar voice of the coyote, and grinned sheepishly. And just outside of the lighted circle the coyote was probably grinning, too. They are the most daring, saucy, impudent, lovable rascals in the world (unless a man has sheep or chickens, in which event the coyote is a fiend incarnate).

So it was natural that during these long evenings, while we exhausted most of the subjects of conversation, we should find ourselves dwelling on the predicament of men who had been wrongfully imprisoned.

Freedom is, after all, only relative. No man has absolute freedom. We are bound by economic chains, by ties of personal dependency. We have telephones, taxicabs and taxes; work, worry and war. Down there in Baja California life and living became unbelievably simplified. We ate, we slept, and we traveled. We had nothing else to do. There was no schedule, no telephones, no illumination at night save the light of the gasoline lantern which was used sparingly when supper was late.

Against this environment of extreme freedom from care and restraint, the life of a man condemned to live behind barred doors, within gray walls, became a persistent nightmare which colored even our waking hours.

The problem of getting firewood helped determine the length of our sleep at night. We would conscientiously save out enough wood for a breakfast fire, and burn the rest at night. When the evening campfire began to die down to coals we would move closer, until, at length, the last of the flames flickered out. Then we would watch the bed of coals until even the coals began to dull. By that time we would be ready for our sleeping bags.

Many times during those silent watches of the night I lay awake for half or three-quarters of an hour thinking about the problems inherent in the wise administration of justice. And the more I came to revel in my own liberty to go where I wanted to, whenever I wanted to, the more I found myself thinking of innocent men cooped up in cells. It was a nagging worry which I could and sometimes did push into the back of my mind—but not very far back, and it wouldn't stay there.

So one day I mentioned how I felt to Harry Steeger, and I discovered he had been experiencing the same reaction. Every time he wakened at night he found himself speculating on the problem, wondering what he as a publisher could do about it.

On one occasion when we discussed the situation, Harry reached a decision.

'Erle,' he said, 'if you ever find any other case where you think the man has been wrongfully convicted, *Argosy* will donate enough space to see that the case is given ample publicity, and we'll see what the public reaction is.

'You know what I'm trying to do with *Argosy*. When we purchased it from the Munsey Company it was an old-time adventure magazine printed on wood pulp paper. We've turned it into an illustrated magazine for men, and people are beginning to notice it. Of all the magazines we publish I think *Argosy* would be the most available vehicle for this sort of thing.'

In the nights which followed that talk we began to carry this thought to its logical conclusion and to explore possibilities.

Some months previous to this we had discussed the peculiar fact that there was no popular magazine devoted to justice, and yet all of our vaunted American way of life was founded upon our concept of justice.

So, down there in Baja California, we began to speculate on the idea of welding those thoughts together—testing the reaction of the American people to find out if they were really interested in the cause of justice and at the same time using space-to correct some specific instance of an injustice.

Night after night, we planned just how a case could be presented to the American people, what their reactions would be and what the effect of those reactions would be upon the governmental agencies who had the final say in the matter.

We realized early in the game that it would never do for a magazine with a national circulation to come out and say in effect, 'This man claims he's innocent. He's been convicted of murder. Erle Stanley Gardner thinks there may be something in the man's contentions, therefore we want the governor to grant a pardon.'

We knew that we'd need facts, and these facts would have to be presented to the reading public in a form that would incite interest. No matter how much space *Argosy* donated to some worthy case, no good would be done unless people read what was printed in that space. And, even then, merely reading about the case wouldn't help unless people became sufficiently aroused to *do* something about it.

Public opinion must be molded, but it must be an enlightened public opinion based on facts, otherwise we would be charged, and justly charged, with the tactics of the rabble rousers.

It is customary in legal circles to refer to the highest tribunal in any jurisdiction as 'the court of last resort.' Out there in the wide open spaces of Baja California, we came to the conclusion that in a country such as ours no officially organized tribunal ever could be the *real* court of last resort. The real court of last resort, we felt, was the people themselves. It was a new and daring concept, yet it was essentially sound. Under our theory of law the people are superior to any department of the government, legislative, executive or judicial. They must, of course, exercise their wishes in accordance with the methods prescribed in the Constitution, but once those methods have been complied with, the will of the people is the supreme law of this land.

That didn't mean that in order to decide whether John Doe had been wrongfully convicted we needed to have the people pass an initiative measure, or, if we decided that John Doe had been wrongfully convicted that we needed to present a Constitutional amendment to get him liberated.

The constitutions of the various states provide that the governors have the power of pardon. The governors, on the other hand, are responsible to the people. Every four years they come up for re-election. They have to stand on their record. If any material thinking segment of a state's population should decide that John Doe had been wrongfully convicted and that the governor's pardoning prerogative was being unjustly withheld, that governor would be faced with a political liability at election time. Governors are not prone to assume political liabilities unless there is a corresponding political credit to be entered on the other side of the ledger.

But how could anyone present a case to the people without following the tactics of the rabble rousers? In the case of John Doe, how could we get the facts, how could we properly marshal those facts, how could we get the public to take a sufficient interest in those facts? How could we persuade a substantial segment of population to take a real interest in John Doe? It was a problem we discussed at length. We felt that we were on the right track if we could once find the proper approach; but the proper approach required that the public should understand the facts, should correlate them, and should then want to take action.

We knew that most magazine readers like detective stories. How about letting the readers study the case of John Doe, fact by fact, until they reached an intelligent opinion?

That would mean investigators in whom the readers would have confidence, and who could unearth those facts. It would mean that reader interest must be kept alive.

Was there any method by which all of this could be accomplished?

Gradually the idea of *Argosy's* board of investigators came into existence.

The basic idea was to get men who were specialists in their line, men who had enough national reputation so readers could have confidence in their judgment, men who would be public-spirited enough to donate their services to the cause of justice (because any question of financial reward would immediately taint the whole proceedings with what might be considered a selfish motivation). We also needed men who had achieved such financial success in their chosen professions that they were in no particular need of personal publicity. Moreover, the aggregate combination must be such that it would be virtually impossible for any prisoner to deceive these men as to the true issues in a case.

It was, of course, a pretty large order.

We thought at once of Dr LeMoyne Snyder.

Dr LeMoyne Snyder is one of the outstanding authorities on homicide investigation in the country. He is not only a doctor of medicine but he is an attorney at law, and he has for some years specialized in the field of legal medicine. His book *Homicide Investigation* is one of the most authoritative technical books on the subject in the country, and is at once a guide for peace officers as well as a treatise for those who are interested in the more highly technical aspects of the subject.

We decided to put the whole idea up to Dr Snyder. Next, we needed some outstanding detective. So we thought of Raymond Schindler.

Raymond Schindler is perhaps the best-known private detective in the country. I had first met him when we were both in the Bahamas. He was then working on the famous case of Alfred de Marigny, who had been accused of murdering his wealthy father-in-law, Sir Harry Oakes. I was covering the case for the New York *Journal-American* and some of its allied newspapers.

Raymond Schindler's career as a private detective dates back to 1906 when he first started work in San Francisco. Later on, it was through the efforts of Raymond Schindler that the

Erle Stanley Gardner: founder of the Court of Last Resort.

corruption which existed in San Francisco under Abe Rueff and 'Big Jim' Gallagher was cleaned up.

Many of Schindler's exploits have found their way from time to time into print, and a year or so ago Rupert Hughes, in a volume entitled *The Complete Detective*, gave a biographical summary of Schindler's life which has, of course, been exceedingly colorful.

So much for the detective end. If Schindler would work with us, we felt he'd be ideal for the job.

It also occurred to us that we'd want to have absolutely accurate information for our own guidance. We had to know whether the men we were talking with were telling the truth. That brought up a consideration of Leonarde Keeler's work with the lie detector. Keeler had not only done a great deal to develop the polygraph but was probably the outstanding polygraph operator in the country. (Before we were able to avail ourselves of Keeler's services to any great extent, he became ill and passed away. His place was taken by Alex Gregory, a man who has an excellent background as an investigator, a careful, conscientious worker, a former member of the Detroit police force, a keen student of psychology.)

There is, of course, some question as to the efficacy of the 'lie detector.'

To my mind the question of, 'How accurate is a lie detector?' is equivalent to asking, 'How good is a camera?'

The answer is, of course, the camera doesn't take the pictures. The photographer takes the pictures. Some photographers using a medium-priced camera can take pictures that win national awards. Some merely take mediocre pictures; others forget to turn the film and so get double exposures, or forget to pull the slide from the plateholder and so get nothing.

I think the same holds true with the polygraph. The polygraph is a scientific instrument. It determines certain specific reactions on the part of the subject. The problem of coordinating the graph of these reactions so as to know whether the subject is or is not telling the truth depends upon numerous factors—the questions which are asked, the manner in which they are asked, the manner in which the subject is prepared for the test, and the skill on the part of the operator.

It is quite possible that Alex Gregory, for instance, won't always be able to tell whether a man is guilty or innocent. But I feel that Alex Gregory would never say that an innocent man was guilty. He might say he didn't know. But if he said a man was definitely guilty, I wouldn't want to run against his judgment. And similarly if Alex Gregory assures us that a man who says he is innocent is telling us the truth, I for one am all in favor of going ahead and launching an investigation which may run into hundreds of hours of time spent.

So much for the polygraph angle.

So far as the legal appraisal was concerned, I promised Steeger I would study the transcripts of testimony in the various cases, and bring to bear such knowledge as I had acquired in twenty-five years of trial work.

Later on this investigating committee was to receive very substantial reinforcements in the persons of Tom Smith and Bob Rhay.

Tom Smith was at the time the warden of the Washington State Penitentiary at Walla Walla. Bob Rhay was working under him, and as presently will be seen, our first case brought us into intimate contact with both of these men. Later on they were destined to become exceedingly interested in the social significance of the program we had undertaken, and when suitable opportunity arose, to affiliate themselves with it.

However, that page in our adventures in justice had not then been written. We were primarily concerned with the problem of getting together a board of investigors who would have enough prestige to influence public opinion, who would have a sufficient love of justice to be willing to donate a large portion of their time, and who had the proper technical qualifications to strip aside all fabrications and arrive at the right answer.

So we worked our way down the peninsula of Baja California, talking around every campfire of plans for our Court of Last Resort, wondering what, if anything, it could accomplish, but each day becoming more and more determined that we would find out by actual experiment just what it could accomplish.

Within a matter of weeks after Steeger and I returned from Baja California I had occasion to consider the case of Clarence

Boggie, prisoner #16587, confined in the Washington State
Penitentiary at Walla Walla, serving a life sentence for murder.

Boggie had written a letter enclosing copies of documents
compiled by the Reverend Arvid Ohrnell, Protestant chaplain
of the Washington State Reformatory at Monroe. This letter
had been acknowledged, but was buried in a pile of similar
appeals from prisoners sent in from all over the country.

Then I received a communication from the Reverend W.A.
Gilbert, a part-time voluntary chaplain at Walla Walla, asking
me for an appointment at my ranch.

Gilbert was the rector of St Paul's Episcopal Church at
Walla Walla. He also did a great deal of voluntary prison
chaplain work purely as an extracurricular activity, donating
his time furnishing spiritual guidance to prison inmates.

Bill Gilbert was attending a church convention in Santa
Barbara. He drove the two hundred odd miles down to my
ranch through Sunday traffic in order to confer with me about
the Boggie case and then drove back that afternoon—nearly
five hundred miles of Sunday driving in order to try and enlist
my aid in the cause of a penniless unfortunate who had then
been incarcerated in the Walla Walla prison for some thirteen
years, and who was scheduled to remain there the rest of his
life.

Bill Gilbert's devotion to a philanthropic cause seemed an
unusual sacrifice of time and energy to me then. Now I have
seen enough of the work done by prison chaplains to know that
it is merely an ordinary incident in their lives.

A book could—and should—be written about the activities
of these men. They sacrifice their own time, their own funds,
pile up mileage on their automobiles, trying to do what they can
to assist in the spiritual and material welfare of prisoners, many
of whom shamelessly take advantage of this unselfish devotion
to a self-imposed duty.

The best of prison chaplains never worry about what a man
has done. They are only interested in trying to see how they can
help the man prepare for the future. They know that for the
most part they are carving in rotten wood, but they keep
carving nevertheless, hoping that when they have stripped
away the layers of mental and moral disease they will come to a

basic foundation which can take and hold a permanent impression.

In a surprising number of instances they are successful.

At that time I personally had no realization of the extent to which prison inmates are isolated behind a curtain of steel and concrete. I had no realization that their correspondence was limited in many instances as to quantity, and in nearly every instance to a chosen list of approved correspondents.

As a practicing attorney any letters I cared to write to prisoners had been delivered and answered. That, as it turned out, is because an exception is made in the case of attorneys. Prisoners are permitted to correspond freely with attorneys. On the other hand, as a general rule, prisoners are not permitted to correspond at all with representatives of the press, and their personal correspondence is very, very limited.

Since I had left the active practice of law my correspondence with prison inmates had been somewhat limited, and in most of the instances my status as attorney had resolved the doubt in my favor and the correspondence had gone through, but once when I tried to find out something about the facts in a case I had been curtly refused permission to correspond with the inmate.

These instances had served to arouse my ire and I had determined that if we started investigating a case with *Argosy* Magazine behind us, we were going to engage in a verbal slugging match if we weren't premitted to interview the prisoner.

So I explained to Bill Gilbert that I would fly up to Walla Walla to interview Boggie. I told Gilbert to explain this to the warden of the penitentiary and to tell him that I didn't want to have a lot of red tape thrown at me when I arrived.

I remember that I explained to Bill Gilbert that heretofore we had been trying to catch our flies with molasses. I was tired of that, and had decided it might be more effective to catch them with a fly swatter.

Gilbert told me that he felt quite certain I would have no trouble in interviewing Clarence Boggie, but he would sound out the warden in the matter.

Bill Gilbert returned to Walla Walla and wired me that I would have no difficulty.

That was a masterpiece of understatement.

Tom Smith, as has been previously mentioned, was the warden. He was more than ready to meet us halfway.

'Now look,' he said finally, 'you're not going to meet any red-tape opposition up here. If Clarence Boggie is innocent we want to find it out just as much as you do. Bill Gilbert has told me about your organization. I know something about the reputation of these men who are associated with you in the work you're doing. If you're going to make an impartial investigation of the Boggie case, and if it isn't going to cost the State anything, I'll do everything in my power to facilitate the investigation. I also think you'll find the State officials here will have a similar attitude. Anything I can do to help promote such an attitude I'll be glad to do. Now, then, you take over from there.'

In short, I found Tom Smith to be entirely different from the type of warden I had expected to find.

In the intimate association with him which was to come later I learned to know the man's big heart, his almost naïve idealism, and his passionate desire for justice.

At the time, I was surprised to find a warden who had absolutely no resemblance to the type of warden fiction writers are too prone to create. There was nothing of the sadistic disciplinarian about him. He was intensely human, eager to learn everything he could about prison administration, to apply what he had learned, and to see that every man had complete justice.

Later on that day I met the incredible Clarence Boggie.

I refer to him as 'incredible' because everything about the man was completely and utterly incredible. Virtually every time I talked with him I discovered some new facet of the man, some new twist of his background, some episode which seemed to be absolutely incredible, yet which later turned out to be the truth.

For instance, Boggie, a penniless prisoner serving a life sentence, with two previous convictions behind him, maintained stoutly that he had never been guilty of any crime.

That, of course, seemed absurd.

Yet subsequent investigations indicated the man's story might well be true. In each instance of a prior conviction he had received a pardon apparently predicated upon the fact that an investigation showed he had been wrongfully convicted.

The man, of course, had some sort of a prison neurosis. He also had a very strong love for his mother which made him place her on a pedestal. He was emotionally unstable, given to sudden spells of crying, particularly if someone would mention his mother. He had been incarcerated long enough so that he had the mental outlook that is sometimes referred to as being 'stir simple.'

Yet here was this penniless man who would, at a later date, casually mention to us that he was the owner of a copper mine worth several million dollars.

I don't know when he first made that statement. We took it as a complete fairy tale, something that had been conjured up in his dreams during the long period of his confinement.

The story of the copper mine was very interesting. The mine, he explained, had been given to him by a woman whom he had never seen, but she wanted to get rid of her earthly property so she had deeded Boogie the mine. The deed had been lost.

You listen to a story like that from a two-time loser serving a life term in a penitentiary for murder, and it is enough to make you want to forget the whole thing. The guy is not only a crook but a liar. You kick yourself for having traveled twelve or fifteen hundred miles to act the part of a gullible sucker.

Yet essentially this story was true.

It wasn't until we happened to stumble onto certain facts that we learned the background of the story, and I mention it at this time because it is so completely typical of Clarence Boggie.

As mentioned above, Boggie worshiped the ground his mother walked on, and any woman more than twenty years his senior would promptly arouse in him a like feeling of worship.

During the great depression, Boggie, a lumberjack, was out of work, walking the streets of Portland, Oregon, when he saw a frail, white-haired woman, being, as Boggie expressed it, "abused" by the police.

It seemed that a police officer had stopped in front of the woman's house and was pointing out to her that the roots of a tree which was growing at the curb had broken up the cement sidewalk.

The woman apparently either was short of cash or else didn't know how to go about having the repairs made, because she was trying to get an extension of time from the officer, but the officer, according to Clarence Boggie, was "pushing her around."

Boggie said he hung around for a minute or two, listening to the conversation. The woman, he explained, was "a little sweetheart, just a dear little white-haired woman, frail and helpless, but just as sweet as she could be, and the officer was abusive.'

So Boggie, big strapping lumberjack that he was, entered into the argument. As he explained it, he 'chased the officer.'

Apparently what he did was to tell the officer that he, Boggie, would see that the matter was straightened out, to quit annoying the woman and go on about his business. She'd been given a warning and that was all there was to it. The officer had no further business there. The sidewalk would be fixed that afternoon. How did Boggie know? Hell, Boggie was going to fix it himself.

Boggie marched up town, where he went into one of the pool halls, rounded up a squad of lumberjacks who were out of work and weren't doing anything anyway, got some sledge hammers, a crowbar and an ax, and went back to the house of the 'white-haired sweetheart.'

Those lumberjacks put on a job of work that was rarely seen within the city limits. They smashed up the sidewalk, cut the offending roots of the tree, smoothed down the ground, poured cement, erected barriers, kept the cement properly moistened, and within a little more than twenty-four hours had a perfectly brand-new sidewalk, smooth and level.

The 'white-haired sweetheart' was, of course, grateful, but Boggie refused to take a cent. Despite the fact that the lumber-jacks were all broke and 'on their uppers,' none of them would take a dime. They wouldn't even let her pay for the cement, which had been procured 'here and there.'

Boggie, of course, was the ringleader and probably the spokesman, but undoubtedly the men all felt very much the same way.

However, the woman did get Boggie's name and address.

It turned out that this woman in turn had a friend in the East who was wealthy and quite elderly. This friend had come to the conclusion that before she died it would be much better for her to strip herself of her property, feeling that worldly wealth and spiritual solace were incompatible.

Looking around for worthy objects of benefaction, she remembered the letter which had been received from her friend in Portland, Oregon. She looked up this letter, and, sure enough, there was the name and address of Clarence Boggie, the man who had made such a chivalrous restoration of the sidewalk.

So the woman promptly made out a deed to Clarence Boggie, giving him title to a piece of ground on which copper had been discovered.

The deed was sent to Boggie at that address. Boggie at that time, however, was in prison. Someone attempted to record the deed and it was lost in transit. Boggie didn't hear about it until some time later. By that time the woman who had made the deed was dead, relatives were in possession of the property, the copper mine had been developed into one of the big copper mines in the country, and Boggie apparently 'didn't have a leg to stand on.' He couldn't even produce the deed, or even testify that he himself had actually seen it.

However, such investigation as we were able to make indicated that he was absolutely truthful in his statement of the facts of the case. The deed actually had been executed and mailed to him, and then, by someone who was trying to record it, had been misaddressed and lost.

Boggie, moreover, told us great stories of his prowess as a logger. These stories made him sound like a reincarnated Paul Bunyan. They were, of course, digested with a tolerant smile. Boggie had been in prison for a long time and doubtless as he thought back over his exploits he kept gilding the lily and painting the rose.

Boggie told us that he could take a crew of men and move more logs in less time, with less expense and greater efficiency, than the average expert.

It is an ironical twist that everyone thought Boggie, because of his emotional instability, his background and his mannerisms, was simply drawing on his imagination in everything that he told us about his background, for a man who is 'stir simple' frequently tries to impress people with tales of his former prowess.

Eventually we learned a lot more about Boggie's abilities, but that is, of course, an entirely different story. What I am trying to convey at this time is a picture of Clarence Boggie as we first saw him, a man with a prison neurosis, a mother fixation, and a well-defined emotional instability.

We found it exceedingly hard to believe his story. However, we had determined to make an investigation of the case, and it was, after all, the case rather than the man that we were primarily interested in.

It was at the time of this first meeting that Boggie turned over to me what, for want of a better name, I have come to refer to as an inmate's 'heartbreak file.'

Just as a girl will keep a hope chest, so does an inmate frequently keep a file which contains the records of his attempts to gain freedom. It is really a heartbreak file.

Here are held the notations on when he is to come before the state parole board, documents setting forth facts in the prisoner's favor, carbon copies of correspondence hopefully sent out. Then the heartbreak. Parole application decision deferred for another year—letters unanswered.

In Boggie's case the heartbreak file was about the most voluminous and the most pathetic I have ever seen.

It is not a simple matter for a prison inmate to write a letter to an official who he thinks may be interested in his case. In the first place there are as a rule only a few typewriters within the walls, and the men who know how to use them are a favored class. A prisoner who wants to have a letter typed must make certain concessions by way of trade.

Money, of course, is contraband within prison. Too many things can be accomplished with money. So the prisoner must make his purchases through the limited credit allowances which can be made by transferring money from his prison account, except, of course, in the case of business transactions which then must have the approval of the warden.

The average prisoner, in order to get a letter written, must turn over his cigarette allowance, or go without some little prison luxury.

For thirteen years Boggie had been forgoing his prison luxuries, getting people to type letters for him. Only by the wildest stretch of imagination could a prisoner have felt that these letters would do any good. They were letters to senators and representatives, even an occasional letter to the President. They had all been neatly typed and had been mailed hopefully whenever Boggie could arrange for the typing and get enough to cover postage. Whenever a new official was elected to office, he could count on receiving a letter from Clarence Boggie.

It was the replies that were heartbreaking. Letters obviously typed by a secretary and signed without reading. Letters that were signed with rubber stamp signatures. Letters that were from secretaries advising Boggie that the matter was being placed in an important file and would be called to Mr Bigboy's attention at the earliest possible moment, that Mr Bigboy, it must be remembered, was swamped with problems incident to his election and a national crisis, but Boggie could rest assured his letter would receive Mr Bigboy's attention just as soon as the matter could be investigated.

In most of the modern penitentiaries a prisoner would not have been permitted to mail the letters that Boggie sent out, but because these were appeals to public officials, to attorneys, and because they were based on Boggie's assertions of complete innocence, the wardens had permitted these letters to be mailed, and the replies to be received.

In one way it was a pathetic heartbreak. In another way it had given Boggie the encouragement necessary to carry on. There was always the hope that one of these days, now that Mr Bigboy had got caught up with the problems incident to assuming his new office, he would remember his promise and turn his attention to the case of Clarence Boggie. . . . So Boggie carried on and waited. Why not? Didn't Boggie have letters over Mr Bigboy's signature assuring that such would be the case?

Then there was Boggie's transcript.

The State of Washington insisted that furnishing a transcript of testimony for use on appeal was a private matter, and as such, entirely up to the defendant.

Without the transcript there could be no appeal. Without

money there could be no transcript.

Boggie had no money. It appeared that the transcript was going to cost some seven hundred and fifty dollars.

Boggie, inside the prison pulled every wire he could think of trying to get money enough to defray the cost of a transcript. His parents were in no position to help. They were elderly and having a hard time to make ends meet. Boggie was penniless— and who was going to help a convicted murderer to the extent of seven hundred and fifty dollars? No one.

Then, after a lapse of some ten years, a peculiar thing happened.

A man who had some few thousand dollars was convicted of crime and sent to the penitentiary. The crime of which this man was convicted is a violation of the moral law and of the statutes. By all man-made standards of conduct this individual is reprehensible.

Yet within the prison this man has done much to help out here and there. Quietly, unostentatiously, he has done the best he could to alleviate the lot of a good many of the inmates. He heard about Clarence Boggie's problem. He heard Clarence Boggie's protestations of innocence. He put up the seven hundred and fifty dollars which enabled Boggie for the first time since his conviction to get a transcript of the testimony taken at the trial. So, when I called on Boggie, he was able to hand me this transcript.

The study of that transcript testimony was a long, uphill job, but reading it, I began to get a picture of the Boggie case.

The case itself was fully as incredible as any of the other things connected with Clarence Boggie.

On June 26, 1933, Moritz Peterson, an elderly recluse seventy-eight years old, was rooming at a private boarding house in Spokane, Washington. He owned a little shack some distance away at the rear of a deep lot on East 20th Avenue in Spokane. There was an occupied dwelling house on the front of this lot, and also one on the adjoining lot.

Peterson was in the habit of leaving his boarding house in the morning, taking a street car to the little shack, and there spending the day puttering around in the garden, taking care of his chickens, pulling weeds, etc. In the evening he'd go back to the place where he boarded. Most of his clothes were kept in the little shack house.

Peterson, in common with most of the world, was in rather straitened circumstances at the time. He had a diamond ring which he believed to be worth five hundred dollars, but he had been trying in vain to sell it for one hundred dollars. (This was at the time when the country was in the depths of a depression and ready money was a very tight commodity.)

The man's financial circumstances are mentioned because it would be almost out of the question to think that anyone who actually knew Moritz Peterson would contemplate trying to rob him. On the other hand there is the distinct possibility that someone who didn't really know him might have thought this eccentric old man, living an ordered life, could well have laid by a little ready cash which he could have kept concealed in his shack or on his person.

Sometime on Saturday night, June 24, 1933, someone broke into Moritz Peterson's shack during the night and made a most thorough job of ransacking the place. Towels having been pinned over the windows so that people in the nearby houses would not notice any light, the intruder proceeded to search every nook and cranny, opening boxes, scattering canceled checks and documents all over the floor.

If one could judge from external appearances the intruder must have been searching for a particular document of some sort. Canceled checks would ordinarily be kept in neat bundles, and it is hardly possible that an intruder would have opened these bundles of checks and strewn the papers over the floor in a search for money, yet that could have been the case. The burglar could well have reasoned that the money might have been secreted in the most unlikely places.

Sunday morning, when Peterson arrived at the shack, he was confronted with the wreckage and complete disorder. He was, of course, very much upset, but he refused to allow the police to be notified. He even went so far as to state that he knew the identity of the intruder and didn't want anything done about it.

Peterson put in Sunday straightening up the place. By afternoon he told the neighbors that the only things which had been taken were a pair of coveralls and a pair of black shoes.

If anyone had wanted to hold up or assault Moritz Peterson the worst day that could possibly have been selected would have been Monday, the conventional washday.

Yet apparently someone was concealed in the Peterson house on Monday, the 26th day of June, 1933, waiting for him to arrive.

The neighbors of course didn't see this person enter, but they did hear the sound of a terrific struggle emanating from the little shack. The time was probably between ten and twenty-five minutes after ten in the morning.

The sounds of that struggle attracted a great deal of attention. Housewives and children ran from their houses. They were in time to see a stocky, heavy-set, bushy-haired individual, who ran with a peculiar 'sideways gait,' running from the house. They chased this individual for some two or three blocks. Then the man disappeared in a wooded area. No one had been able to get a look at his face.

While one of the housewives and some children were chasing the individual who ran away from Moritz Peterson's shack, one of the other women had looked in at his door, found Peterson lying, moaning, with his head virtually beaten in. She dashed to her house and telephoned the police.

What happened after that was what might be called a tragedy of errors.

The little party who were running after the fugitive, trying to keep him in sight, followed him until he entered a thicket of underbrush, whereupon they turned back.

The first officer to arrive on the scene was a motorcycle officer, who came tearing up with siren screaming, and came to a stop before the house at the front of the lot.

The excited audience explained to the motorcycle officer what had happened. The motorcycle officer promptly decided that his duties were along other lines and in other fields. He dashed away from there, fast.

Police officers from the central station tore through the streets with sirens screaming, to come to the Peterson shack.

Apparently it was at this time that the officers found Moritz Peterson lying on the floor, his head so terribly smashed that one of the eye sockets had been completely broken. A homemade weapon was on the floor beside the dying man.

The officers were told by the boys that the assailant had jumped into the brush a couple of blocks up the street, so the officers valiantly permitted themselves to be guided to the spot where the murderer had disappeared, at which time they suddenly discovered they had 'forgotten their guns.' So they returned to their automobile, and, with siren screaming, went tearing back to get their guns.

In the meantime an ambulance had been summoned and the ambulance, also accompanied by the sound of sirens, went to the scene of the crime to pick up Moritz Peterson and transport him to a hospital. The officers, by this time having fully armed themselves, came dashing back to the scene of the crime.

A description of all this confusion and particularly the noise of the sirens is important for reasons which will presently become apparent.

After Peterson had been removed to the hospital, the police made a rather cursory examination of the premises and took into their possession the weapon with which the crime had been committed. It was a homemade bludgeon which had been fashioned with considerable skill and ingenuity, and consisted of a round, water-washed rock wrapped in burlap. This burlap had been tightly twisted and stitched so that the long twisted burlap made a semi-flexible handle. The whole thing was a most potent, deadly weapon, which could strike terrific blows. The assailant had repeatedly struck Moritz Peterson on the head with this weapon.

Strangely enough, however, despite the fact that Peterson had received these fatal injuries, he still remained conscious. The dying man apparently experienced a sensation of great pressure on his brain and thought there was a weight still on his head, but by the time he reached the hospital he was able to talk. He kept complaining of this terrible weight that was crushing his head.

Sometime after reaching the hospital Moritz Peterson's daughter was summoned, and at the bedside of her dying father asked him in the presence of witnesses if he knew who had done this thing to him.

Peterson admitted that he did but didn't want to mention the man's name. The daughter kept insisting, and finally Peterson stated that if she would take the terrific weight off of his head he would tell her; and then, after further questioning, mentioned a name, a name which was heard very distinctly by the daughter.

This name was not the name of Clarence Boggie, nor could that name at any time ever be connected in any way with him. At the time there was nothing to connect Clarence Boggie with Moritz Peterson or with the burglary of the Peterson shack.

The police, in the course of their investigation, were reported to have arrested a suspect who was positively identified by the witnesses who had seen the man running away from the Peterson shack, but after a while the police announced that this man had a perfect alibi and he was released.

This fact, mentioned casually in the local press, was subsequently to assume a very great significance, but at the time it appeared as one of the various diversions, and was snowed under by the conjectures and surmises and press releases given out by the police in order to show that they were diligently working on the case.

Then gradually the case petered out. The police ran down clues, gave the usual optimistic statements to newspaper reporters, and wound up by getting nowhere.

Moritz Peterson died shortly after being admitted to the hospital, and had lost consciousness a very short time after making the statement to his daughter in which he had named his assailant.

At this time, Clarence Boggie was on the streets of Portland, Oregon.

The time, it will be remembered, was during the depression. People who didn't have cash had virtually no way of getting any. People who did have cash didn't know what to do with it. Banks were failing. People were being laid off. Jobs were scarce.

Boggie had no job, and he did have a criminal record.

He had been convicted of a bank robbery in Oregon.

Boggie's story of how he happened to be convicted of that bank robbery is as completely incredible as any of the other Boggie stories. We have never even investigated to find out whether this story was true because apparently the Oregon authorities had made such an investigation and had granted him a pardon—not a parole but a full pardon.

Boggie's story was that he had been camped in the 'jungles' under a bridge across a little creek bed, that a car dashed by at wild speed above the bridge, and someone threw a coat over the bridge. The car went hurtling down the road, and after the car, the sound of screaming sirens indicated pursuing police.

Boggie thought somebody was being pinched for speeding.

He went over and picked up the coat. It was a good fit, and Boggie was badly in need of a coat.

About the time Boggie had nicely adjusted himself to the coat, the creek bed began to swarm with officers. They grabbed Boggie and searched him on suspicion, and in the pockets of the coat they found a lot of currency which had been taken in a bank robbery.

Boggie was convicted. Months passed. Boggie kept protesting his innocence and asking for an investigation. Evidently such an investigation was finally made. He was pardoned, but only after he had spent some years in the Oregon penitentiary.

Now, at about this time, there enters the picture a very interesting character whom we shall refer to as Convict X. This man is, so far as I know, still serving a term in a penitentiary. He is a shrewd, ingenious operator, a clever opportunist, and he may be possessed of a quiet sense of humor. I don't know. I do know that when I was trying to interview him he was completely hostile. He didn't want to talk with me. He didn't want to answer questions.

One of my associates said to him, 'Don't you know who this man is? This is Erle Stanley Gardner. He'll give you a square deal. Haven't you ever read any of his books?'

Convict X twisted his lip in a sneer. 'Bah!' he said. 'Escape fiction.'

This convict came across Boggie on the streets of Oregon at a time when the convict was looking for accomplices. Boggie's story as to why the man wanted them is a story in itself.

In a little town in the state of Idaho the ex-chief of police knew that, because of the instability of the banks, certain relatively affluent citizens were keeping money in large quantities concealed in their houses. Boggie insisted this ex-officer had conceived the idea that if stick-up men should rob one of these houses and should take in a good haul of ready cash, it would be a bad thing for the victim, but it might be turned into a good thing for the ex-chief of police.

The former officer is supposed to have known that a certain individual had thirty thousand dollars concealed in his house. This citizen kept his house carefully locked at all times and had resorted to elaborate safeguards against robbery.

According to Boggie, word went out through the underworld that this ex-chief of police would like to have a sociable talk with some thoroughly competent men who could pull a smooth job. The word trickled through the devious channels of organized crime and reached the ears of Convict X, who promptly got in touch with the former officer. A deal was made.

And this is one place where Boggie's story to us may have been somewhat colored. There is evidence indicating that at the start Boggie may have been the one who passed the story of the ex-chief of police on to Convict X. The history of what happened and what Boggie claimed happened have some variations which are probably significant.

In any event, Convict X and the ex-chief made a deal.

The ex-chief agreed to call on the man who distrusted banks. He would very conveniently leave his car, with its tank filled with gas, on the outside, and the ignition keys would be in the car.

The former official also agreed that when he entered the house he would manage to turn back the spring lock and snap the catch which would hold it back, so that anyone could enter the door by simply turning the knob and pushing.

It was that simple.

Convict X and an accomplice were making the haul, but they wanted someone to sit outside as a watchman. They wanted someone who was so simple that he would follow instructions, so dumb that he could be used as a fall guy in the event anything went wrong.

At this point, stir-simple Clarence Boggie with his mother-complex enters the picture. Boggie was made to order.

According to Boggie's story, the men were to take a trip to Idaho. Boggie was to go along. Some time later he got cold feet. He tried to back out, then he tried to escape. The men wouldn't let him go, but Boggie finally did get away from them.

He started hitchhiking. He was picked up by a man who gave him a ride in return for Boggie's promise to do some of the driving.

So he rode along with this gentleman until it became dark. Then it turned out the man's lights wouldn't work. Boggie decided there was a shorted wire somewhere. He stopped at a sort of service station and general merchandise store and went to work. He had located a short in the wire and was making repairs with tape when another car pulled in and pilloried Boggie in the white lights.

This was the car driven by Convict X; the identical car from which Boggie had made his escape.

There was a short, quiet talk. Convict X quite apparently had associated with Boggie long enough in the Oregon prison to know Boggie's weakness. If Boggie didn't come along and do exactly as they said, Convict X assured him they were going to hunt up 'Mummy' and kill her.

Even after a lapse of some fifteen years, Boggie couldn't tell about this without becoming hysterical. Up to this point he could control himself, but when he reached this phase of the story tears streamed down his cheeks and he completely lost his self-control.

There was never any question in the mind of anyone who talked with Boggie that his fear that these men would have killed his dear 'Mummy' was an actual, tangible force. So far as Boggie was concerned, he accepted it as a basic fact that these men would do exactly what they threatened, and the only way he could save 'Mummy's' life was to go along in absolute docility no matter what happened. From that time on Boggie was their man.

Boggie, Convict X and another accomplice, went to the little town in Idaho which had been picked for the robbery. At the appointed time the ex-chief of police drove up and parked his car. He explained to the owner of the house that he wanted to listen to his radio set for a while.

He was duly admitted and, according to plan, as he stepped inside he turned the spring lock on the door so that anyone could walk right in. Then he carefully closed the door.

Boggie was to be the lookout man. He was to signal the others if anything started to go wrong.

Convict X and his accomplice glided quietly up to the door and tried the knob to make certain that the officer had been able to manipulate the lock. Finding that he had done so, they suddenly pushed the door open and jumped into the room with drawn guns.

It was part of the plan that the former chief, despite the menace of the guns, was to put up a valiant battle.

Convict X told me about all this, a little at a time. For the most part, getting information out of him was pretty much of a job. He was inclined to answer questions in monosyllables or not answer them at all, but when he came to the point where he described the battle with the former chief of police he needed no urging. His eyes lit with enthusiasm. That was one part of the job that he thoroughly enjoyed and he loved to tell about it.

It seemed the two criminals really did a job on the former officer. He had asked to be beaten up, and these boys carried out that part of their assignment with an enthusiastic zeal that gave the man everything he had asked for—and more. He had wanted to be marked up enough so that it would be perfectly apparent he had struggled valiantly against overpowering odds.

'Boy, oh, boy,' Convict X said ecstatically in telling me about it, 'we hung a couple of beautiful shiners on that so-and-so.'

The ex-officer, having been overpowered, was immunized by one of the convicts who held a gun pointed at the man's stomach, while the other intruder went to work on the householder and his wife, trying to find out the place where the thirty thousand dollars were secreted.

Now the story develops a touch of grim humor.

The victim explained to the holdup men that they were acting on a wrong tip, that he didn't have any money in the house. He was supposed to have money concealed but he was too smart for that trap. He preferred to take a chance on a bank despite the fact that there was some chance the bank might fail.

He pulled a checkbook out of his pocket. He showed check stubs to the robbers. And he was so absolutely convincing that he talked them out of it.

Imagine the feelings of the ex-chief of police, standing there with his hands in the air, his face badly banged up, his eyes swelling shut, listening to what was going on, hearing the man who he knew full well had thirty thousand dollars concealed on the premises talking the bandits into believing he had nothing. How he must have wanted to enter the discussion by shouting to the bandits, 'You poor fools. Don't let him talk you out of it. I told you he had thirty thousand dollars here and I wouldn't have told you that unless I'd known. Get busy and find that money, you poor bungling amateurs!'

But the ex-chief, forced to act out the part of a valiant officer, who had been overpowered, beaten up, slugged, and was now facing the gun of a trigger-happy desperado, could only stand there and listen.

The householder, apparently very much frightened, was perfectly willing to surrender 'all the money he had on the premises,' a few hundred dollars. He was so frightened that if he had had any more he would unquestionably have given it up. He put on quite an act. Convict X believed him. So did the other man. They took the money that was available and made a dash out of the front door, piled helter-skelter into the waiting car and took off.

The man who had been held up was nobody's fool. Certain things about the holdup caused him to become suspicious. It had been a little too opportune.

The bandits were apprehended, the whole story came out, and Convict X and Clarence Boggie found themselves facing a long prison term in Idaho.

Boggie made a statement. He wanted to turn State's evidence.

Convict X told him grimly, 'You rat on us and we'll frame something a lot worse than this on you.' (Later on a deputy sheriff, who had overheard this and other remarks, was to make an affidavit that from what he had overheard he had every reason to believe Convict X had framed Boggie for the Peterson murder—and the authorities were to brush that affidavit aside.)

Boggie, Convict X and the accomplice were all sentenced to terms in the Idaho State Penitentiary.

It appeared that on his way north to pull this job Convict X had stopped for a short time in Spokane. Boggie had some people he wanted to see and Convict X wanted to make preparations for a job he was to do.

This was but a short time after Moritz Peterson had been murdered.

Through a fortuitous chain of circumstances Convict X had an absolutely perfect alibi for the Peterson murder. He had been serving a term in a Canadian prison and had been released from that prison on the day *following* the death of Moritz Peterson. Therefore, so far as that crime was concerned, Convict X was in the clear and knew it.

On the other hand, Convict X, who had an adroit, ingenious mind, studied the local newspapers while he was stopping over in Spokane and gave a lot of thought to the Peterson murder, reading about the various clues the police were 'running down.' He noticed the police were going in circles while issuing the usual optimistic reports that they were confident the culprit would be in custody within a short time, etc. So Convict X decided that the Peterson murder might come in very handy in case of necessity.

Just how handy will presently become apparent.

Convict X needed funds and he was a very desperate man. As he explained the matter to me later in a burst of indignation, the Canadian prison had turned him loose with a prison suit of clothes and a Canadian ten-dollar bill in his pocket. 'Why, that wasn't enough,' he charged bitterly, 'for operating capital.'

I asked him what he meant by 'operating capital.'

'Not enough to buy a "rod" with,' he retorted, still angry at this evidence of Canadian lack of hospitality.

So Convict X was in urgent need of 'operating capital.' By the time he reached Spokane he had remedied the defect as far as the 'rod' was concerned, but he was still short of money.

Spokane officers believed he had participated in a robbery and kidnaping while in Spokane, and under the so-called 'Lindbergh Laws' which were being passed by the various states in a wave of indignation over kidnapings, Convict X could have been extradited from Idaho to Washington, and sentenced to death.

The Washington authorities went up to Idaho with the idea of extraditing Convict X to Washington, trying him and demanding the death penalty.

This, it is to be remembered, was after Convict X had been arrested in Idaho but before he had been convicted there. If Idaho was willing to release him to Washington, Washington could prosecute him, and, if convicted, could execute him.

Convict X didn't like that prospect.

At this point it becomes necessary to put two and two together and rely upon a certain amount of surmise and circumstantial evidence. But the indications are quite plain and there is considerable evidence that Convict X said to the officers, 'If you boys will let me stay up here in Idaho and take the rap on this robbery charge without extraditing me back to Washington, I'll do you a favor; I'll solve the Peterson murder for you.'

In any event, and regardless of what actually did happen, the fact remains that the Washington authorities after a talk with Convict X did not extradite him. They let him remain and take the rap in Idaho, and they *did* claim that they now knew the identity of the real murderer of Moritz Peterson. There is reason to believe they returned with a pair of coveralls and a pair of black shoes, which Convict X assured them had been given him by Boggie, and which Boggie had told him were the property of 'the old man.'

Perhaps there was no trade. Perhaps it was all merely coincidental.

The fact remained that the crestfallen officers found that they didn't have a case, because the coveralls did not belong to Moritz Peterson, and the shoes were not the right size.

Rumor has it that on careful investigation the police found a laundry mark in the coveralls, and that this laundry mark established an entirely different chain of ownership.

It is, therefore, apparent that Convict X had formulated some pretty definite plans in his shrewdly ingenious mind. From his viewpoint the Peterson murder case represented an ideal opportunity to buy his way out of any jam in the state of Washington.

The Spokane police were anxious to solve the murder. People

were indignant over the idea of a harmless, inoffensive, well-liked citizen being bludgeoned to death by a murderer who had only a relatively short start on the police and who was never apprehended. Spokane police wanted very much to solve that murder case.

Convict X had an unshakable alibi.

Therefore if Convict X could offer the Spokane police a 'solution' of the Peterson murder, he would be in a marvelous trading position. For a man of Convict X's temperament, personality and occupation, being in a good trading position with the police was well worth the investment in a couple of stage props—a pair of secondhand coveralls and some old shoes.

Of course, Convict X needed just a little more than that. He needed a fall guy, and a man looking for a fall guy couldn't have found anyone more made to order than Clarence Boggie.

So, putting two and two together, it would seem that Clarence Boggie had served several purposes on that fateful trip north from Portland.

And the story that Convict X is known to have told the officers is weird in the extreme. Boggie, he said, had boasted of killing Peterson, had taken Convict X to a place where he had buried the 'loot', had there dug up a small coffee can, had taken off the cover and extracted a worn, empty billfold which he had offered to Convict X and which Convict X had taken.

Thus a pattern of double-crossing chicanery emerged—the dog-eat-dog attitude of factual occurrences in everyday life as opposed to the version that is handed out to the public.

Of course, the Spokane police didn't give up that easily.

They looked up Boggie from all conceivable angles, but all that they had to connect Boggie with the crime was the word of Convict X, and Convict X, of course, with his long criminal record, his extremely personal interest in the matter, would hardly make a witness on whom a district attorney would like to depend.

There must have been a shrewd suspicion in the minds of the officers that they had been taken for a ride by a quick-thinking, fast-talking convict, but if that was the case the officers couldn't do anything about it without publicizing their own gullibility, and Convict X kept assuring them of his complete good faith. Clarence Boggie, he insisted, was the man who committed the crime, even if Boggie had lied about the coveralls and the shoes, and the officers could rest assured that Convict X was giving them the real low-down. If there had been any prevarication about the coveralls and the shoes, it had been Boggie's lie and not that of Convict X, etc.

The Moritz Peterson case went into the unsolved file. The officers busied themselves about other matters; but, always in the back of their minds was the feeling that Clarence Boggie had perhaps outsmarted them in some way and had juggled the evidence. They felt that he was the man who had committed the murder.

Not only did Convict X say that Boggie had confessed to him, but later another Idaho convict claimed Boggie had confessed to him while in the Idaho penitentiary—had, in effect, walked right up to him, and without preliminary conversation said, 'I killed Moritz Peterson,' and then turned and walked away. It was that simple.

In this way, Convict X was able to assure the Washington officers of his entire good faith in the matter. He was never returned to Washington and tried on the kidnap case.

Then, many months later and 'on a tip,' the officers went to a place near a small Oregon town where Boggie had stayed for a while, and there they found an overcoat. There was some evidence that Boggie had worn this overcoat to the house when he arrived. The overcoat had been left there. It had received rather hard usage and was in a dilapidated state.

However, that overcoat was identified by the daughter of Moritz Peterson as having been an overcoat worn by her father during his lifetime.

That did it. The officers came down on Boggie like a thousand ton of bricks.

The murderer of Moritz Peterson had been identified as a person having wild-looking bushy black hair. Clarence Boggie, apparently from the time when he was brought under suspicion, started slicking his hair smoothly down with quantities of hair oil.

This didn't stop the officers. They would bring him in, ruffle his hair up, ask witnesses to identify him, and then take Boggie's picture. Naturally, some of these pictures of Boggie with his thickly greased long hair, pulled up high above his head, resembled the pictures in Frye's geography of a Dyak of Borneo. These pictures were given to the press.

Boggie's story about how he came by the overcoat was incredible.

He had, he said, been in a secondhand clothing store in Portland, Oregon. A man came in with an overcoat, a pretty good-looking overcoat, with a pair of slippers in the pocket. He offered to sell this coat to the proprietor of the store. He wanted a dollar for it. The proprietor hadn't liked the looks of the man and had refused to buy the overcoat.

Boggie spoke up. '*I'll* give you a dollar for it.'

It made the proprietor angry. He didn't think Boggie had any right to interfere in that way. If he had been dickering in the hope the seller would make a lower offer, Boggie's interference would have lost him a good purchase.

The man who was offering the overcoat for sale promptly and eagerly accepted Boggie's dollar. So Boggie bought himself a one-way ticket to a life sentence in the Washington State Penitentiary at Walla Walla.

Little things, which may or may not have been significant so far as the jury were concerned, indicated the background of the Boggie trial. The prosecution, for instance, was permitted to show by witnesses that Boggie had been in a car, with a revolver, and that Boggie's statement explaining the ownership and possession of the revolver was that the authorities had given it to him so he could protect himself.

This, of course, was greeted with the equivalent of hoots of derision.

Later on, the defense tried to prove the actual ownership of the revolver and the reason it was in the car with Boggie by no less person than Fred C. May, the deputy sheriff of Shoshone County, Idaho. The court refused to permit such testimony to go in, on the ground that it was irrelevant.

In vain did counsel protest. The court stated that questions concerning the revolver had been completely irrelevant, and charged the attorneys for the defense that if they permitted irrelevant matter to be brought in by the prosecution they could not thereby make an issue of it. Such are the technicalities of law.

It is to be remembered that the running murderer had a peculiar, 'sideways gait.' Boggie did not have any such gait, but he did have a very slight limp. No one of the witnesses had seen the murderer's face, but witnesses were called upon to identify Boggie as 'looking like' the man who had been seen running away from the scene of the murder two years earlier.

It is to be noted that the witnesses who had seen the murderer running away from the scene of the crime were not given an opportunity to look at Boggie when the police had first had reason to suspect him of the murder. It was not until a lapse of some two years (after the overcoat had been located) that the witnesses were called on to make an identification, and then there was no line-up or anything of that sort. The witnesses were simply brought in to see Boggie and asked if that was the man. There is, in fact, considerable evidence in the record itself that the identification, made in this way, could not have been made if the defendant had been in a line-up.

A junk dealer stated that he had seen Boggie visiting Peterson on the Friday before the murder. Another witness, who had one of the houses in the front of the lot, insisted that she had seen a man whom she thought was Boggie visiting there on a Friday, but on cross-examination, when the witnesses had been separated, it appeared that each was testifying to a different Friday.

It is to be noted that the man who was seen running away from the scene of the murder that twenty-sixth day of June, was not carrying an overcoat, nor, in the heat of a Spokane summer, was he wearing any overcoat. Virtually the entire case against Boggie hinged on the identification of an overcoat, and that identification was made some two years after the crime had been committed.

The murderer, running away from Moritz Peterson's shack that June day, had been followed by one of the housewives who had been doing her washing, and some of the children. The other housewife had been telephoning the police. No one had seen the murderer's face, but one woman had been close enough to see a part of his cheek, the color of his skin, and had observed the running figure closely.

At the time of the trial the prosecution had called her as a witness and the examination had been rather peculiar. For one thing, the prosecution did not ask her to identify Clarence Boggie as the man whom she had seen running away from the house; and when the attorney for the defense cross-examined her, he, probably fearing a trap, was careful not to give her any opportunity to make a positive identification. So this woman was in effect asked a few general questions about hearing the struggle in the shack, seeing the man run away, following him for a couple of blocks, and then she was excused.

One of the other witnesses was much more positive in her identification of Boggie, but there were certain circumstances which tended to weaken the identification. Among other things was the intimation that she had previously identified another person, only to retract that identification when she found out that she must have been mistaken.

There were, of course, other angles to the case. A couple of days after the murder Boggie had been bumming a ride in Pendleton, Oregon. He had spoken in enthusiastic terms of the hunting near a certain place in Oregon, a place where he lived at the time. The driver of the car had expressed a wish to go hunting with Boggie, and Boggie had thoughtfully given him his name and address.

Later on, reading in the newspapers that Boggie was wanted for murder, the driver of the car got in touch with the police.

The prosecution contended that Boggie had made a headlong 'flight' from the scene of the murder. (A strange flight by a man who makes it a point to impress his personality upon the individual with whom he is riding, and gives his name and address.)

However, when Boggie tried to explain away the situation and tell his story, he was asked an impeaching question. Wasn't it true that he had twice been convicted of a felony?

Boggie was forced to admit that such was the case; and that was all there was to it.

Boggie was convicted, and, fortunately for him, escaped the gallows. He was sentenced to life imprisonment. . . .

In summarizing the facts in this case it seems remarkable that even with the urging of the chaplain we would have wasted time investigating the Boggie case. His story was incredible. The case against him, while not particularly sturdy, was, nevertheless, a pretty good case. The penitentiaries are filled with people against whom the prosecution didn't have as good cases as they had against Clarence Boggie. And, on the other hand, there was virtually nothing to establish Boggie's innocence except his word that he wasn't guilty.

The prosecution was able to show that Boggie, with a long criminal record, had the dead man's property in his possession, and had confessed to Convict X, and to another convict in Idaho, that he had killed Moritz Peterson. Witnesses who had seen the murderer running away from the scene of the crime had identified Boggie as being the man.

Despite this positive evidence each link in the chain of evidence had certain weaknesses. Convict X had a definite interest in the matter, or could well have had, if he had made a trade with the Spokane police. The overcoat had not been picked up until two years after the murder. It had been hanging in a barn, and was a fairly worn-out garment by the time it was shown to the daughter of the murdered man for identification. Boggie had not been identified in a line-up, but had simply been exhibited to witnesses who were asked if this was the man they had seen running away from the house at the time of the murder.

Identification evidence is a most tricky subject. The subconscious mind frequently plays tricks upon witnesses who are acting in the greatest good faith, and in the Boggie case witnesses were not called upon to identify him until two years after the date of the crime.

However, as I have said, we can go to any penitentiary in the country and find hundreds of cases where the evidence on which the man was convicted is no more solid than the evidence on which Boggie was convicted.

There was one factor in Boggie's favor. Boggie had made an application for *habeas corpus* and a hearing duly came up in a Federal court. Hon. Lloyd L. Black, the Federal judge before whom that hearing was held, is a patient, a kindly individual who is prone to try to get at the facts of a case and not rush through these numerous *habeas corpus* applications in order to 'clear his calendar.'

He became very much interested in the case when the daughter of Moritz Peterson, the same woman who had been present at the time the dying man had made a statement that he would name the person who had killed him, stated very definitely and positively that she did not believe Clarence Boggie had killed her father or knew anything about the murder, that she simply didn't believe Boggie was known to her father.

Judge Black found no reason to grant the writ of *habeas corpus* but he was very much impressed by the sincerity of the daughter and by her declaration. He at least intimated in open court that he would like to see some further investigation made in the case.

And so those were the facts which confronted me when I arrived in Walla Walla, talked with Tom Smith, met Clarence Boggie, talked with him, went over his heartbreak file and then studied the evidence in the case.

I decided that considerable investigative work was going to be needed and got on the long-distance telephone to Raymond Schindler in New York. I found that he was at the moment in Los Angeles, and was on the point of taking a plane back to New York. I persuaded him he had better fly up to join me, so he took a night plane and arrived in Walla Walla, where I had a chartered plane ready. We flew to Spokane.

Obviously one of the highlights of the case from a legal standpoint was the manner in which the prosecution had interrogated the housewife who had seen the murderer running away from the Peterson shack, yet who wasn't specifically asked to point out Boggie.

My courtroom experience indicated that there must have been a very definite reason for the peculiar type of questions which had been asked this woman on the witness stand. The prosecution had asked all of the usual questions, had got her right up to the point in her testimony where the next logical question would have been to ask her to point out the murderer, and then veered off into a detour from which the attorneys had never returned to the main highway of ordinary procedure.

Frequently those things happen when a prosecutor lays a trap for the defense attorney. Knowing that he has a very positive witness whose testimony would be damning, the prosecutor pretends to fumble around and leaves a beautiful 'opening' for the cross-examiner. The cross-examiner sticks his head through that opening and promptly has it chopped off.

But somehow as Schindler and I read and discussed this woman's testimony, we didn't feel that it had been a trap. We felt that there was something in the background, some reason that the prosecution had pretended to fumble the ball.

Of course, many years had elapsed since the trial, but we felt that if it was still possible to find this woman, we wanted to talk with her.

We found her, and when we did we uncovered a shocking story.

This witness and her young son had seen the murderer emerge from the Peterson shack. They had followed as he ran down the street, not trying to overtake him but trying to keep him in sight. They had never seen his face. (None of the witnesses had ever seen the face of the fleeing man.) But this woman had been in a position to see the side of his cheek and had noticed the color of his skin.

A considerable time after the murder, and apparently at a time when Boggie was under arrest, this woman had seen a man prowling around the vicinity of the Peterson shack. (It is to be noted in passing that long after the time of the murder several other homemade lethal weapons had been found in the bushes nearby, the over-all characteristics being somewhat similar to the murder weapon in the Peterson case.)

This woman felt absolutely certain in her own mind that the man she saw was the same man she had seen running away from the scene of the murder. She went to the telephone and called the police, telling them excitedly that the man who killed Moritz Peterson was outside and to come and pick him up.

The police told her to forget it, that the man who had killed Moritz Peterson was Clarence Boggie, that Boggie had been arrested and was safe in jail awaiting trial.

The woman insisted that this man was the murderer, that in any event he was a prowler who had no business there, and she wanted the police to come out and arrest him.

The police hung up.

After a while the prowler went away.

Nor was this all. The day before Clarence Boggie was to be tried, the deputy prosecutor had gone to the school where this woman's twelve-year-old son was in attendance.

According to this woman the deputy prosecutor painted a very glittering picture. The boy was told he was to be a very important witness. He was to be excused from classes the next day. A big police car with a driver was to come to school and get him. The boy was to go to court. He was to stand up and be sworn as a witness, and for this he would receive witness fees which would be entirely his own money, which he could spend any way he wanted to.

The deputy prosecutor, however, wanted him to be sure and identify Boggie, who would be sitting right there in the courtroom. He wanted the boy to mention that he had seen the face of the murderer who was running away from the Peterson shack, and that this man was Boggie.

But the boy protested he *hadn't* seen the murderer's face.

According to this woman's story the deputy prosecutor had then said, 'But I want you to say that you saw the man's face. You know that I am a public official. I wouldn't ask you to do anything that was wrong. That's the thing I want you to do, to say that you saw the man's face.'

The perplexed, bewildered boy shook his head. He couldn't say he had seen the man's face because he hadn't.

In the end the deputy prosecutor warned the boy against saying anything to his mother about the conversation. So the boy went home from school, a very troubled, worried young man who couldn't eat any supper.

The mother questioned him, trying to find out what was wrong, but, mindful of the warning he had received not to talk to his mother about the conversation, he didn't want to tell her. By this time, very much alarmed and sensing that something was radically wrong, she kept after him until finally he broke down and tearfully told her the story.

This mother was a good, straightforward American woman. She took the boy by the hand and walked up to the prosecutor's office, where lights shining through the windows indicated that last-minute preparations for the courtroom battle the next day were going on.

'What,' she indignantly demanded, 'are you trying to do to my son?'

No wonder the prosecution had handled her with gloves. No wonder they hadn't asked her to identify Clarence Boggie. Had they asked her she would have said that she didn't think Clarence Boggie was the man, that she didn't think he had the same build, that she didn't think he had the same complexion, that she thought the real murderer was the man whom she had seen prowling around the premises at a time when Clarence Boggie was in jail and at a time when the police refused even to come out to investigate.

It is to be remembered that more than fifteen years had passed from the time of the Peterson murder to the date of our investigation. We couldn't talk with the boy because he had grown up to be a young man, had gone to war and had given his life for his country.

On the other hand, the deputy prosecutor had cut one corner too many, had been himself convicted of crime and sent to prison.

So there we had a story on our hands that we couldn't verify. The mother, of course, hadn't heard the conversation with the deputy prosecutor. She only knew what the boy had told her, but the mother had confronted the deputy prosecutor with her boy, and so to that extent was a witness who could testify in any court to that much of the story. . . . And what a sordid story it was. A deputy prosecutor trying to suborn perjury, trying to get a young boy just at the threshold of life to do something that he knew was wrong, trying to send a man to the gallows by assuring a twelve-year-old boy, 'I'm a public official. I wouldn't ask you to do something that was wrong, would I?'

Such was our introduction to the investigation of the Boggie case, the first intimation we had that the Court of Last Resort might be a lot more important than we had at first realized and might find some very tightly closed doors leading into some dark and dingy rooms.

When Steeger and I had discussed the manner in which *Argosy* would donate its space to the activities of the investigating committee for the Court of Last Resort, it was agreed that we wouldn't try to carry the investigation through to completion and then publish what we had found out.

We felt that if we were going to do the job we wanted to do it would be necessary to take the reader right along with us. We wanted to get readers interested in the cause of justice. We wanted to get them interested in a case, and in order to get them interested we wanted them to participate in the investigation.

It was decided we'd make only the most cursory preliminary investigation, that we would then start working on the case, not knowing whether the defendant was guilty or innocent, simply knowing that it was a good case for investigative work, and that the readers of *Argosy* could look over our shoulders while we were making it.

In fact, it is to be continually borne in mind that the Court of Last Resort was not the magazine and was not the investigators, but was the public, the readers of the magazine themselves. The board of investigators was nothing more nor less than an investigative board.

For that reason I carried a portable typewriter along with me when I flew to Washington, and each day I made a summary of what our work had disclosed. Each night we carefully studied the transcript in the Boggie case and made an analysis of the evidence. Since there were several volumes of this transcript the schedule which we set ourselves was a hard one. By day we talked with witnesses. At night we studied transcripts, and put together an analysis and the condensation of the evidence. In the small hours of the morning I would whip out copy to send to the magazine, and when enough copy had been sent in for the first installment of the Boggie case, Schindler flew back to New York and I left for my ranch in California, taking the transcript back with me.

A peculiar situation developed. The authorities in Washington suddenly realized that a case which had taken place in their state was being publicized, and the authorities didn't even know what the case was all about, and didn't have any way of finding out.

The attorney general of Washington called me and wanted to know if I would mail the transcript to his office. I told him I didn't feel I could do that, but that I would be very glad to let anyone whom he might designate study it at my ranch.

So Ed Lehan, a special deputy attorney general, flew down from Washington and spent several days going over the transcript.

At the end of that time Lehan concluded that the evidence had not been such as to warrant a conviction.

Ed Lehan returned to Washington to carry on an investigation for the attorney general.

Raymond Schindler and I flew back to Washington and were joined by Harry Steeger. Here we made a supplemental investigation and learned that the proprietor of the secondhand store, where Boggie claimed he had bought the overcoat, was still in business in Portland, Oregon.

We flew down to Portland, located the man and asked him if he remembered the occasion of the overcoat being purchased while he was contemplating whether or not he would buy it.

The proprietor remembered the occasion perfectly. He was still indignant at the manner in which Boggie had stepped into the picture. According to his understanding, Boggie was a customer. His only excuse for being in the store was to buy something that was on display or to offer to sell something. Aside from that he should keep out of any business transactions.

He remembered the man coming in with the overcoat, with the slippers in his pocket, and he didn't like his looks. The overcoat looked 'hot' to him. He couldn't tell us why he felt that way, but it was simply the reaction of a man who had done business with a lot of people, many of whom were crooks. He thought this man was a crook and didn't want to do business with him. He didn't know whether he would have changed his mind if the price on the overcoat had been lowered or not. But while he was debating the matter with himself, Boggie had stepped in, offered a dollar and taken the coat.

This man had been a witness at the time of Boggie's trial and he felt that a deliberate attempt had been made to intimidate him.

For the most part the proprietor of a secondhand store can't do business unless he has the friendship of the police. It was at least intimated to this man, or he thought it was intimated to him, that it would be exceedingly unwise for him to be a witness on behalf of Boggie. However, he took the stand and told what he knew.

The prosecutor had sought to discredit this testimony by showing that two years after the date of the transaction the witness *couldn't identify the overcoat.*

Of course he couldn't.

If he had, it would have been a most suspicious circumstance.

All that this man remembered was his natural feeling of exasperation when Boggie stepped in to buy the overcoat in question.

Steeger, Schindler and I went back to Washington. We had quite a conference with Smith Troy, the attorney general.

I think Smith Troy is one of the most fair-minded attorneys general I have ever met. He puts his cards face up on the table and he calls the turns as he sees them. As a district attorney he was a remarkably able prosecutor. As an attorney general he is popular, well liked and efficient, and as attorney general he decided that if Clarence Boggie had been improperly convicted it was up to his office to take the responsibility of conducting an investigation, and this was done with vigor and absolute fairness.

When Smith Troy was ready to make a report to Governor Monrad C. Wallgren, Raymond Schindler, Harry Steeger, Tom Smith as warden of the penitentiary, and I went to call on the Governor. He invited us to his executive mansion for cocktails and later on for a supper. We spent the entire evening with him.

Ed Lehan was supposed to join us there earlier, but his plane from Spokane was delayed on account of bad weather, and he didn't arrive until later in the evening. He and Smith Troy gave the Governor the facts in the Boggie case as they understood them and stated they were willing to make a definite recommendation.

THE COURT OF LAST RESORT

Governor Wallgren was very much impressed. He said he certainly didn't want an innocent man in prison, but he did want the report from Ed Lehan and Smith Troy to be in writing.

Ed Lehan agreed to put his report in writing, and Smith Troy agreed to take Lehan's report and supplement it with a report and recommendation from his office as attorney general of the State of Washington.

We felt that the case had been completed, and after shaking hands all around started back to our respective domiciles.

Thereafter, however, things began to drag. There were intimations that someone with considerable political influence in the State of Washington wasn't particularly enthusiastic about having Clarence Boggie pardoned.

And then came a peculiar development.

The Seattle *Times* had in its employ a very alert, able reporter named Don Magnuson. Magnuson had, at one time, talked with Clarence Boggie when he was on a trip to the prison at Walla Walla, and may even have read or glanced through the Boggie transcript.

Nothing had been done about it so far as his paper was concerned.

However, when the articles began to appear in *Argosy* publicizing a case which was, so to speak, in the back yard of the Seattle newspapers, Don Magnuson got busy and proceeded to write a series of articles which very nearly duplicated the legal analysis of the testimony in the case which we had left with the various officials in the state of Washington.

At the time we didn't pay a great deal of attention to these articles. We felt that the Governor had given us his word in the Boggie case; that the attorney general had made an investigation which indicated Boggie had been improperly convicted, and that the Governor was going to grant Boggie a pardon; that if the Seattle *Times* wanted to publish an analysis of the Boggie case based upon work that had been done by *Argosy* investigators they were quite free to do so.

But we couldn't understand the peculiar delay, and it bothered us.

When we had originally set up the Court of Last Resort it had been planned that we would take one case and present it to the readers, letting them look over our shoulders as we made the investigation, and then get their reaction. We had assumed that we could take a case and carry it through in a complete presentation to the reader and have the case closed within two or three installments.

We didn't count on the public reaction, and we didn't count upon the series of interminable delays in the Boggie case. We thought that since we had analyzed the evidence in the case, secured new evidence, made a presentation to the attorney general, secured the Governor's promise that if the attorney general's report was favorable Boggie would be released—that was all there was to it.

But the minute *Argosy* began publishing 'The Court of Last Resort,' letters began coming in, and as they continued coming in we found that readers wanted to know more about the developments in the Boggie case. They wanted to have us bring the case to a satisfactory conclusion one way or the other.

By this time, we began to realize only too well that a magazine of general circulation simply can't 'donate' space to a cause. A magazine is in a highly competitive market. People who pay twenty-five cents for a magazine want to get twenty-five cents' worth of recreation, entertainment, amusement and interesting information. If any substantial part of the magazine is filled with something they don't like, the reading public feels that it has to that extent been deprived of its money's worth and is going to turn to some other magazine.

The letters from readers of 'The Court of Last Resort' made it clear that we would either have to discontinue the feature or put it on a permanent basis. Either course presented very grave problems, particularly in view of the fact that things had come to a standstill in the Boggie case.

So I flew up to Olympia, the state capital of Washington, to find out what was happening.

At first I couldn't seem to get anywhere. Then Smith Troy, the attorney general, asked me if our group would be willing to co-operate with the Seattle *Times*. I told him, sure, we'd be glad to co-operate with anyone, but personally I didn't see why the Governor didn't go ahead and grant Boggie a pardon.

Troy told me that there had been new developments in the case which he wasn't in a position to disclose, but felt that if I talked with Henry MacLeod, the city editor, and Don Magnuson, I might receive some startling information. Smith Troy said he felt that these gentlemen would talk with me if we'd promise to co-operate.

I told Troy I'd be only too·glad to talk with them, and telephoned New York to ask Steeger if he would be willing to co-operate with the Seattle *Times*. Steeger said, 'Certainly,' to go right ahead. We'd co-operate with any newspaper that was trying to get at the facts in any case.

So then MacLeod, Magnuson and I sat down for a talk and I learned that when the first article had appeared in print an individual had telephoned the paper and said in effect, 'Why, I know all about the murder of Moritz Peterson. I know who did it. I told the Spokane police about it at the time. I didn't know that anyone had ever been convicted. I know this man Boggie never did have a thing to do with it. It was another person.'

Naturally the *Times* had rushed Don Magnuson out to see this witness.

The witness had been a businessman in Spokane. A certain peculiar character, whom we will refer to as John Doe, came into the store of this witness on several occasions, and, on one occasion shortly before the murder, had in his possession a weapon which had been made by putting a round, water-worn rock in a piece of burlap, wrapping the burlap around and around, so that the various thicknesses of cloth formed a substantial handle, and stitching the burlap tightly around this handle with the end result of a perfect weapon.

As soon as this witness saw a picture of the weapon that had been used to kill Moritz Peterson he recognized it as being the same weapon which had been in the possession of John Doe a short time earlier. He had promptly notified the Spokane police.

So the police had picked up John Doe. They found that John Doe had been in the neighborhood of the Peterson cabin on the morning that the murder was committed.

But had he been at the scene of the murder *when* it was committed? There was the question.

In investigating this case the police found a witness who had seen John Doe some little distance (as I remember it, it was nearly a mile) from the scene of the murder at '*the time that the sirens went by.*'

What sirens?

The police assumed that the statement of the witness related to the time the sirens had signaled the passing of police cars on their way to answer the frantic telephone calls from Peterson's neighbors.

But had that been the time?

In the first place, the police had no way of knowing exactly what time that was. In the second place, the proceedings had certainly been beautifully mixed up. Just recall the procession of police sirens.

The police knew when the call had been received at the police station. It will be remembered, however, that the first man on the job was the speed cop on his motorcycle. He had listened to the excited story poured in his ears by the witnesses who insisted that the murderer had 'gone thataway,' and had vanished in the wooded lot only a few seconds before.

The officer shook his head. Chasing murderers wasn't part of his duty. He jumped on his motorcycle and tore away.

Then came the police. The police heard the story and the children eagerly escorted the police up to the place where the murderer had gone into the brush. The police, you will recall, had forgotten their guns, and they wouldn't go into the brush without them.

So back they went to the police station to get armed.

Some time along in there, and at a time on which police records are silent, an ambulance came and took Moritz Peterson to the hospital.

All in all, there must have been a whole procession of sirens going back and forth, and the fact that some witness had seen John Doe at a certain place '*when the sirens went by*' was hardly the type of evidence which could be used as an alibi. It hardly seems possible that police could have considered '*the time the sirens went by*' as being any sort of an alibi. It simply didn't prove anything.

What sirens? When?

But the police had turned John Doe loose, and, by the time the Seattle *Times* had dug up this witness, were singularly unenthusiastic about reopening the case.

This was, of course, a very interesting development. Mac-Leod, Magnuson and I talked it over in detail, and it was decided that the first thing to do was to try and locate John Doe.

John Doe had been an itinerant, a man who was, according to the Spokane witness, eccentric to the point of being peculiar. He had vanished and left no trail.

So I moved down to Spokane with Magnuson and an assistant reporter from the Seattle *Times*. Raymond Schindler and Shelby Williams, the manager of his New York office, flew out to Spokane.

Schindler, Williams and the two reporters started running down clues, trying to uncover some lead which would disclose the present whereabouts of John Doe.

The trail was fifteen years old and, of course, as so frequently happens in a case of that kind, ninety-nine per cent of the leads that were investigated turned out to be blind alleys.

They found that John Doe had gone to Arizona, then he had disappeared for a while. They found that he had been in prison, and to add to the long chain of coincidences found that he had actually served a term in the Washington state penitentiary at Walla Walla at the same time Boggie was there serving his life sentence.

Naturally, as a writer, the dramatic possibilities appealed to me. Suppose it should appear that the man who actually murdered Moritz Peterson had rubbed elbows in prison with the man who had been erroneously convicted of that murder. What were his feelings? What would he do? Would he hunt Boggie up and try to form a friendship with him to see how Boggie was taking it, or would he avoid him? Or would he be sufficiently callous to go about the even tenor of his ways, completely ignoring Boggie?

I decided that later on I would make an investigation of this and perhaps confront John Doe with Boggie, but in the meantime, since we were working under cover, we dared not breathe a word of any of this to Boggie or even intimate that we were trying to close in on John Doe.

Finally the investigating team struck pay dirt, and after a long and arduous investigation uncovered a clue which they felt would enable them to put their hands on John Doe within thirty days. In other words, they found where John Doe was going to be thirty days from that date and there was every assurance that he would be there.

So Schindler, Shelby and I went home. The newspapermen stayed on the job, and at the end of thirty days did uncover John Doe and had the Spokane police pick him up for questioning. They got precisely no place.

At that time Henry MacLeod rang us up and wanted to have Leonarde Keeler come out with a polygraph to give John Doe a lie detector test.

It turned out, however, that this wasn't going to be a simple matter. From telephone descriptions of John Doe's character, Keeler felt that there was a possibility John Doe might not be a 'good subject.' There was also the very strong chance that by the time Keeler got out there John Doe would refuse to take a lie detector test. Nor did Keeler want to fly out on a matter of that importance and make an immediate test. He wanted to take some time to investigate the man with whom he was dealing and familiarize himself with all details of the case.

By that time *Argosy* had spent many thousands of dollars on the Boggie case, and the outlook didn't seem at all promising. The magazine feature, 'The Court of Last Resort,' had proven terribly expensive, and no one knew for certain whether the readers of the magazine cared a hoot if innocent men were imprisoned or freed, or whether they simply wanted an end to a 'story.'

The investigators were all donating their time, but the traveling and incidental expenses had been enormous. We had put in literally months of work. The long-distance and telegraph bills alone were fantastic.

So, while John Doe was being detained, *Argosy* in New York held telephone conversations with Leonarde Keeler in Chicago, and I kept the wires buzzing to Seattle.

Looking back on it, it is incredible to think that we could so have misjudged the American reading public.

Later on it appeared that readers everywhere had been

following the Boggie case; that the reading public cared very much indeed whether innocent men who had been wrongfully convicted were held in prison.

At the time we weren't aware of this. We were feeling our way. The avalanche of public approval that was to dispel all our doubts was just beginning to form. We had no means of knowing what a terrific power it was to become.

In the meantime the Spokane police stated that they wanted to see whether the witness uncovered by the Seattle *Times* could make an identification of the murder weapon which, it is to be remembered, had then been in their hands for sixteen years. The witness had seen that weapon sixteen years earlier and hadn't seen it since.

The Seattle *Times* agreed to have their witness go to Spokane and make an identification of the weapon.

When the witness arrived the Spokane police tossed out a collection of weapons, all as nearly identical as they could make them, and asked the witness to pick out the one he had seen.

It seemed that the Spokane police had been busily engaged in duplicating the murder weapon.

Here again we have another incredible fact in the Boggie case. The witness sat down and carefully examined each of the weapons, and then *picked out the exact weapon which had been used to murder Moritz Peterson sixteen years earlier.*

'This is the one,' he said.

And he was right.

Nor was that identification merely a matter of chance. It happened that this witness was one of those unusually keen observers, who possessed a remarkable ability to recall what he had seen. Moreover, there was one peculiarity about the murder weapon *which had escaped the notice of the Spokane police but which had clung to the memory of the witness.*

I know that it wasn't merely an afterthought or a coincidence because the witness himself had told me about this peculiarity when Don Magnuson had arranged for me to meet him, a meeting which had taken place some weeks before the interview with the police in Spokane.

Then came another development.

Ed Lehan, the deputy attorney general, whom Smith Troy

had delegated to fly down to my ranch and inspect the transcript in the Boggie case, had been very much interested in subsequent developments. He had worked carefully on the case, had made a report to Smith Troy, who, in turn, had made a report to the Governor.

Digging into police records in Spokane, Lehan found that during the time John Doe had first been arrested by the Spokane police, and prior to the time he had been released because he had an alibi for the time that '*the sirens went by,*' every one of the witnesses who had seen the murderer running from the cabin of Moritz Peterson on that fateful Monday morning had positively identified John Doe as being the man they had seen.

The witness who had at the time of Boggie's trial glibly identified him as the man she had seen, had actually, nearly two years before, when the occasion was fresh in her mind, identified John Doe as being the man who had run away from that cabin and had been so positive, according to police records, that she had made the definite statement, 'I'll stake my life on it.'

It will be remembered that when we examined the transcript in the Boggie case there was indication that this witness had previously made an identification of another man, and that there had been a retraction of the identification when it appeared that the other man had a perfect alibi and couldn't possibly have been connected with the crime.

That man was John Doe and the alibi was merely a statement that he had been seen at a certain place some distance from the scene of the crime '*when the sirens went by.*'

As Smith Troy, the attorney general, succinctly stated, 'The State now has a better case against John Doe than it ever had against Clarence Boggie.'

But who was going to prosecute John Doe?

Certainly not the authorities in Spokane.

Clarence Boggie had been convicted by the authorities in Spokane. It would have been a bitter pill to have to swallow, after all these years, to admit a mistake and seek to convict John Doe.

John Doe seemed to sense that if he 'sat tight' he would come out all right.

He sat tight.

After a while John Doe was quietly released.

Those, generally, are the facts of the Boggie case and the murder of Moritz Peterson. There are certain other facts which I could disclose, but I don't think they would do any particular good at this time.

With the Seattle *Times* and *Argosy* Magazine hammering away at the Boggie case, Governor Wallgren finally granted Boggie a conditional pardon in December, 1948.

Don Magnuson received an award for his outstanding reporting, and the Seattle *Times* was showered with congratulations in the press. No one saw fit to mention that *Argosy* Magazine had been investigating the case for months, and even had a virtual commitment from Governor Wallgren long before the Seattle *Times* had even published a word. Bill Gilbert and some of the others who had known of our work started writing indignant letters.

However, I for one am frank to admit that political pressure might well have prevented any action from ever having been taken if it hadn't been for the work of the Seattle *Times* in uncovering the witness, who, apparently, had never read any of the articles in *Argosy*, but who did read that first article in the *Times*.

As I expressed it at one time, I think perhaps *Argosy* was ninety per cent responsible for proving that Boggie had been improperly convicted, whereas the Seattle *Times* was ninety per cent responsible for proving that a case much stronger than the case against Clarence Boggie could have been made against someone else.

Even at this late date the attorney general's office at Washington is looking for further evidence against John Doe in connection with the murder of Moritz Peterson. It has some hope that it may be forthcoming.

I know that I personally welcomed the assistance of the Seattle *Times* at the time we joined forces, and I welcome it now.

Henry MacLeod, Don Magnuson, and Magnuson's assistant, a newspaper reporter who, by the way, took a violent personal dislike to me, were first-class newspapermen. It was a revelation to see the way these men, with their knowledge of local conditions and the power of a local newspaper behind them, dug into the facts of the case. Their work in the Boggie case is one of the best illustrations I know of why we should have a free press, and why readers and advertisers should support powerful local newspapers. An advertiser who buys space in his local newspaper gets value received in terms of a dollars-and-cents return on his investment. In addition to all this he is making a tax-exempt investment in liberty and in freedom of the press. Without our local newspapers citizens would find themselves in a very sorry plight.

The truth of this is so apparent it seems a waste of time to mention it. Yet, strange as it may seem, this is an angle that many local businessmen and newspaper readers overlook.

I know that in my own case I didn't fully realize what a powerful factor a newspaper could be in safeguarding liberties until I saw the way these men from the Seattle *Times* with their knowledge of local conditions could get information that would have been unavailable to us.

From that time on we realized that whenever possible it would pay to have some local newspaper take an interest in our cases.

So far as the Court of Last Resort was concerned, the Boggie case demonstrated certain problems which, incidentally, we have never been able to solve.

In order to secure a committee the personnel of which would command confidence on the part of the public, would carry sufficient prestige to impress state officials, and at the same time be composed of men who were well established financially so that there was no need of personal publicity, it was necessary to get men who had active business interests. If a man is successful he has numerous demands on his time. If he isn't successful people aren't inclined to accept his opinion.

Dr LeMoyne Snyder's services are in constant demand. Leonarde Keeler was tremendously busy during his lifetime, and Alex Gregory at the present time is working on a crowded schedule. Raymond Schindler has the job of co-ordinating the investigation in countless cases. He is constantly flying back and forth from New York to Los Angeles, up to San Francisco, down to Florida, and occasionally over to Europe.

Harry Steeger, in addition to the responsibilities of supervising the destinies of *Argosy* Magazine, has some three dozen magazines in his publishing string. For my part I am always metering minutes, trying to be in two places at once, and do two things at the same time.

The result was that when we would fly to Walla Walla, Olympia or Spokane, and start an investigation, the long-distance telephone would be hammering out a constant succession of calls concerning some 'emergency' which had developed in our various businesses while we were away.

We could only get away a few days at a time; then we would have to go dashing back and face the discouraging prospect of a desk piled high with mail which had accumulated in our absence.

The members of the investigating committee had agreed to donate their time, the magazine had agreed to defray traveling expenses. But when, for instance, a man has to fly from New York to the Pacific Coast to work a few days on a case, then dash back to his office, expenses pile up.

When three or four such individuals get together for a conference, the bill runs into big money.

Those of us who felt that we could afford to do so stopped sending in vouchers and donated all our expenses as well as our time. But some of us simply weren't in a position to do this; contributing the time alone had been a very great sacrifice.

Such factors made the Court of Last Resort terribly costly, and made it debatable as a cold-blooded business proposition. Despite the fact that the reading public was indicating its approval it was, of course, quite clear that if the money spent on the Court of Last Resort should be used to increase promotional allotments and editorial rates, the expenditures would be far more profitable.

But, offsetting this tremendous expense was the knowledge that the work is a badly needed activity in connection with our whole scheme of justice.

Harry Steeger wanted *Argosy* to stand for something. He wanted the magazine not only to entertain, but to be a constructive force, and he overruled his editors when they pointed out how much more desirable it would be to use the money spent on the Court of Last Resort for promotional purposes.

Harry Steeger has a certain bulldog tenacity, and having started the Court of Last Resort he 'stayed put.'

Had we known what we now know about investigating the cases, the investigation of the Boggie case would have been greatly simplified. We learned a lot from that case.

Before finally leaving it, I think it is only fair to mention certain obvious truths which should be given careful consideration.

The police may not have forced the identification of Clarence Boggie in the manner in which a good card magician forces the man from the audience to pick out one particular card from the deck, but there can be no question that the tactics used by the police were such as to greatly influence the witnesses in making an identification.

One of the witnesses who had 'identified' Boggie as 'looking like' the man seen running from the scene of the murder, was asked if she could have made her identification had she been called upon to pick Boggie out of a line-up.

She admitted, at the time the question was first asked, that this would have been most difficult. Later on she said that she hadn't understood the question.

It is also evident that the jurors were out of sympathy with Clarence Boggie, and paid undue attention to his previous record of convictions. A certain amount of persuasive evidence was marshaled against Boggie, but it is difficult to understand how anyone could have felt that this evidence proved him guilty beyond all reasonable doubt.

Identification evidence, even when asserted with vehemence, should always be considered in the light of surrounding circumstances.

Some persons who are inclined to be positive and opinionated will get on a witness stand and swear with every ounce of sincerity at their command that the defendant in the case is the man they saw at such-and-such a time, at such-and-such a place.

Unfortunately the man who should be the most doubtful is, nine times out of ten, the man who is the most positive.

The fair man, whose testimony is apt to be accurate, is more likely to say, 'Well, I can't be absolutely positive, but I *think* that this is the man. Of course, it's been some time ago, but I think this is the man.'

Defense attorneys are inclined to pounce upon such a witness and by showing that he isn't positive and only 'thinks' the defendant is the man, sneeringly subject the witness to ridicule.

In many instances, such tactics are unfair.

Jurors should not readily condone a fair witness being torn to pieces by a jeering, sarcastic defense attorney who is crucifying the witness upon the cross of his own fairness.

On the other hand, juries should not be too much impressed by the testimony of the man who, after seeing some individual for a few seconds during the excitement attending the commission of a crime, swears positively that the man seated in the courtroom is the criminal. Jurors should consider all the facts.

Carefully conducted experiments show that it is rather difficult to make a positive identification, particularly where the individual was seen casually.

I remember at one time when I was attending one of Captain Frances G. Lee's seminars on homicide investigation at the Harvard Medical School, Dr Robert Brittain, a brilliant Scotsman, one of the shrewdest medicolegal brains in the profession (at present Lecturer in Forensic Medicine at Leeds University in England) was lecturing to a class of some fifteen state police officers, men who had been chosen for the course because of aptitude and ability.

Dr Brittain was commenting on description and identification. Abruptly he ceased his lecture, turned to the assembled group and said, 'By the way, how tall am I? Will someone speak up, please?'

Someone said, 'Five foot eight.'

Dr Brittain was like an auctioneer. 'Anyone here who thinks I'm taller than five foot eight?' he asked.

There was something in his voice that made it appear the estimate might have been on the short side, so someone promptly said, 'Five foot eight and a half,' and then someone went to five foot nine.

After a while Dr Brittain said, 'Well, who thinks I'm *shorter* than five foot eight?'

That immediately drew a customer.

Then Dr Brittain went on to the question of his weight and his age. Before he got done he had a series of descriptions which were simply meaningless. Between the extreme estimates there was a margin of difference that represented some fifteen years in age, some twenty pounds in weight and some four inches in height, and it is to be remembered that these descriptions were furnished not by men who were excited because they were being held up, or by men who were getting a fleeting glimpse of an individual in a dim light—they were sitting there looking directly at Dr Brittain, whose figure was only partially obscured by a table, and they were trained observers, men who made it their business to classify and describe.

But what of Clarence Boggie? What of the man himself?

Boggie, it is to be remembered, had been convicted and sent to prison in Idaho for the robbery which had been perpetrated by Convict X.

Boggie had served considerable time in Idaho, always protesting his innocence, and finally, because of various factors in the case, including an affidavit by a sheriff who had overheard conversations which made him believe Boggie might have been forced into the crime, the authorities had launched an investigation.

An investigator had actually found the place where Boggie had been repairing the lights which had short-circuited on the car of the man who had given him a ride. The attendant of that service station remembered that another car had drawn up and Boggie had been forced to get into it. Then the car had driven away.

The Governor of Idaho granted Boggie a pardon, but Boggie never had an opportunity to enjoy even five minutes of liberty under that pardon. The Washington authorities had grabbed him at the moment the pardon was delivered and had whisked him away to try him for the murder of Moritz Peterson, to convict him of that murder and to send him to prison for life.

Boggie at the time of his release found himself in a world that was all but strange to him. He had been in prison for nearly twenty years, and the outside world had made a good many strides during that time.

It was also difficult for him to make an emotional adjustment to freedom.

Moreover Boggie had received quantities of fan mail.

We had relied on publicity to get justice done in his case and the publicity had swelled into a tide which threatened to sweep Boggie off his feet.

Lawyers inspired him with the idea that he could sue the State of Washington for a huge sum of money for false imprisonment. People wrote to Boggie wishing him luck. Some of these fan letters were from women.

Boggie, who had spent some twenty years of his life entirely removed from the company and companionship of women, had placed his mother upon a pedestal and idolized her.

It was no time at all until Boggie was engaged to be married.

The power of the press had brought about Boggie's liberation, and from the moment of Boggie's release he became 'good copy.' Practically everything he did, every floundering mistake made in attempting to adjust himself to his newfound liberty, was publicized in the newspapers.

Then he found himself. He married a childhood sweetheart. He settled down, and finally found someone who had enough confidence in him to put him in charge of a logging crew.

Boggie's previous statements to us that he was one of the best aerial loggers in the country had been taken with a grain of salt and a barrel of pepper. His similar statements to prospective employers had apparently been dismissed as not even worthy of serious consideration.

Now Boggie had a chance to show what he could do.

That was the last unbelievable thing about the unbelievable Boggie. He was just as good as he said he was.

Boggie started breaking all records for handling logs. He tore into the work with a fervor and an efficiency that amazed everyone.

And then just when Boggie had adjusted himself to life on the outside, when he had married and established a home, when he had demonstrated his ability to handle a responsible job of putting out logs, the problem of physical adjustment proved too much for him.

Boggie had one triumphant day in which he broke all previous records for an output of logs.

His heart, which had been weakened by twenty years of confinement within walls, twenty years of routine prison diet, couldn't stand the strain that was thrown on it. Boggie came home. He told his wife that he had broken every previous existing record at the camp for moving logs.

Smiling his tired, twisted smile, Boggie went to the bathroom to wash his hands and fell over dead.

ROBERT GRAVES

New Light on an Old Murder

When, some twenty-five years ago, I wrote a two-volume novel about the Emperor Claudius, my pseudo-autobiographical approach obliged me to break off the story just before he died. However, not to keep my readers guessing, I printed as an epilogue the three main Classical accounts of Claudius's murder, those of Suetonius, Tacitus, and Dio Cassius. For good measure, I added a satire attributed to the Emperor Nero's tutor, the Spanish philosopher and playwright Seneca: 'The *Apocolocyntosis* of Claudius.' *Apocolocyntosis* has always been read as a humorous portmanteau word combining *apotheosis* (deification)—because Claudius was deified immediately after his death—and *colocynthos* (pumpkin)—presumably because Seneca regarded Claudius as a pumpkin-headed fool. The agreed translation therefore is 'Pumpkinfication,' and it never occurred to me that the word could have any other meaning.

Claudius's murder was engineered by his wife Agrippina. He had recently adopted Nero, her seventeen-year-old son by a former marriage, and named him joint-heir to the Empire with twelve-year-old Britannicus, his own son by Messaline. Agrippina decided to oust Britannicus from the succession; Nero's gratitude on becoming sole Emperor ought, she reckoned, to secure her supreme power behind the throne. Meanwhile she did all she could to turn Claudius against Britannicus and kept the two as far apart as possible. At last, fearing that Claudius suspected her of treachery and unfaithfulness, she planned to get rid of him without delay.

In 1949, Dr Valentina Wasson, a New York physician, wrote to enquire whether I had any views on the exact circumstances of the murder, which she and her husband, R. Gordon Wasson,

a vice-president of J.P. Morgan and Company, were investigating from the mycological angle. I looked up the sources
again, and here they are in what I believe to be the order of their
historic trustworthiness:

> Most people think that Claudius was poisoned; but when, and by
> whom, is disputed. Some say that the eunuch Halotus, his official
> taster, administered the drug while he was dining with the priests of
> Jupiter in the Citadel; others, that Agrippina did so herself at a family
> banquet, poisoning a dish of mushrooms, his favourite food. An equal
> discrepancy exists between the accounts of what happened next.
> According to many of my informants, he lost his power of speech,
> suffered frightful pain all night long, and died shortly before dawn. A
> variant version is that he fell into a coma but vomited up the entire
> contents of his stomach and was then poisoned a second time, either by a
> gruel—the excuse being that he needed food to revive him—or by means
> of an enema, the excuse being that his bowels must be emptied too.
> Claudius's death was not revealed until all arrangements had been
> completed to secure Nero's succession. As a result, people made vows
> for his safety as though he still lived, and a troop of actors were
> summoned, under the pretence that he had asked to be diverted by
> their antics. He died on October 13th, 54 A.D., during the consulship of
> Asinius Marcellus and Acilius Avola, in his sixty-fourth year, and the
> fourteenth of his reign. He was given a princely funeral and officially
> deified, an honour which Nero later neglected and then cancelled; but
> which Vespasian restored.
>
> Suetonius: *XII Caesars (tr. Robert Graves)*

> Agrippina had long decided on murder. Now she saw her opportun-
> ity. Her agents were ready. But she wanted advice about poisons. A
> sudden, drastic effect would give her away. A gradual, wasting recipe
> might make Claudius, faced with death, love his son again. What was
> needed was something subtle that would upset the Emperor's faculties
> but produce a deferred fatal effect. An expert in such matters was
> selected—a woman called Locusta, recently sentenced for poisoning
> but with a long career of imperial service ahead of her. By her talents, a
> preparation was supplied. It was administered by a eunuch who
> habitually served the Emperor and tasted his food.
> Later, the whole story became known. Contemporary writers stated
> that the poison was sprinkled on a particularly succulent mushroom.
> But because Claudius was torpid—or drunk—its effect was not at first
> apparent; and an evacuation of his bowels seemed to have saved him.
> Agrippina was horrified. But when the ultimate stakes are so alarming-
> ly large, immediate disrepute is brushed aside. She had already
> secured the complicity of the Emperor's doctor Xenophon; and now
> she called him in. The story is that, while pretending to help Claudius
> to vomit, he put a feather dipped in a quick poison down his throat.
> Xenophon knew that major crimes, though hazardous to undertake,
> are profitable to achieve.
>
> Tacitus: *Annals (tr. Michael Grant)*

Claudius was angered by Agrippina's actions, of which he was now becoming aware, and sought for his son Britannicus, who had purposely been kept out of his sight by her most of the time (for she was doing everything she could to secure the throne for Nero, inasmuch as he was her own son by her former husband Domitius); and he displayed his affection whenever he met the boy. He would not endure her behaviour, but was preparing to put an end to her power, to cause his son to assume the *toga virilis*, and to declare him heir to the throne. Agrippina, learning of this, became alarmed and made haste to forestall anything of the sort by poisoning Claudius. But since, owing to the great quantity of wine he was forever drinking and his general habits of life, such as all emperors as a rule adopt for their protection, he could not easily be harmed, she sent for a famous dealer in poisons, a woman named Locusta, who had recently been convicted on this very charge; and preparing with her aid a poison whose effect was sure, she put it in one of the vegetables called mushrooms. Then she herself ate of the others, but made her husband eat of the one which contained the poison; for it was the largest and finest of them. And so the victim of the plot was carried from the banquet apparently quite overcome by strong drink, a thing that had happened many times before; but during the night the poison took effect and he passed away, without having been able to say or hear a word. It was the thirteenth of October, and he had lived sixty-three years, two months and thirteen days, having been emperor thirteen years, eight months and twenty days.

Dio Cassius: *Book LXI (tr. E. Cary)*

Mr and Mrs Wasson had gone a long way towards solving their detective problem. The mushrooms, nowhere described as being themselves poisonous, were almost certainly of the wholesome and delicious variety now known, in Claudius's honour, as the *amanita caesarea*. They have round, orange-coloured caps primrose-yellow spores and stalks, and grow plentifully throughout Southern Europe in October, the month of his death. The Wassons believed that Locusta, the professional poisoner employed by Agrippina, made Halotus, the official taster, doctor the mushrooms handed to Claudius with the juice of another mushroom of the same genus—the deadly *amanita phalloides*. The *phalloides* has a yellowish-white slightly pointed cap, white spores and stalk, and grows plentifully near Rome at the same season as the *caesarea*. It seems that Claudius's family and friends were served from a single large dish; and their survival would suggest that he had been unfortunate enough to eat a single poisonous *phalloides* included among the *caesarea* by mistake. Nor was there any chance of

Claudius's detecting the poison—for which no remedy was then, or is now, known—by its taste. All those luckless people who have ever eaten *amanita phalloides* agree (before they die) that it tastes most delicious. They have quite enough time to make this observation, since the ill-effects seldom occur until six hours have elapsed. Sometimes nothing happens for as long as twenty hours. Yet once the poison takes a firm hold, the victim is in no condition to think of anything but his excruciating stomachic pains, which gradually carry him off. One hears vague talk about survivors, but I can find no certain instance of one. Claudius's inability to collect his wits before he died was, Tacitus notes, a condition of the poisoning on which Agrippina insisted.

That Seneca knew the peculiar properties of *amanita phalloides*, the Wassons deduced from a letter he wrote some nine years later to his friend Lucilius the Stoic. While condemning Claudius's gluttony, he exclaims:

> 'Good gods! How many men are employed in the service of a single belly! But can you believe that the tasty poison of those mushrooms does not operate secretly, even if no ill-effect is immediately experienced?'

This seems to me pretty conclusive proof of Seneca's complicity in the murder, and at the same time it explains how Locusta's apparently flawless plot miscarried. Claudius's gross habit, elsewhere attested by Suetonius, of drinking too much and then ridding his stomach of the excess, nearly saved his life. It seems that, soon after being carried from the table dead drunk, he vomited up a part of his meal; which put Agrippina in a most awkward position. (Tacitus's 'an evacuation of the bowels seemed to have saved him' makes no sense and can refer only to the vomiting.) Agrippina had no means of judging how much poison, if any, remained in her husband's stomach; nor, apparently, of preparing the same meal again, even if he could be persuaded to make a second attempt at downing it. Meanwhile, plans had been concluded for Nero's acclamation as the sole Emperor; and, if Claudius were to recover, the news of her attempted coup might well leak out—in which case he would probably appoint Britannicus, who was (according to Suetonius) now officially of age, his co-Emperor, and execute Nero and herself without trial.

The Emperor Claudius: poisoned by a mushroom?

Agrippina and her assistants moved quickly. The best hope of saving their skins lay in reinforcing the action of whatever poison remained in Claudius's system, by administering another drug of the same general effect. A *post-mortem* could then show him to have died by mischance from that single deadly mushroom. So they bribed, or forced, the imperial physician Xenophon to finish his master off. According to Tacitus, Xenophon put a feather smeared with venom down Claudius's throat; but this sounds both difficult and dangerous. The Wassons preferred Suetonius's less melodramatic account, according to which the poison was administered by enema. We were left to discover precisely what drug Xenophon could have chosen and procured at short notice to ensure the desired results.

Then it occurred to me that I had been as stupid as all the long line of Classical scholars who studied these texts before me. The Greek word *colocynthos* does not only mean 'pumpkin'; it also means the wild gourd mentioned in that exciting Biblical passage (II Kings 4: 38–41) about the college of prophets who shredded vegetables into the communal stew and discovered too late that some ignoramus had added a lapful of sliced wild gourd. They cried in agony to their master Elisha: 'O man of God, there is death in the pot!'

Colocynth, though a useful purge in minimal doses, and notorious as the active agent of the powerful No. 9 pill employed by M.O.'s to cure malingerers during the First World War, is a virulent alkaloid poison. Scribonius Largus, the apothecary, in a valuable book of medical prescriptions published around A.D. 45, acknowledges indebtedness for the colocynth recipe to his friend the late Paccius of Antioch. Paccius's No. 9 pill soon became very popular among the Roman aristocracy, most of whom (then as now) ate far too much, slept far too much, and took far too little exercise. But though Xenophon could easily lay his hand on colocynth without exciting suspicion, it tastes exceedingly bitter; and how to make Claudius accept a decisive dose in gruel (as Agrippina seems to have suggested), was a delicate problem. Xenophon's ingenious alternative, that of rectal administration under colour of giving his patient a good turn-out, proved effective.

Hence Seneca's subsequent coinage of the word *Apocolocynto-sis*, the real meaning of which was: 'Deification by means of colocynth.' He celebrated this cruel murder with a light-hearted satire on Claudius's physical and intellectual failings, and it is difficult to forgive the joke about Claudius's miserable last words: *'Vae me, puto me concacavi!'*—'Alas, I think I have messed myself badly!' Seneca writes that Claudius always *did* make a mess of everything. However, to die from colocynth poisoning is at least a swifter and less agonizing fate than to die from *amanita phalloides*.

The farce of pretending, several hours after the end, that Claudius was still alive and being amused by a variety troupe, seems to have been dictated by the change of drugs. Claudius ate his late meal on October 12th, A.D. 54, at about 2:30 P.M. The first gripings from *phalloides* poisoning should have come on between 9 P.M. and midnight; but the 'deferred fatal effect' could not be hoped for until the following evening. Xenophon's colocynth acted far more rapidly. Claudius died before dawn, and Agrippina found herself uncomfortably ahead of schedule. It looks as if the new arrangements for Nero's acclamation as Emperor had been agreed with the Guards Colonel who would begin his turn of duty at noon; because it was not until then that Nero came out from the Palace to receive the soldiers' homage. Agrippina afterwards excused the delay as due to astrological considerations. How much Nero himself already knew about the plot is uncertain; but on a later occasion he laughingly quoted the Greek proverb: 'Mushrooms are the food of the gods,' and added that mushrooms had, in fact, made a god of his predecessor.

Agrippina satisfied herself that Locusta's *amanita phalloides* was a wonderfully effective drug, when (according to Dio Cassius) she killed her enemy Marcus Julius Silanus with a dose of the poison that had been prepared for Claudius. Nor does this seem to have been her last use of it. Tacitus reports that Annaeus Serenus, Commander of Nero's Bodyguard (whom we meet elsewhere as an intimate friend of Seneca's) assisted Nero's secret liaison with a slave-girl named Acte; and that Nero appealed to Seneca for help when Agrippina got wind of the affair. But Tacitus omits to mention Agrippina's revenge of Serenus, and we must turn to Pliny's *Natural History* for the information:

> The safest fungi are those, the flesh of which is red, the colour being more pronounced than that of the mushroom. The next best are the white ones, the stems of which have a head very similar to the cap worn by the Flamens; and a third kind are the *suilli* ('piglets'), very conveniently adapted for poisoning. Indeed, it is but very recently that they have carried off whole families, and all the guests at a banquet; Annaeus Serenus, for instance, the commander of Nero's Guard, together with all the tribunes and centurions. What great pleasure, then, can there be in partaking of a dish of so doubtful a character as this?

Pliny meant, I suppose, that *amanita phalloides* can readily be smuggled into a harmless dish of *amanita caesarea*, with no chance of immediate discovery, and with spectacular success, especially if one does not care how many others, besides the intended victim, die horribly from it.

> *From the distant past to an even more remote future. Up to here we have concentrated on fairly practical solutions to crimes, but here at the end let's allow the imagination to fly a little. Robert Graves' recreation of Ancient Rome in his two novels about Claudius constitutes an imaginative reconstruction of the first rank; Harlan Ellison's leap into the future is something else again, and not for the squeamish.*
>
> *Unsolved! opened with perhaps the greatest of all the classic murderers, Jack the Ripper, and to close Solved! the wheel is brought full circle, and posits another kind of solution altogether: the flight of fantasy inspired by real events — a whole genre, and perhaps another collection. Hope to see you there. Meanwhile, here is the inimitable Mr Ellison...*

HARLAN ELLISON

The Prowler in the City At the Edge of the World

First there was the City, never night. Tin and reflective, walls of antiseptic metal like an immense autoclave. Pure and dust-free, so silent that even the whirling innards of its heart and mind were sheathed from notice. The city was self-contained, and footfalls echoed up and around—flat slapped notes of an exotic leather-footed instrument. Sounds that reverberated back to the maker like yodels thrown out across mountain valleys. Sounds made by humbled inhabitants whose lives were as ordered, as sanitary, as metallic as the city they had caused to hold them bosom-tight against the years. The city was a complex artery, the people were the blood that flowed icily through the artery. They were a gestalt with one another, forming a unified whole. It was a city shining in permanence, eternal in concept, flinging itself up in a formed and molded statement of exaltation; most modern of all modern structures, conceived as the pluperfect residence for the perfect people. The final end-result of all sociological blueprints aimed at Utopia. Living space, it had been called, and so, doomed to *live* they were, in that Erewhon of graphed respectability and cleanliness.

Never night.

Never shadowed.

. . . a shadow.

A blot moving against the aluminium cleanliness. The movement of rags and bits of clinging earth from graves sealed ages before. A shape.

He touched a gunmetal-gray wall in passing: the imprint of dusty fingers. A twisted shadow moving through antiseptically pure streets, and they become—with his passing—black alleys from another time.

Vaguely, he knew what had happened. Not specifically, not with particulars, but he was strong, and he was able to get away without the eggshell-thin walls of his mind caving in. There was no place in this shining structure to secrete himself, a place to think, but he had to have time. He slowed his walk, seeing no one. Somehow—inexplicably—he felt . . . safe? Yes, safe. For the first time in a very long time.

A few minutes before he had been standing in the narrow passageway outside No. 13 Miller's Court. It had been 6:15 in the morning. London had been quiet as he paused in the passageway of M'Carthy's Rents, in that fetid, urine-redolent corridor where the whores of Spitalfields took their clients. A few minutes before, the foetus in its bath of formaldehyde tightly-stoppered in a glass bottle inside his Gladstone bag, he had paused to drink in the thick fog, before taking the circuitous route back to Toynbee Hall. That had been a few minutes before. Then, suddenly, he was in another place and it was no longer 6:15 of a chill November morning in 1888.

He had looked up as light flooded him in that other place. It had been soot silent in Spitalfields, but suddenly, without any sense of having moved or having *been* moved, he was flooded with light. And when he looked up he was in that other place. Paused now, only a few minutes after the transfer, he leaned against the bright wall of the city, and recalled the light. From a thousand mirrors. In the walls, in the ceiling. A bedroom with a girl in it. A lovely girl. Not like Black Mary Kelly or Dark Annie Chapman or Kate Eddowes or any of the other pathetic scum he had been forced to attend . . .

A lovely girl. Blonde, wholesome, until she had opened her robe and turned into the same sort of slut he had been compelled to use in his work in Whitechapel . . .

A sybarite, a creature of pleasures, a Juliette she had said, before he used the big-bladed knife on her. He had found the knife under the pillow, on the bed to which she had led him—how shameful, unresisting had he been, all confused, clutching his black bag with all the tremors of a child, he who had moved through the London night like oil, moved where he wished, accomplished his ends unchecked eight times, now led toward sin by another, merely another of the tarts, taking advantage of him while he tried to distinguish what had happened to him and where he was, how shameful — and he had used it on her.

That had only been minutes before, though he had worked very efficiently on her.

The knife had been rather unusual. The blade had seemed to be two wafer-thin sheets of metal with a pulsing, glowing *something* between. A kind of sparking, such as might be produced by a Van de Graaff generator. But that was patently ridiculous. It had no wires attached to it, no bus bars, nothing to produce even the crudest electrical discharge. He had thrust the knife into the Gladstone bag, where now it lay beside the scalpels and the spool of catgut and the racked vials in their leather cases, and the foetus in its bottle. Mary Jane Kelly's foetus.

He had worked efficiently, but swiftly, and had laid her out almost exactly in the same fashion as Kate Eddowes: the throat slashed completely through from ear-to-ear, the torso laid open down between the breasts to the vagina, the intestines pulled out and draped over the right shoulder, a piece of the intestines being detached and placed between the left arm and the body. The liver had been punctured with the point of the knife, with a vertical cut slitting the left lobe of the liver. (He had been surprised to find the liver showed none of the signs of cirrhosis so prevalent in these Spitalfields tarts, who drank incessantly to rid themselves of the burden of living the dreary lives they moved through grotesquely. In fact, this one seemed totally unlike the others, even if she had been more brazen in her sexual overtures. And that knife under the bed pillow . . .) He had severed the vena cava leading to the heart. Then he had gone to work on the face.

He had thought of removing the left kidney again, as he had Kate Eddowes's. He smiled to himself as he conjured up the expression that must have been on the face of Mr.

George Lusk, chairman of the Whitechapel Vigilance Committee, when he received the cardboard box in the mail. The box containing Miss Eddowes's kidney, and the letter, impiously misspelled:

> *From hell, Mr. Lusk, sir, I send you half the kidne I took from one woman, prasarved it for you, tother piece I fried and ate it; was very nice. I may send you the bloody knif that took it out if you only wate while longer. Catch me when you can, Mr. Lusk.*

He had wanted to sign *that* one "Yours Truly, Jack the Ripper" or even Spring-Heeled Jack or maybe Leather Apron, whichever had tickled his fancy, but a sense of style had stopped him. To go too far was to defeat his own purposes. It may even have been too much to suggest to Mr. Lusk that he had eaten the kidney. How hideous. True, he *had* smelled it . . .

This blonde girl, this Juliette with the knife under her pillow. She was the ninth. He leaned against the smooth steel wall without break or seam, and he rubbed his eyes. When would he be able to stop? When would they realize, when would they get his message, a message so clear, written in blood, that only the blindness of their own cupidity forced them to misunderstand! Would he be compelled to decimate the endless regiments of Spitalfields sluts to make them understand? Would he be forced to run the cobbles ankle-deep in black blood before they sensed what he was saying, and were impelled to make reforms?

But as he took his blood-soaked hands from his eyes, he realized what he must have sensed all along: he was no longer in Whitechapel. This was not Miller's Court, nor anywhere in Spitalfields. It might not even be London. But how could *that* be?

Had God taken him?

Had he died, in a senseless instant between the anatomy lesson of Mary Jane Kelly (that filth, she had actually *kissed* him!) and the bedroom disembowelment of this Juliette? Had Heaven finally called him to his reward for the work he had done?

The Reverend Mr. Barnett would love to know about this. But then, he'd have loved to know about it *all*. But "Bloody Jack" wasn't about to tell. Let the reforms come as the Reverend and his wife wished for them, and let them think their pamphleteering had done it, instead of the scalpels of Jack.

If he was dead, would his work be finished? He smiled to himself. If Heaven had taken him, then it must be that the work *was* finished. Successfully. But if *that* was so, then who was this Juliette who now lay spread out moist and cooling in the bedroom of a thousand mirrors? And in that instant he felt fear.

What if even God misinterpreted what he had done?

As the good folk of Queen Victoria's London had misinterpreted. As Sir Charles Warren had misinterpreted. What if God believed the superficial and ignored the *real* reason? But no! Ludicrous. If anyone would understand, it was the good God who had sent him the message that told him to set things a-right.

God loved him, as he loved God, and God would know.

But he felt fear, in that moment.

Because who was the girl he had just carved?

"She was my granddaughter, Juliette," said a voice immediately beside him.

His head refused to move, to turn that few inches to see who spoke. The Gladstone was beside him, resting on the smooth and reflective surface of the street. He could not get to a knife before he was taken. At last they had caught up with Jack. He began to shiver uncontrollably.

"No need to be afraid," the voice said. It was a warm and succoring voice. An older man. He shook as with an ague. But he turned to look. It was a kindly old man with a gentle smile. Who spoke again, without moving his lips. "No one can hurt you. How do you do?"

The man from 1888 sank slowly to his knees. "Forgive me. Dear God, I did not know." The old man's laughter rose inside the head of the man on his knees. It rose like a beam of sunlight moving across a Whitechapel alleyway, from noon to one o'clock, rising and illuminating the gray bricks of soot-coated walls. It rose, and illuminated his mind.

"I'm not God. Marvelous idea, but no, I'm not God. Would you like to meet God? I'm sure we can find one of the artists who would mold one for you. Is it important? No, I can see it isn't. What a strange mind you have. You neither believe nor doubt. How can you contain both concepts at once ... would you like me to straighten some of your brain-patterns? No. I see, you're afraid. Well, let it be for the nonce. We'll do it another time."

He grabbed the kneeling man and drew him erect.

"You're covered with blood. Have to get you cleaned up. There's an ablute near here. Incidentally, I was very impressed with the way you handled Juliette. You're the first, you know. No, how could you know? In any case, you *are* the first to deal her as good as she gave. You would have been amused at what she did to Caspar Hauser. Squeezed part of his brain and then sent him back, let him live out part of his life and then—the little twit—she made me bring him back a second time and used a knife on him. Same knife you took, I believe. Then sent him back to his own time. Marvelous mystery. In all the tapes on unsolved phenomena. But she was much sloppier than you. She had a great verve in her amusements, but very little *éclat*. Except with Judge Crater; there she was—" He paused, and laughed lightly. "I'm an old man and I ramble on like a muskrat. You want to get cleaned up and shown around, I know. And *then* we can talk.

"I just wanted you to know I was satisfied with the way you disposed of her. In a way, I'll miss the little twit. She was such a good fuck."

The old man picked up the Gladstone bag and, holding the man spattered with blood, he moved off down the clean and shimmering street. "You *wanted* her killed?" the man from 1888 asked, unbelieving.

The old man nodded, but his lips never moved. "Of course. Otherwise why bring her Jack the Ripper?"

Oh my dear God, he thought, *I'm in Hell. And I'm entered as Jack.*

"No, my boy, no no no. You're not in Hell at all. You're in the future. For you the future, for me the world of now. You came from 1888 and you're now in—" he stopped, silently speaking for an instant, as though computing apples in terms of dollars, then resumed "—3077. It's a fine world, filled with happy times, and we're glad to have you with us. Come along now, and you'll wash."

In the ablutatorium, the late Juliette's grandfather changed his head.

"I really despise it," he informed the man from 1888, grabbing fingerfuls of his cheeks and stretching the flabby skin like elastic. "But Juliette insisted. I was willing to humor her, if indeed that was what it took to get her to lie down. But what with toys from the past, and changing my head every time I wanted her to fuck me, it was trying; very trying."

He stepped into one of the many identically shaped booths set flush into the walls. The tambour door rolled down and there was a soft *chukk* sound, almost chitinous. The tambour door rolled up and the late Juliette's grandfather, now six years younger than the man from 1888, stepped out, stark naked and wearing a new head. "The body is fine, replaced last year," he said, examining the genitals and a mole on his right shoulder. The man from 1888 looked away. This was Hell and God hated him.

"Well, don't just *stand* there, Jack." Juliette's grandfather smiled. "Hit one of those booths and get your ablutions."

"That isn't my name," said the man from 1888 very softly, as though he had been whipped.

"It'll do, it'll do ... now go get washed."

Jack approached one of the booths. It was a light green in color, but changed to mauve as he stopped in front of it. "Will it—"

"It will only *clean* you, what are you afraid of?"

"I don't want to be changed."

Juliette's grandfather did not laugh. "That's a mistake," he said cryptically. He made a peremptory motion with his hand and the man from 1888 entered the booth, which promptly revolved in its niche, sank into the floor and made a hearty *zeeeezzzz* sound. When it rose and revolved and opened, Jack stumbled out, looking terribly confused. His long sideburns had been neatly trimmed, his beard stubble had been removed, his hair was three shades lighter and was now parted on the left side, rather than in the middle. He still wore the same long dark coat trimmed with astrakhan, dark suit with white collar and black necktie (in which was fastened a horseshoe stickpin) but now the garments seemed new, unsoiled of course, possibly synthetics built to look like his former garments.

"Now!" Juliette's grandfather said. "Isn't that much better? A good cleansing always sets one's mind to rights." And he stepped into another booth from which he issued in a moment wearing a soft paper jumper that fitted from neck to feet without a break. He moved toward the door.

"Where are we going?" the man from 1888 asked the younger grandfather beside him. "I want you to meet someone," said Juliette's grandfather, and Jack realized that he was moving his lips now. He decided not to comment on it. There had to be a reason.

"I'll walk you there, if you promise not to make gurgling sounds at the city. It's a nice city, but I live here, and frankly, tourism is boring." Jack did not reply. Grandfather took it for acceptance of the terms.

They walked. Jack became overpowered by the sheer *weight* of the city. It was obviously extensive, massive, and terribly clean. It was his dream for Whitechapel come true. He asked about slums, about doss houses. The grandfather shook his head. "Long gone."

So it had come to pass. The reforms for which he had pledged his immortal soul, they had come to pass. He swung the Gladstone and walked jauntily. But after a few minutes his pace sagged once more: there was no one to be seen in the streets.

Just shining clean buildings and streets that ran off in aimless directions and came to unexpected stops as though the builders had decided people might vanish at one point and reappear someplace else, so why bother making a road from one point to the other.

The ground was metal, the sky seemed metallic, the buildings loomed on all sides, featureless explorations of planed space by insensitive metal. The man from 1888 felt terribly alone, as though every act he had performed had led inevitably to his alienation from the very people he had sought to aid.

When he had come to Toynbee Hall, and the Reverend Mr. Barnett had opened his eyes to the slum horrors of Spitalfields, he had vowed to help in any way he could. It had seemed as simple as faith in the Lord, what to do, after a few months in the sinkholes of Whitechapel. The sluts, of what use were they? No more use than the disease germs that had infected these very same whores. So he had set forth as Jack, to perform the will of God and raise the poor dregs who inhabited the East End of London. That Lord Warren, the Metropolitan Police Commissioner, and his Queen, and all the rest thought him a mad doctor, or an amok butcher, or a beast in human form did not distress him. He knew he would remain anonymous through all time, but that the good works he had set in motion would proceed to their wonderful conclusion.

The destruction of the most hideous slum area the country had ever known, and the opening of Victorian eyes. But all the time *had* passed, and now he was here, in a world where slums apparently did not exist, a sterile Utopia that was the personification of the Reverend Mr. Barnett's dreams—but it didn't seem . . . *right*.

This grandfather, with his young head.

Silence in the empty streets.

The girl, Juliette, and her strange hobby.

The lack of concern at her death.

The grandfather's expectation that he, Jack, *would* kill her. And now his friendliness.

Where were they going?

[Around them, the City. As they walked, the grandfather paid no attention, and Jack watched but did not understand. But this was what they saw as they walked:

[Thirteen hundred beams of light, one foot wide and

seven molecules thick, erupted from almost-invisible slits in the metal streets, fanned out and washed the surfaces of the buildings; they altered hue to a vague blue and washed down the surfaces of the buildings; they bent and covered all open surfaces, bent at right angles, then bent again, and again, like origami paper figures; they altered hue a second time, soft gold, and penetrated the surfaces of the buildings, expanding and contracting in solid waves, washing the inner surfaces; they withdrew rapidly into the sidewalks; the entire process had taken twelve seconds.

[Night fell over a sixteen block area of the City. It descended in a solid pillar and was quite sharp-edged, ending at the street corners. From within the area of darkness came the distinct sounds of crickets, marsh frogs belching, night birds, soft breezes in trees, and faint music of unidentifiable instruments.

[Panes of frosted light appeared suspended freely in the air, overhead. A wavery insubstantial quality began to assault the topmost levels of a great structure directly in front of the light-panes. As the panes moved slowly down through the air, the building became indistinct, turned into motes of light, and floated upward. As the panes reached the pavement, the building had been completely dematerialized. The panes shifted color to a deep orange, and began moving upward again. As they moved, a new structure began to form where the previous building had stood, drawing—it seemed—motes of light from the air and forming them into a cohesive whole that became, as the panes ceased their upward movement, a new building. The light-panes winked out of existence.

[The sound of a bumblebee was heard for several seconds. Then it ceased.

[A crowd of people in rubber garments hurried out of a gray pulsing hole in the air, patted the pavement at their feet, then rushed off around a corner, from where emanated the sound of prolonged coughing. Then silence returned.

[A drop of water, thick as quicksilver, plummeted to the pavement, struck, rebounded, rose several inches, then evaporated into a crimson smear in the shape of a whale's tooth, which settled to the pavement and lay still.

[Two blocks of buildings sank into the pavement and the metal covering was smooth and unbroken, save for a metal tree whose trunk was silver and slim, topped by a ball of foliage constructed of golden fibers that radiated brightly in a perfect circle. There was no sound.

[The late Juliette's grandfather and the man from 1888 continued walking.]

"Where are we going?"

"To van Cleef's. We don't usually walk; oh, sometimes; but it isn't as much pleasure as it used to be. I'm doing this primarily for you. Are you enjoying yourself?"

"It's . . . unusual."

"Not much like Spitalfields, is it? But I rather like it back there, at that time. I have the only Traveler, did you know? The only one ever made. Juliette's father constructed it, my son. I had to kill him to get it. He was thoroughly unreasonable about it, really. It was a casual thing for him. He was the last of the tinkerers, and he might just as easily have given it to me. But I suppose he was being cranky. That was why I had you carve up my granddaughter. She would have gotten around to me almost any time now. Bored, just silly bored is what she was—"

The gardenia took shape in the air in front of them, and turned into the face of a woman with long white hair. "Hernon, we can't wait much longer!" She was annoyed.

Juliette's grandfather grew livid. "You scum bitch! I *told* you pace. But no, you just couldn't, could you? Jump jump jump, that's all you ever do. Well, now it'll only be feddels less, that's all. Feddels, damn you! I set it for pace, I was *working* pace, and *you* . . . !"

His hand came up and moss grew instantly toward the face. The face vanished, and a moment later the gardenia reappeared a few feet away. The moss shriveled and Hernon, Juliette's grandfather, dropped his hand, as though weary of the woman's stupidity. A rose, a water lily, a hyacinth, a pair of phlox, a wild celandine, and a bull thistle appeared near the gardenia. As each turned into the face of a different person, Jack stepped back, frightened.

All the faces turned to the one that had been the bull thistle. "Cheat! Rotten bastard!" they screamed at the thin white face that had been the bull thistle. The gardenia-woman's eyes bulged from her face, the deep purple eye-shadow that completely surrounded the eyeball making her look like a deranged animal peering out of a cave. "Turd!" she shrieked at the bull thistle-man. "We all agreed, we all said and agreed; you *had* to formz a thistle, didn't you, scut! Well, now you'll see ..."

She addressed herself instantly to the others. "Formz now! To hell with waiting, pace fuck! Now!"

"No, dammit!" Hernon shouted. "We were going to *paaaaace!*" But it was too late. Centering in on the bull thistle-man, the air roiled thickly like silt at a river-bottom, and the air blackened as a spiral began with the now terrified face of the bull thistle-man and exploded whirling outward, enveloping Jack and Hernon and all the flower-people and the City and suddenly it was night in Spitalfields and the man from 1888 was *in* 1888, with his Gladstone bag in his hand, and a woman approaching down the street toward him, shrouded in the London fog.

(There were eight additional nodules in Jack's brain.)

The woman was about forty, weary and not too clean. She wore a dark dress of rough material that reached down to her boots. Over the skirt was fastened a white apron that was stained and wrinkled. The bulbed sleeves ended midway up her wrists and the bodice of the dress was buttoned close around her throat. She wore a kerchief tied at the neck, and a hat that looked like a wide-brimmed skimmer with a raised crown. There was a pathetic little flower of unidenti-fiable origin in the band of the hat. She carried a beaded handbag of capacious size, hanging from a wrist-loop.

Her step slowed as she saw him standing there, deep in the shadows. Saw him was hardly accurate: sensed him.

He stepped out and bowed slightly from the waist. "Fair evenin' to ye, Miss. Care for a pint?"

Her features—sunk in misery of a kind known only to women who have taken in numberless shafts of male blood-gorged flesh—rearranged themselves. "Coo, sir, I thought was 'im for true. Old Leather Apron hisself. Gawdamighty, you give me a scare." She tried to smile. It was a rictus. There were bright spots in her cheeks from sickness and too much gin. Her voice was ragged, a broken-edged instrument barely workable.

"Just a solicitor caught out without comp'ny," Jack assured her. "And pleased to buy a handsome lady a pint of stout for a few hours' companionship."

She stepped toward him and linked arms. "Emily Matthewes, sir, an' pleased to go with you. It's a fearsome chill night, and with Slippery Jack abroad not safe for a respectin' woman such's m'self."

They moved off down Thrawl Street, past the doss houses where this drab might flop later, if she could obtain a few coppers from this neat-dressed stranger with the dark eyes.

He turned right onto Commercial Street, and just abreast of a stinking alley almost to Flower & Dean Street, he nudged her sharply sidewise. She went into the alley, and thinking he meant to steal a smooth hand up under her petticoats, she settled back against the wall and opened her legs, starting to lift the skirt around her waist. But Jack had hold of the kerchief and, locking his fingers tightly, he twisted, cutting off her breath. Her cheeks ballooned, and by a vagary of light from a gas standard in the street he could see her eyes go from hazel to a dead-leaf brown in an instant. Her expression was one of terror, naturally, but commingled with it was a deep sadness, at having lost the pint, at having not been able to make her doss for the night, at having had the usual Emily Matthewes bad luck to run afoul this night of the one man who would ill-use her favors. It was a consummate sadness at the inevitability of her fate.

I come to you out of the night.
The night that sent me down
all the minutes of our lives
to this instant.
From this time forward, men will
wonder what happened

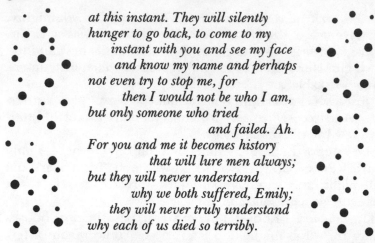

*at this instant. They will silently
hunger to go back, to come to my
instant with you and see my face
and know my name and perhaps
not even try to stop me, for
then I would not be who I am,
but only someone who tried
and failed. Ah.
For you and me it becomes history
that will lure men always;
but they will never understand
why we both suffered, Emily;
they will never truly understand
why each of us died so terribly.*

A film came over her eyes, and as her breath husked out
in wheezing, pleading tremors, his free hand went into the
pocket of the greatcoat. He had known he would need it,
when they were walking, and he had already invaded the
Gladstone bag. Now his hand went into the pocket and came
up with the scalpel.

"Emily . . ." softly.

Then he sliced her.

Neatly, angling the point of the scalpel into the soft flesh
behind and under her left ear. *Sternocleidomastoideus.* Driving
it in to the gentle crunch of cartilage giving way. Then,
grasping the instrument tightly, tipping it down and drawing
it across the width of the throat, following the line of the
firm jaw. *Glandula submandibularis.* The blood poured out
over his hands, ran thickly at first and then burst spattering
past him, reaching the far wall of the alley. Up his sleeves,
soaking his white cuffs. She made a watery rattle and sank
limply in his grasp, his fingers still twisted tight in her
kerchief; black abrasions where he had scored the flesh. He
continued the cut up past the point of the jaw's end, and
sliced into the lobe of the ear. He lowered her to the filthy
paving. She lay crumpled, and he straightened her. Then he
cut away the garments laying her naked belly open to the
wan flickering light of the gas standard in the street. Her
belly was bloated. He started the primary cut in the hollow

of her throat. *Glandula thyreoeidea.* His hand was sure as he drew a thin black line of blood down and down, between the breasts. *Sternum.* Cutting a deep cross in the hole of her navel. Something vaguely yellow oozed up. *Plica umbilicalis medialis.* Down over the rounded hump of the belly, biting more deeply, withdrawing for a neat incision. *Mesenterium dorsale commune.* Down to the matted-with-sweat roundness of her privates. Harder here. *Vesica urinaria.* And finally, to the end, *vagina.*

Filth hole.

Foul-smelling die red lust pit wet hole of sluts.

And in his head, succubi. And in his head, eyes watching. And in his head, minds impinging. And in his head titillation

for a gardenia
   a water lily
   a rose
   a hyacinth
   a pair of phlox
   a wild celandine
and a dark flower with petals of obsidian, a stamen of onyx, pistils of anthracite, and the mind of Hernon, who was the late Juliette's grandfather.

They watched the entire horror of the mad anatomy lesson. They watched him nick the eyelids. They watched him remove the heart. They watched him slice out the fallopian tubes. They watched him squeeze, till it ruptured, the "ginny" kidney. They watched him slice off the sections of breast till they were nothing but shapeless mounds of bloody meat, and arrange them, one mound each on a still-staring, wide-open, nicked-eyelid eye. They watched.

They watched and they drank from the deep troubled pool of his mind. They sucked deeply at the moist quivering core of his id. And they delighted:

Oh God how Delicious look at that It looks like the uneaten rind of a Pizza or look at That It looks like lumaconi *oh god IIIIIwonder what it would be like to Tasteit!*

See how smooth the steel.

He hates them all, every one of them, something about a girl, a venereal disease, fear of his God, Christ, the Reverend Mr. Barnett, he . . . he wants to fuck the reverend's wife!

Social reform can only be brought about by concerted effort of a devoted few. Social reform is a justifiable end, condoning any expedient short of decimation of over fifty percent of the people who will be served by the reforms. The best social reformers are the most audacious. He believes it! How lovely!

You pack of vampires, you filth, you scum, you . . .

He senses us!

Damn him! Damn you, Hernon, you drew off too deeply, he knows we're here, that's disgusting, what's the sense now? I'm withdrawing!

Come back, you'll end the formz . . .

. . . back they plunged in the spiral as it spiraled back in upon itself and the darkness of the night of 1888 withdrew. The spiral drew in and locked at its most infinitesimal point as the charred and blackened face of the man who had been the bull thistle. He was quite dead. His eyeholes had been burned out; charred wreckage lay where intelligence had lived. They had used him as a focus.

The man from 1888 came back to himself instantly, with a full and eidetic memory of what he had just experienced. It had not been a vision, nor a dream, nor a delusion, nor a product of his mind. It had happened. They had sent him back, erased his mind of the transfer into the future, of Juliette, of everything after the moment outside No. 13 Miller's Court. And they had set him to work pleasuring them, while they drained off his feelings, his emotions and his unconscious thoughts; while they battened and gorged themselves with the most private sensations. Most of which, till this moment—in a strange feedback—he had not even known he possessed. As his mind plunged on from one revelation to the next, he felt himself growing ill. At one concept his mind tried to pull back and plunge him into darkness rather than confront it. But the barriers were down, they had opened new patterns and he could read it all, remember it all. *Stinking sex hole, sluts, they have to die.* No, that wasn't the way he thought of women, any women, no matter how low or common. He was a gentleman, and women were to be respected. *She had given him the clap. He remembered.* The shame and the endless fear till he had gone to his physician father and confessed it. The look on the man's face. He remembered it all. The way his father had tended him, the way he would have tended a plague victim. It had never been the same between them again. He had tried for the cloth. *Social reform hahahaha.* All delusion. He had been a mountebank, a clown ... and worse. He had slaughtered for something in which not even he believed. They left his mind wide open, and his thoughts stumbled ... raced further and further toward the thought of

EXPLOSION!IN!HIS!MIND!

He fell face forward on the smooth and polished metal pavement, but he never touched. Something arrested his fall, and he hung suspended, bent over at the waist like a ridiculous Punch divested of strings or manipulation from above. A whiff of something invisible, and he was in full possession of his senses almost before they had left him. His mind was forced to look at it:

He wants to fuck the Reverend Mr. Barnett's wife.

Henrietta, with her pious petition to Queen Victoria— "Madam, we, the women of East London, feel horror at the dreadful sins that have been lately committed in our midst ..."—asking for the capture of himself, of Jack, whom she would never, not *ever* suspect was residing right there with her and the Reverend in Toynbee Hall. The thought was laid as naked as her body in the secret dreams he had never remembered upon awakening. All of it, they had left him with opened doors, with unbounded horizons, and he saw himself for what he was.

A psychopath, a butcher, a lecher, a hypocrite, a clown.

"You did this to me! Why did you do this?"

Frenzy cloaked his words. The flower-faces became the solidified hedonists who had taken him back to 1888 on that senseless voyage of slaughter.

van Cleef, the gardenia-woman, sneered. "Why do you think, you ridiculous bumpkin? (Bumpkin, is that the right colloquialism, Hernon? I'm so uncertain in the mid-dialects.) When you'd done in Juliette, Hernon wanted to send you back. But why should he? He owed us at least three formz, and you did passing well for one of them."

Jack shouted at them till the cords stood out in his throat. "Was it necessary, this last one? Was it important to do it, to help my reforms . . . was it?"

Hernon laughed. "Of course not."

Jack sank to his knees. The City let him do it. "Oh God, oh God almighty, I've done what I've done . . . I'm covered with blood . . . and for *nothing*, for *nothing* . . ."

Cashio, who had been one of the phlox, seemed puzzled. "Why is he concerned about *this* one, if the others don't bother him?"

Nosy Verlag, who had been a wild celandine, said sharply, "They do, all of them do. Probe him, you'll see."

Cashio's eyes rolled up in his head an instant, then rolled down and refocused—Jack felt a quicksilver shudder in his mind and it was gone—and he said lackadaisically, "Mm-hmm."

Jack fumbled with the latch of the Gladstone. He opened the bag and pulled out the foetus in the bottle. Mary Jane Kelly's unborn child, from November 9th, 1888. He held it in front of his face a moment, then dashed it to the metal pavement. It never struck. It vanished a fraction of an inch from the clean, sterile surface of the City's street.

"What marvelous loathing!" exulted Rose, who had been a rose.

"Hernon," said van Cleef, "he's centering on you. He begins to blame you for all of this."

Hernon was laughing (without moving his lips) as Jack pulled Juliette's electrical scalpel from the Gladstone, and lunged. Jack's words were incoherent, but what he was saying, as he struck, was: "I'll show you what filth you are! I'll show you you can't do this kind of thing! I'll teach you! You'll die, all of you!" This is what he was saying, but it came out as one long sustained bray of revenge, frustration, hatred and directed frenzy.

Hernon was still laughing as Jack drove the whisper-thin

blade with its shimmering current into his chest. Almost
without manipulation on Jack's part, the blade circumscribed
a perfect 360° hole that charred and shriveled, exposing
Hernon's pulsing heart and wet organs. he had time to
shriek with confusion before he received Jack's second
thrust, a direct lunge that severed the heart from its attach-
ments. *Vena cava superior. Aorta. Arteria pulmonalis. Bronchus
principalis.*

The heart flopped forward and a spreading wedge of
blood under tremendous pressure ejaculated, spraying Jack
with such force that it knocked his hat from his head and
blinded him. His face was now a dripping black-red collage
of features and blood.

Hernon followed his heart, and fell forward, into Jack's
arms. Then the flower-people screamed as one, vanished,
and Hernon's body slipped from Jack's hands to wink out of
existence an instant before it struck at Jack's feet. The walls
around him were clean, unspotted, sterile, metallic, uncaring.

He stood in the street, holding the bloody knife.

"Now!" he screamed, holding the knife aloft. "Now it
begins!"

If the city heard, it made no indication, but

[Pressure accelerated in temporal linkages.]

[A section of shining wall on the building eighty miles
away changed from silver to rust.]

[In the freezer chambers, two hundred gelatin caps were
fed into a ready trough.]

[The weathermaker spoke softly to itself, accepted data
and instantly constructed an intangible mnemonic circuit.]

and in the shining eternal city where night only fell when
the inhabitants had need of night and called specifically for
night . . .

Night fell. With no warning save: *"Now!"*

In the City of sterile loveliness a creature of filth and
decaying flesh prowled. In the last City of the world, a City
on the edge of the world, where the ones who had devised
their own paradise lived, the prowler made his home in
shadows. Slipping from darkness to darkness with eyes that

saw only movement, he roamed in search of a partner to dance his deadly rigadoon.

He found the first woman as she materialized beside a small waterfall that flowed out of empty air and dropped its shimmering, tinkling moisture into an azure cube of nameless material. He found her and drove the living blade into the back of her neck. Then he sliced out the eyeballs and put them into her open hands.

He found the second woman in one of the towers, making love to a very old man who gasped and wheezed and clutched his heart as the young woman forced him to passion. She was killing him as Jack killed her. He drove the living blade into the lower rounded surface of her belly, piercing her sex organs as she rode astride the old man. She decamped blood and viscous fluids over the prostrate body of the old man, who also died, for Jack's blade had severed the penis within the young woman. She fell forward across the old man and Jack left them that way, joined in the final embrace.

He found a man and throttled him with his bare hands, even as the man tried to dematerialize. Then Jack recognized him as one of the phlox, and made neat incisions in the face, into which he inserted the man's genitals.

He found another woman as she was singing a gentle song about eggs to a group of children. He opened her throat and severed the strings hanging inside. He let the vocal cords drop onto her chest. But he did not touch the children, who watched it all avidly. He liked children.

He prowled through the unending night making a grotesque collection of hearts, which he cut out of one, three, nine people. And when he had a dozen, he took them and laid them as road markers on one of the wide boulevards that never were used by vehicles, for the people of this City had no need of vehicles.

Oddly, the City did not clean up the hearts. Nor were the people vanishing any longer. He was able to move with relative impunity, hiding only when he saw large groups that might be searching for him. But *something* was happening in the City. (Once, he heard the peculiar sound of metal grating on metal, the *skrikkk* of plastic cutting into plastic—and he instinctively knew it was the sound of a machine malfunctioning.)

He found a woman bathing, and tied her up with strips of his own garments, and cut off her legs at the knees and left her still sitting up in the swirling crimson bath, screaming as she bled away her life. The legs he took with him.

When he found a man hurrying to get out of the night, he pounced on him, cut his throat and sawed off the arms. He replaced the arms with the bath-woman's legs.

And it went on and on, for a time that had no measure. He was showing them what evil could produce. He was showing them their immorality was silly beside his own.

But one thing finally told him he was winning. As he lurked in an antiseptically pure space between two low aluminium-cubes, he heard a voice that came from above him and around him and even from inside him. It was a public announcement, broadcast by whatever mental communications system the people of the City on the edge of the World used.

OUR CITY IS PART OF US. WE ARE PART OF OUR CITY. IT RESPONDS TO OUR MINDS AND WE CONTROL IT. THE GESTALT THAT WE HAVE BECOME IS THREATENED. WE HAVE AN ALIEN FORCE WITHIN THE CITY AND WE ARE GEARING TO LOCATE IT. BUT THE MIND OF THIS MAN IS STRONG. IT IS BREAKING DOWN THE FUNCTIONS OF THE CITY. THIS ENDLESS NIGHT IS AN EXAMPLE. WE MUST ALL CONCENTRATE. WE MUST ALL CONSCIOUSLY FOCUS OUR THOUGHTS TO MAINTAINING THE CITY. THIS THREAT IS OF THE FIRST ORDER. IF OUR CITY DIES, WE DIE.

It was not an announcement in those terms, though that was how Jack interpreted it. The message was much longer and much more complex, but that was what it meant, and he knew he was winning. He was destroying them. Social reform was laughable, they had said. He would show them.

And so he continued with his lunatic pogrom. He butchered and slaughtered and carved them wherever he found them, and they could not vanish and they could not escape and they could not stop him. The collections of hearts grew to fifty and seventy and then a hundred.

He grew bored with hearts and began cutting out their brains. The collection grew.

For numberless days it went on, and from time to time in the clean, scented autoclaves of the City, he could hear the sounds of screaming. His hands were always sticky.

Then he found van Cleef, and leaped from hiding in the darkness to bring her down. He raised the living blade to drive it into her breast, but she

van   ished

He got to his feet and looked around. van Cleef reappeared ten feet from him. He lunged for her and again she was gone. To reappear ten feet away. Finally, when he had struck at her half a dozen times and she had escaped him each time, he stood panting, arms at sides, looking at her.

And she looked back at him with disinterest.

"You no longer amuse us," she said, moving her lips.

Amuse? His mind whirled down into a place far darker than any he had known before, and through the murk of his blood-lust he began to realize. It had all been for their amusement. They had *let* him do it. They had given him the run of the City and he had capered and gibbered for them.

Evil? He had never even suspected the horizons of that word. He went for her, but she disappeared with finality.

He was left standing there as the daylight returned. As the City cleaned up the mess, took the butchered bodies and did with them what it had to do. In the freezer chambers the gelatin caps were returned to their niches, no more inhabitants of the City need be thawed to provide Jack the Ripper with utensils for his amusement of the sybarites. His work was truly finished.

He stood there in the empty street. A street that would *always* be empty to him. The people of the city had all along been able to escape him, and now they would. He was finally and completely the clown they had shown him to be. He was not evil, he was pathetic.

He tried to use the living blade on himself, but it dissolved into motes of light and wafted away on a breeze that had blown up for just that purpose.

Alone, he stood there staring at the victorious cleanliness of this Utopia. With their talents they would keep him alive, possibly alive forever, immortal in the possible expectation of needing him for amusement again someday. He was stripped to raw essentials in a mind that was no longer anything more than jelly matter. To go madder and madder, and never to know peace or end or sleep.

He stood there, a creature of dirt and alleys, in a world as pure as the first breath of a baby.

"My name isn't Jack," he said softly. But they would never know his real name. Nor would they care. *"My name isn't Jack!"* he said loudly. No one heard.

"MY NAME ISN'T JACK, AND I'VE BEEN BAD, VERY BAD, I'M AN EVIL PERSON BUT MY NAME ISN'T JACK!" he screamed, and screamed, and screamed again, walking aimlessly down an empty street, in plain view, no longer forced to prowl. A stranger in the City.

SOURCES AND ACKNOWLEDGEMENTS

'Death in Silk Stockings' by Ellery Queen is from *Deadlier Than The Male* (Corgi, 1967).

The Case of Mr George Edalji' by Sir Arthur Conan Doyle was first published as a series in the *Daily Telegraph* in 1907, subsequently reprinted as a booklet by T. Harrison Roberts, 1907, and later collected in *The Story of Mr George Edalji* (Grey House Books, 1985). The publishers are most grateful to Richard Whittington-Egan, the editor of that collection, for his help with this book, and to Camille Wolff, its publisher.

'Coppolino Revisited' by John D. Macdonald, from *I, Witness* (Times Books, 1978) is reprinted by kind permission of The Mystery Writers of America.

'The Invisible Man' by Julian Symons also from *I, Witness*, is reprinted by kind permission of Curtis Brown Ltd, London.

'The 'Perfect' Crime That Was Unspeakably Dumb' by Damon Runyon, is reprinted by kind permission of King Features, Inc.

'The Trial of Madeleine Smith' by F. Tennyson Jesse and 'The Gorse Hall Mystery' by Freeman Wills Crofts were first published in *Great Unsolved Crimes* (Hutchinson, n.d.).

The Court of Last Resort by Erle Stanley Gardner was first published by William Sloane Associates, 1952; revised edition published by Pocket Books, Inc., 1954.

'New Light on an Old Murder' by Robert Graves was first published in *Food for Centaurs* (Doubleday & Co., Inc., 1960).

'The Prowler In the City At the Edge of the World' originally appeared in DANGEROUS VISIONS; copyright © 1967 by Harlan Ellison. Reprinted by arrangement with, and permission of, the Author and the Author's agent, Richard Curtis Associates, Inc., New York. All rights reserved. This preferred text from THE ESSENTIAL ELLISON (1987).

While every effort has been made to trace authors and copyright holders, in a few cases this has proved impossible; the publishers would be glad to hear from any such parties so that these omissions can be rectified in future editions of the book.

Thanks are due to the following for permission to reproduce the photographs and illustrations of the following pages:

20, courtesy of Richard Whittington-Egan. BBC Hulton Library 25; The Bettmann Archive 119; Topham Picture Library 139, 149, 163; Syndication International 114, 199, 205; William Morrow & Co., Inc 235; Mary Evans Picture Library 291, 294.